THE FARMER'S TOOLS
AD 1500-1900

THE
FARMER'S TOOLS

The history of British farm implements,
tools and machinery
AD 1500-1900

by G. E. FUSSELL

ORBIS PUBLISHING · LONDON

First published in Great Britain by
Andrew Melrose Limited, London 1952;
this edition by Orbis Publishing Limited,
London 1981

© G. E. Fussell 1952, 1981

Printed in Singapore

ISBN: 0–85613–359–0

DEDICATED

BY THE AUTHOR

TO

ALL INVENTORS, DESIGNERS,

MANUFACTURERS AND USERS

OF FARM MACHINERY

CONTENTS

LIST OF ILLUSTRATIONS

PREFACE

THE NEW SYSTEM of power haulage provided by the tractor has allowed the engineer much greater scope in the design of complex farm machines. Such machines could hardly have been hauled by animals, nor could they have been operated had it not been for the power units supplied by small internal combustion engines.

Steam power had proved very useful in the nineteenth century, but it was cumbersome and was only practical where very large implements could be used economically, and where supplies of solid fuel and water could be obtained without too much difficulty.

There had been great developments before the tractor came, though they cannot really be said to have begun until the printed word was available to make ideas widely known, so that the literate could discuss them with their less literate, but possibly more practical-minded, contemporaries, as well as with their equally learned compeers. That is why this study is begun at about 1523, when Fitzherbert's *Boke of Husbandrye* was first issued.

The factory production of implements and machines could not, of course, be introduced until the coming of the industrial revolution. It did not, in fact, get into full swing until well into the nineteenth century, but a great deal of what may be called preliminary work had been done a long time before then and had been fairly continuous. Fruitful ideas had come to many persons, who had done their best either to set them down in their theoretic and didactic farming publications, or to create them in practical and usable form. In this way progress had been made in such things as drainage ploughs, tillage ploughs, horse hoes and other cultivation implements, the seed-drill and the threshing machine, while the reaper had been foreshadowed. These things are, it is hoped, adequately discussed in the body of this work.

The plan of the book is to follow the seasons throughout the year, from seed-time to harvest, and to tell the story of the progress made in improving the implements and machines used for each season's work during the four centuries under discussion. Clearly it is impossible to avoid some overlapping here and there because farm operations have a habit of overlapping each other.

Little reference will be made to general history, though some reference to the surrounding circumstances at particular times will be necessary. The stress of the times, economic changes, and the increase in population all played their part in encouraging improved farming, and better implements and machines were a most essential part of improved farming. I shall, therefore, try to indicate the stimulus that these factors applied to men's minds beyond the natural desire of all ingenious men in rural society to simplify and cheapen farm work.

I feel obliged to lay down one mechanical definition that I have adopted; I hope it will be acceptable. In this study an implement is regarded as something inert, having no internal working parts essential to its operation, such as a plough, a harrow or a roller, while a machine will be taken to be something that has moving parts within itself essential to its operation, like a seed-drill, a reaper or a threshing machine.

I must acknowledge my indebtedness and gratitude to the Leverhulme Fellowship Committee for a grant that has enabled me to complete this study. Both Mr. N. D. Waring of the National Institute of Agricultural Engineering and Mrs. Patricia Baxter have done a great deal to help in the collection of material, the former at the Institute and the latter at the Bodleian. To them I owe my sincere thanks. My wife has assisted me during the last year of the work, by reading and by secretarial work. Without her help I doubt if this book could have been finished. I am also grateful to the many firms of manufacturers who have supplied material information, and to the librarians and others, too numerous to mention, who have kindly placed their resources and knowledge at my disposal.

Aye, an old Wooden Plough, and they say, to be sure,
As the wideawake farmer mun use 'em no more,
They mun all be of iron, and wood there's no trade for,
Why, what do the fools think as Ash Trees were made for?

Anon., 18*th Cent.*

CHAPTER ONE

FIELD DRAINAGE

WET LAND MAY have some advantages, but few British farmers would care to consider them. The first thing necessary to make land productive is to lay it dry; this is a problem that has preoccupied farmers all over Europe from time immemorial. The cultivated crops of the temperate zone can only be grown successfully on land that has been drained of superfluous moisture.

Nothing except hand tools was used for this purpose until the eighteenth century, when one or two draining ploughs were invented; the only methods of field drainage known in the Middle Ages were the open water furrow and the ditch.[1] The covered drain was, however, known in classical times, and is described by Palladius, an author who was familiar to medieval scholars, but to nobody else in those days. These drains may have been introduced during the Roman occupation, and it is possible that some knowledge of them was handed down by farm workers from father to son after the Romans left, in the same way, described so genially by W. H. Hudson, as the secrets of the shepherd were passed along.[2]

Palladius was translated into the vernacular early in the fifteenth century, and it is easy to believe that the English version of the poem describes both the classical practice, and, with some reservations, that

B

of late medieval times. There are instructions for making the covered drain that sound extraordinarily like advice, given so recently as 1925 by the Ministry of Agriculture, on how to make bush or faggot drains.[3]

The translation told the farmer to make:

> A furrow three feet deep thy lands thorough,
> With gravel or with little pebble stones
> Unto the midward filled.

And to see that:

> . . . the hedes of hem alle
> Into some greet ditche pitchelonges falle.

If the farmer had no stones on his land, or near enough to fetch cheaply, "sarment," straw or lop could be used to fill the drain.[4] Five hundred years later the Ministry advised the use of overgrown hedge clippings, since the hedges have to be cut in any case. The butts should be placed towards the outfall and when pressed down the brush filling should not be more than six or seven inches deep. Above the wood, straw, rushes, or hedge brushings were to be laid to a depth of two or three inches. This filling is not so deep as that recommended by Palladius, but the system is the same, and has survived the vicissitudes of climate and conquest through some two thousand years at least. These widely separated references are naturally not isolated; they do not exist in solitary splendour with an immense space of time between them, but, on the contrary, British farming literature repeatedly returns to the subject, and continuously advises the adoption of the system in terms that differ but little.

Fitzherbert, the author of the first English printed work on farming, *Boke of Husbandrye*, 1523, must have been acquainted with Palladius, because the classics were a necessary part of the education of such a man in early Tudor days when enthusiasm for the new scholarship of the Renascence was running like a fire in stubble across Europe; but curiously enough he did not subscribe to the stone or brush filled drains of his predecessors and successors. Ditches, he says, must be wide and deep, and the width must be proportionate to the depth, e.g. four feet wide for two and a half feet, five feet wide for three feet deep and so on.[5] This is odd, because Fitzherbert certainly puts on record the practices of his own day, the early sixteenth century, and probably his work also represents the best medieval farming. In his other work, *Surveyinge*, he tells us that if open drains "wylle not make the marres grounde drie, then you must make a soughe undernethe the erthe, as men do to get cole, yron, leade or tynne."[6] How this was to be done, he does not say, but it is very likely that the "soughe" was made in the same way as it was in Staffordshire in the sixteenth century. In that county "Mr. Sylvester, of Welford, first digs a hole deep and large enough to receive a *Man* together with his instrument like a shovel, then he excavates the *hollow black earth* as far as his instrument will reach both ways, i.e. about eight foot besides the diameter of the hole, leaving the upper turf thick above it, then at the same distance on a line from eight foot to eight foot, he makes other holes, and so on as the work requires, and then putting in Alders—or other fit materials, as *brush wood* to keep the earth from falling in, and choking the Sough, it will drain the ground to that rate that many times it will sink a yard or more."[7]

Thomas Tusser, the other great Tudor farming writer, does not even mention "soughs" as a means of draining, though he was acquainted with Essex, a county later in the forefront of draining innovations, and also Suffolk. The sum total of his advice on draining is to

> Trench, hedge, and furrow
> That water may thorough,

in September, and after

> Seed sown, draw a furrow, the water to drain,
> And dyke up such ends, as in harm do remain.

Again, in May

> The fen and the quagmire, so marish be kind,
> And are to be drained, now win to thy mind;
> Which yearly undrained, and suffered uncut,
> Annoyeth the meadows, that thereon do but.[8]

His contemporaries, and many others until the end of the seventeenth century, adhered to this system,[9] which, of course, is still in the main the method of field drainage where it efficiently carries off surface water. And the control of surface water by open furrows and ditches led to its use for watering meadows as well as freeing them from "annoyance." The earliest recommendation to do this that I have so far found, comes from a work in French. "If the ground of the meadow be withered and dry, it will be a marvelious commoditie unto it," wrote Estienne and Liebault in 1600, "to drawe into it all the winter long, at the least some small brooke, for the watering and moisturing of it, seeing that moisture the naturall nourishment of haie, and this woulde be done speciallie during the moneths of November, December, Januarie and Februarie; afterward when the earth hath drunke her full stoppe the way whereby the water of the brooke runneth."[10] More detailed advice is added, but is not relevant here.

At this time there were so-called water meadows in Tan Deane (Taunton Dean), on the Severn, Crediton, and near Welshpool, but these, like others in different parts of the country, were merely riverside meadows that got flooded in the ordinary course of affairs. These floods "do feed them fat," and gave heavy yields of feed. John Norden, who remarks upon this natural effect, suggests that stopping rivers artificially and governing the flooding would be a help to all meadows where there was sufficient water. Already in his day this was a type of husbandry "much used in *Somerset, Devon and Cornwall*."[11] This process had also been developed by Rowland Vaughan in Worcester some little time before 1600,[12] and, at a later date, water meadows had been made in an extensive tract of country from Marlborough to Hungerford, Ramsbury and Littlecot.[13]

It was both for the construction of water meadows and the cutting of trenches in which to make hollow or covered drains that special tools were first designed. Perhaps it was the greater number of trenches and channels required for water meadows than for any other meadows, or arable lands, that first encouraged some unknown person to design these tools. They are described at some length by Walter Blith, who gives a careful explanation of their use. Blith's method later received the approbation of the first specific treatise on water meadows[14] and the subject continued to claim space in general books of farming lore in the seventeenth and eighteenth centuries.[15]

The difficulty that confronted the open-field farmer in trying to drain his land has aroused little comment amongst historians, who have found other reasons for condemning the system; but it must have been a severely practical problem to the farmer. Blith saw that if the winter water remained on the land, it bred rushes and foulness, and gnawed out its heart and strength. Experience showed that "where great

Baulkes betwixt Lands, Hades, Meares, or Divisions betwixt Land and Land are left, and one Furlong butting or Hadlanding upon the other Furlongs, makes such a stoppage of the free passage of the water, that a great part of the land lyeth as it were drowned a great part of the year, that it overcomes that backing many times till near Midsummer, when other sound Lands have yielded a full half yeares profit. . . ."

Such conditions must be overcome if the land is to be farmed so as to attain the highest degree of fertility and grow the heaviest possible crops. Blith's remedy was the covered drain. He recommended drains three to four feet deep, in which the lowest level was filled with faggots of willow, alder or lime, covered by a layer of turf and then fifteen inches of stones, the remaining depth of the trench being filled with the soil.[16] Other writers gave different admixtures of materials as their favourite prescriptions. In Oxfordshire "an ingenious *Husbandman*, that having dug his trenches about a yard deep and two foot over, first laid at the bottom green *Black-thorn* bushes, and on them a *stratum* of large round stones, or at least such as would not lie close; and over them again another *stratum* of *Black-thorn*, and upon them *straw* to keep the dirt from falling in between, and filling them up; by which means he kept his trench open, and procured so constant and durable a drain, that the *land* is since sunk a foot or eighteen inches and become firm enough to support carriages."[17]

From laying stones so that there were gaps between them through which the water could flow, to placing flat stones or bricks so as to form a channel, is a natural step. Hollow brick drains were made in the early years of the eighteenth century by laying bricks crosswise at the bottom of the trench, others being laid lengthwise at the sides and these again covered with a crosswise layer.[18]

Switzer, who describes this way of making a hollow drain, had in mind the construction by hand labour of something that was very like a modern mole drain. It was "the best and cheapest Method of drayning Clayey Land," and "and will do as well in Pasture, Arable or Wood Lands as in Gardens." He advised digging a trench with draining spades of different widths, the tools commonly used in making trenches for filled hollow drains, "and at every twenty Foot as under, if the Ground lye near a Level (which is the worst case that can attend this Method) dig a narrow Trench of about ten Inches or a Foot wide at most quite through your Gardens . . . and a full Foot and a half within the Clay ; take a wooden Rowl of about five Inches diameter at one End, of four Foot long, and four Inches diameter at the other; and placing this Rowl at the bottom of your Trench, take the Clay you had before dug out, and with a Rammer ram it in round the Rowl which will form a perfect Tube; and the Rowl being bigger at one end than the other you may by the help of a Chain fastened to the bigger End pull it out of the Tube so that proceeding four Foot at a time, you may go through your whole Trench or Trenches from End to End and all over your Garden; taking great Care to keep your Drains or Ditches on the Extremity of your Gardens, and the Ends of the Tubes open.

"I should also have set down that before you move this Rowl you take a Puncher made in the form of a Pyramid a little broke off at the Top, about three Foot long, three Inches Diameter at the great End, and one at the small, with which Instrument (made of wood as it is) you are to punch a Hole through the ramm'd Clay upon the Top of your Rowl, through which perforation all the water is to pass, that comes from the Ground above, down into the under ground Drain or Tube below.

"And in order to keep this perforated Hole open, and not to be choaked up by the Earth's tumbling into it, you are to take some small Faggot-wood or Furze-bushes, and chopping them short, you are to cover the Hole therewith, adding to the Top a broad Tile to secure it from any impression that may come from above."[19]

The result of this system, says Switzer, would be to make the land "as hollow and as unfit to retain stagnated water as a Sieve." Even in arable lands this system of hand-made mole drains would be favourable. He states that he has known such drains to last twelve years, and that building them cost only twenty shillings an acre.

This method of forming a mole drain did not find favour with many people, and it was another three-quarters of a century before the mole plough was invented. The mole drain was even said to have been tried in Lancashire and found useless, but the "Rowl" was apparently effective, for it is mentioned under the title of "plug" draining,[20] especially at the end of the century and later. Nevertheless, the popular methods throughout all this time were the normal open drains arranged in accordance with the needs of the situation, and the brush, stone or furze filled hollow drain.[21]

These drains were constantly noticed with satisfaction by Arthur

Young as he travelled about the country exploring the methods adopted by farmers living in different districts. He saw them in Suffolk,[22] and at Braintree, in Essex, found the cost of this kind of draining so low as 2d. per rod and small beer to the workmen. He came across them near Kettering, Harborough, Keddleston, Chesterfield, Bawtry, Barnsley, Bromford, Dunmow, Ware, Mitcham, and "on Mr. Arbuthnot's farm," Richmond; he also found them in Hampshire, in Dorset, and on Edmund Burke's farm at Beaconsfield.[23] He notes that Mr. Turner, of Bignor Park, Sussex, whose land was a stiff clay, found that hollow training "was no sort of use." Young was taken to a field "drained twelve years ago, at the expense of 30 l; the drains well cut and filled with stones; and yet the land to this day as wet as ever." This is one of the few unfavourable notices I have been able to discover relating to the method.

Young came across an indication of the antiquity of the usage at Hook, Hampshire, where a Mr. Poole had acted as a pioneer in reviving the hollow drain. This gentleman told Young that nearly a hundred years before "a very large oak, 200 years old, was cut down" and "in digging a ditch through the spot where the old stump was, on taking up the remains of it, a drain was discovered under it, filled with alder branches, and it is very remarkable that the alder was perfectly sound; the greenness of the bark was preserved and even some leaves were found; on taking them out they presently dropped to powder. It is from hence very evident that underground draining was practised more than 300 years ago in this kingdom."

Mr. Turner, who found that hollow draining failed on his land, was convinced that the only method "of use, is the open ones to take the water that runs on the surface; and for making of which he bought Mr Knowle's drain plough." This was one of many cumbersome draining ploughs that were tried out. They were the first step in mechanizing land drainage work. It does not seem that they were effective machines. Their draught was too great for them to be economical, because they required so many as eight, twelve and even twenty horses to draw them. Draining ploughs of this kind, however, continued to be used at least until 1836.[24]

A hundred years before Ellis had observed that the Cambridgeshire plough used for draining had been tried unsuccessfully in Lancashire because "it is always running up in a short time."[25] The

Cambridgeshire draining plough was described by John Mortimer. It was a bigger and stronger version of an ordinary plough, but fitted with pieces of wood joined to the beam through which two coulters could be fixed. These coulters were opposite each other and bent inwards at the points "to cut each side of the trench. The Share is very broad and flat and cuts off the bottom of the Trench. The Mould-board is three times the length of other Ploughs, to cast the Turf a great way off the Trench. This Plough cuts a Trench a Foot wide at the bottom, a Foot and a half broad at the Top, and a Foot deep." This plough was drawn by twenty horses and cost £3. Mortimer reckoned that it answered the charge.[26] It was evidently the forerunner of Clarke's draining plough. The Royal Society of Arts later in the century were not as enthusiastic and offered premiums for a satisfactory design of a plough for this job, but no really practical implement seems to have been evolved.

There was great competition between the "inventors" of the different designs, but the main principle was much the same in all. It was that of the Cambridgeshire draining plough, the underlying idea being to set two coulters parallel at whatever width it was desired to make the trench, and to clear the spoil by two long mouldboards, the share making a level sole. These ploughs, when the land allowed them to be hauled, would make a trench a foot deep and eighteen to twenty inches wide at the surface. The idea of them may well have originated in Blith's trenching plough, which cut out the trench in two operations, one for each side of the cut.[27]

Knowles, of the Isle of Wight, and Cuthbert Clarke of Belford, Northumberland, competed in the 1760's for the premiums offered by the Royal Society of Arts for implements of this type, and both received an award of fifty guineas.[28] One of Clarke's ploughs was purchased by the Society. The inventor was a little jealous of his production; he said that the Society were "so exceeding cautious in deciding the claim" (as between him and others) "that they appointed a time for the trial of each candidate's machine, made in full size."[29] The implement, which is shown in a plate at the end of Clarke's book, is depicted in even more emphatic detail in an engraving in *The Complete Farmer*.[30] It had three coulters and was fitted with a wheel, or rather roll, which prevented the plough going deeper into the earth. This roll, which was in front of the coulters, was divided into

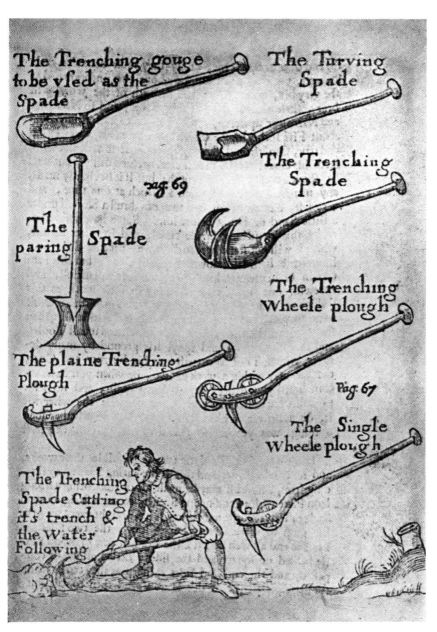

1. Seventeenth-century Draining Tools. From Walter Blith, *English Improver Improved*, 3rd. ed., 1653.

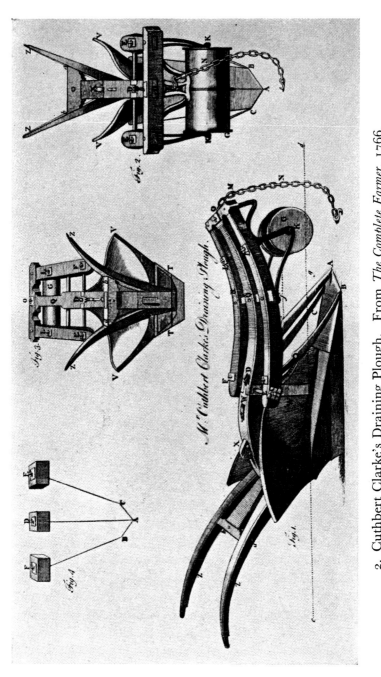

2. Cuthbert Clarke's Draining Plough. From *The Complete Farmer*, 1766.

Great Drain Plough.

Fig. 1.

3. Great Drain Plough. From Arthur Young, *General View of the Agriculture of . . . Essex*, 1807.

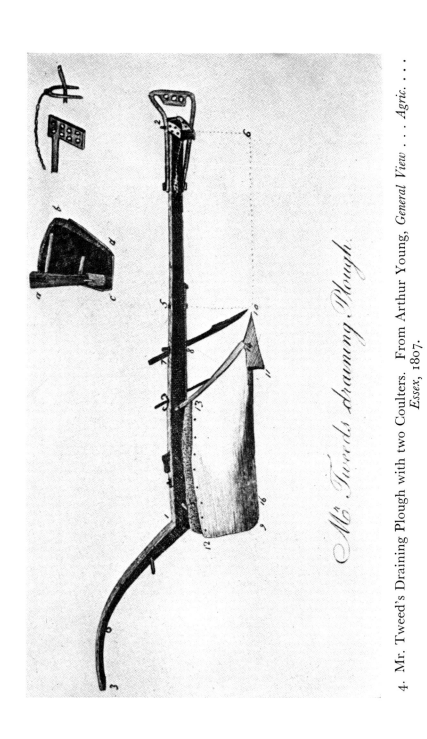

Mr. Tweed's draining Plough.

4. Mr. Tweed's Draining Plough with two Coulters. From Arthur Young, *General View ... Agric. ... Essex,* 1807.

5. Mr. Vaisey's Mole Plough. From Arthur Young, *General View . . . Agric. . . . Essex*, 1807.

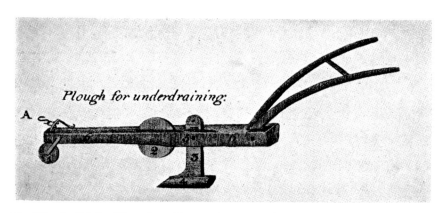

Plough for underdraining.

6. Watt's Mole Plough. From *Letters and Communications to the Bath and West Soc.*, 1799, ix., p. 110.

7. Fowler's Mole Plough with Pipes. *Jour. R.A.S.E.*, 1851, p. 640.

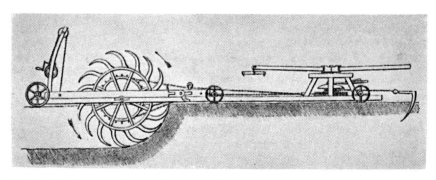

8. Paul's Rotary Drain Cutter. From J. C. Morton, *Cyclopaedia of Agriculture, c.* 1856.

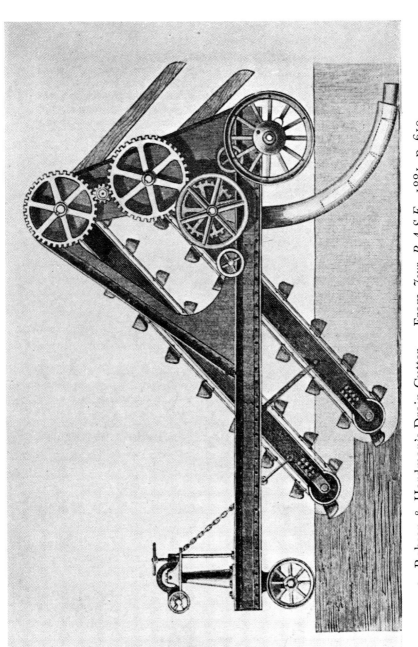

9. Robson & Hardman's Drain Cutter.   From *Jour. R.A.S.E.*, 1881, p. 619.

Ploughing

10. Ploughing with one Horse and two Oxen. From an early nineteenth-century engraving in the author's collection.

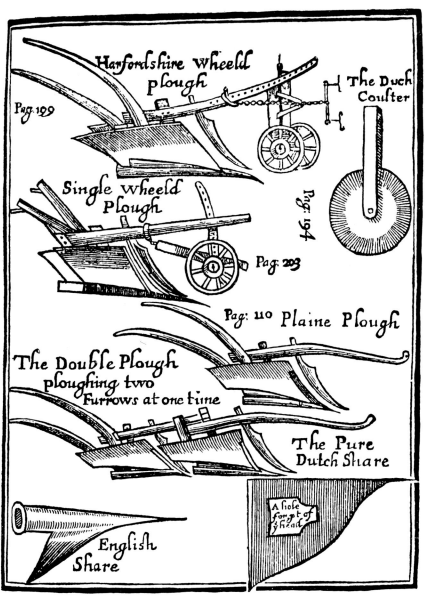

11. Seventeenth-century Ploughs. From Walter Blith, *English Improver Improved*, 3rd. ed., 1653.

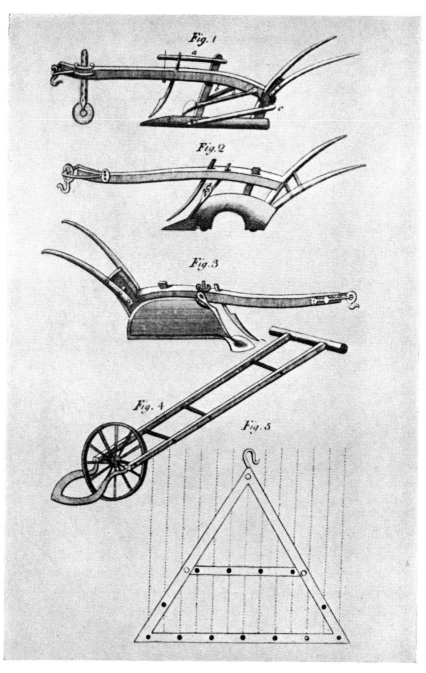

12. Kentish Turnwrist, Improved Sowing and Ridging Ploughs. From *Complete English Farmer*, 1771.

13. Small's Chain Plough. From J. Allen Ransome, *Implements of Agriculture*, 1843.

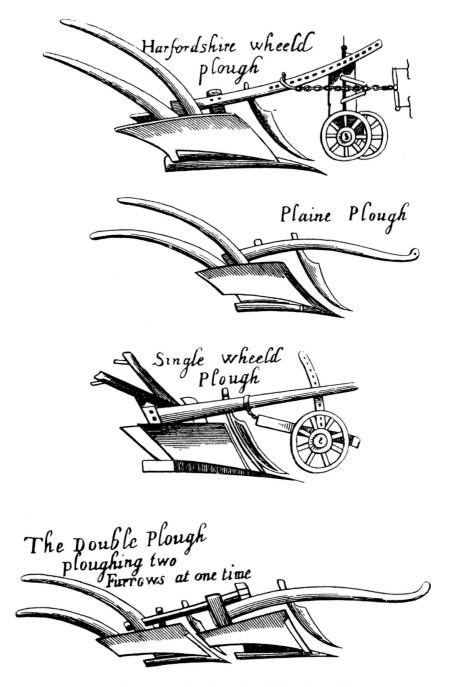

14. Lord Somerville's reproduction of Blith's plate (No. 11 above) showing how little changed the common ploughs were after 150 years. From Somerville, *Facts and Observations Relative to Sheep, Wool, &c.*, 1809.

15. Brand's Plough. From J. Allen Ransome, *Implements of Agriculture*, 1843.

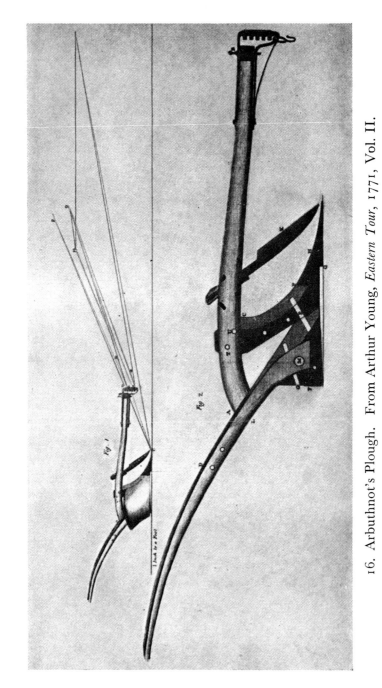

16. Arbuthnot's Plough. From Arthur Young, *Eastern Tour*, 1771, Vol. II.

three parts by circular pieces of iron that projected beyond the roll and cut the turf. The coulters followed in the same track, and completed this part of the work. The beams shown are of massive timber; it is little wonder that it would not do in heavy clay.

Dossie reported that after the premium had been awarded, more than twenty Knowles' ploughs were made by one person in London[31] but they still would not do. Although Arthur Young was favourably impressed by them,[32] they did not afford all the advantages over hand labour that had been so glibly claimed for them. Young thought that they performed better in the tests than in actual work.[33] At the same time Mr. Ducket (of whom more anon) was awarded £50 for a trenching plough and a three-furrow plough.

Another invention of this type that gained a measure of approbation was Grey's draining plough. This was fitted with a centre coulter and two land wheels which ran on either side of the drain and regulated the depth of the cut. Lawson thought much more of this plough than he did of Clarke's, but probably it might just as well have been included with the latter, in his category of "appliances that have been invented, but not found generally useful."[34]

All the time that these experiments in the use of heavy draining ploughs were being made, drains were being dug by hand, as Young constantly reported; but every attempt was made to lighten the labour of digging by the invention of special tools, like those that Walter Blith had depicted a century or more before. Spades of different widths were used, with narrower blades as the trench was made deeper. In addition there was the special spade, which, judging from the illustration, was pushed before the worker like a breast plough. It was rounded and had two horn-like projections at the sides. These were sharp, and were intended to cut off the turf like the wing or "mouldboard" of a breast plough. This horned spade was used at Gorton near Manchester in 1764[35] in just the same form as it is shown in Blith's plate. It is also mentioned by the Society of Gentlemen, authors of *The Complete Farmer*. Great proficiency was gained by the workers in the use of these draining spades, and in the nineteenth century it was remarked that a drain four feet deep with absolutely smooth sides could be made by some of them, but the horned spade had quite disappeared by then.

Towards the end of the eighteenth century, and throughout the nineteenth, drains were opened by this method for setting in tiles. The use of tiles had developed from the suggestions thrown out by Switzer; they were the logical result of the attempt to find an improved method, superior to the brush and stone filled drains that had been known for so long, and which continued to be used concurrently with the newer methods.

Earthenware pipes were known in the seventeenth century, and were used for conveying water supplies, notably the New River water from Islington to London, and from the well at Shrewsbury through that city.[36] These pipes were advertised in the *Weekly Miscellany for the Improvement of Husbandry*, August 22, 1727, but it does not seem to have occurred to anyone that they might be used for draining land. Indeed, a direct caveat was entered against them by a correspondent in the same issue of the *Weekly Miscellany*, when Mr. Edwards, an inventor, whose pipes were to be sold by Aaron Mutchell, potter at Vauxhall, suggested using them for this purpose.

It was only at the end of the eighteenth century that tile draining began to find favour. Semi-circular bricks, which might rest on the earth, or upon flat tiles, were then introduced, and were sometimes placed edge to edge to form a circular pipe. A somewhat similar brick arch, made like a ridge tile, was used in Shropshire, but anything of a shape that could be used in building was hampered by the excise of 2s. 6d. a thousand levied on common bricks. Plug draining was still practised at the end of the eighteenth century in Lancashire mosses, but was thought to be "better calculated for the purpose of an aqueduct, or conveyance for the water, than for drying the soil." Such is the obliquity of men's vision that the same thing was felt to be true of the "pipes of clay, about eighteen inches long, with an opening of three or four inches diameter," that were used in Essex and other counties before the end of the eighteenth century. This was some fifty years before Josiah Parkes produced his one-inch diameter tubular tile that so astonished Lord Spencer and his friends.[37] The pipe tile cannot, however, have been very widely used at this time because Joseph Elkington's system of tapping springs, which had been awarded £1,000 by the Board of Agriculture,[38] was all the rage. No more mechanical an object than a crowbar was required for his method.

A large variety of specially shaped bricks was, however, designed and produced which singly or together would form variously shaped pipe drains.[39] These were bound to give place to the tubular pipe which was finally recognized as cheaper and most effective, although the Royal Agricultural Society awarded Silver Medals for oval, horseshoe and angular tiles so late as 1843.[40] The horseshoe shape had been used in Oxford and found not to answer in 1855, while in the same year the happily placed Blackmore Vale in Dorset was reported to be making tiles of its own clay to drain its clay lands.

Before the Union in 1707, farming in Scotland had been very backward, but all through the eighteenth century Scottish landowners and farmers had been changing their methods to those of the more advanced systems followed by their peers in South Britain; and by the end of the eighteenth century the farming of the Border and the Lothians in particular, had absorbed the new methods. In some respects, indeed, it had improved upon them. In the first decade of the nineteenth century it was recognized as the best farming in Great Britain.

One result of the general interest in these improvements was that an enterprising and inventive Scotsman rediscovered and became the protagonist of hollow draining, assisted by his new subsoil plough. He called it "thorough" draining. Like many another who has introduced valuable innovations, perhaps only by the recognition and improvement of long-established processes, he was really an amateur of farming. James Smith of Deanston was as absorbed in agriculture as only an enthusiastic amateur can be. When he took over Deanston Farm of one hundred and eighty-nine acres, he reintroduced and perfected the parallel drain system of Palladius. The farm was quite unpromising— a thin soil, studded with boulders, over a strong subsoil, wet and flourishing with aquatic plants except where it was dry enough to grow heath, fern and broom.

His drainage system was complex but effective. The main drains were four feet deep, the receiving drains three feet deep and the parallel field drains two feet six inches at distances varying between sixteen and twenty-one feet apart. They were dug in the shape of a V and piled up to eighteen inches from the surface with broken boulder stones collected on the farm itself. Deep ploughing followed, but was found unsuccessful because it mixed the subsoil with the surface soil. So Smith invented his subsoil plough which broke up the subsoil without bringing it to the surface. At the same time the whole of each field was laid flat, and an ingenious system of supplying the water from the drains for livestock was installed. In Lord Ernle's picturesque phrase, "By his system of drainage and deep ploughing, he converted a rush-grown marsh into a garden."[41]

Naturally enough, Smith's neighbours, observing the success of his system, imitated him and got the same results. One of them, Mr. A. Forbes, in telling the story of the drainage of his farm at Rettie, Banff, said that stone drains were first made about the year 1825, and followed by muggs or tiles of half-moon shape, which were used in tracks about two feet deep and put on pieces of wood where the bottom of the trench was soft. The consequent improvement was so great that a large part of the farm was drained in this way, but the drains proved too shallow and the pipes too small, being only one to two inches in diameter. Some twenty years before Forbes had become tenant of the farm and had drained it systematically on the herringbone pattern of drains with protected outlets. As a result a field formerly covered with rushes had become one of the best growing fields on the farm.[42]

This indicates that hollow draining was not unknown in Scotland before Smith of Deanston became its hearty propagandist, but Smith was certainly the man who secured widespread publicity for it. He rendered the system much more effective by his invention of the subsoil plough which broke up the retentive hard pan without bringing the dead earth to the surface. In 1831 the pressure of his growing fame made it necessary for him to describe his method in writing, and he then published his first pamphlet, *Remarks on Thorough Draining and Deep Ploughing*.

By 1836 the farming depression that had lasted ever since the victory at Waterloo was beginning to lift, but it was still serious, and the complaints were so loud that the Government of the day appointed yet another Select Committee on Agricultural Distress. Smith was called upon to give evidence. The only means of increasing yields and output that he could recommend was his system of drainage. C. Shaw Lefevre, M.P., was greatly impressed and spread further Smith's fame, reporting that his system "was the only one likely to promote the general improvement of agriculture and to aid the farmers in overcoming their difficulties." This was an exaggerated claim, but the subject was becoming of increasing importance, especially to the owners and tenants of heavy wet lands. When the first volume of the *Journal of the*

Royal Agricultural Society of England was published in 1840, field drainage was dealt with in three contributions and repeatedly in the succeeding volumes.[43]

Just before Smith's pamphlet appeared in 1831 Josiah Parkes (1793–1871) returned from France and began his career as an agricultural engineer. He was interested in drainage, particularly in the reclamation of bogs. In 1833 he was working on the drainage of Chat Moss, Lancashire. Here his work led him to the conclusion that deep drainage was more successful than the rather shallow system of field drains employed by Smith and his disciples. He advocated the four-feet drain and the five-feet drain.

These two partisans and their disciples proceeded to engage in a lengthy controversy that lasted for some decades of the nineteenth century. The matter for a pretty argument in a pre-scientific farming age was readily assembled by either party. There was no patent in Smith's subsoil plough. At the first show of the English (later the Royal) Agricultural Society at Oxford in 1839, Sir Edward Strachey of Rackheath Hall, Norwich, exhibited a competing type,[44] and others were reported as time went on. Useful as these ploughs were for their proper purpose, the popularity of the pipe drain was not yet established.

Several tile-making machines had been invented by 1843 when the Tweeddale Patent Tile and Brick Company, London, was awarded a silver medal for a hand tile-making machine invented by the Marquis of Tweeddale. Another medal was awarded to F. W. Etheridge, of the Woodlands, near Southampton, for his patent machine, but neither of these were tubular pipes. Ransome's of Ipswich won a silver medal for a Beart's brick machine improved by A. Stickney of Ridgemount, Holderness. John Read, 35, Regents Circus, Piccadilly, also received a medal for his cylindrical or pipe tiles.

Parkes in 1843 thought that pipes had nowhere been used for more than thirty-five years. John Read, however, made them when employed as a farm servant to the Rev. Dr. Marriott of Horsmonden in Kent, at the end of the eighteenth century. Read's pipes were about three inches in diameter and were made by bending a sheet of clay over a wooden cylindric mandril. The narrow slit left by this imperfect method along the length of the tile was then thought necessary to admit the water. Philip Pusey, secretary to the Royal Agricultural Society, and a contemporary of Parkes, puts the time of origin at 1795, when Mr. Reid (presumably the same man) was pipe draining in Sussex. Reid also invented a subsoil plough. By 1843, ten tileries for making his type of pipe had been set up by the farmers of Kent; but "the preparation of a perfect cylindric tile, as now [1843] made by machine, seems to have originated in Essex, whence it travelled into Suffolk and Sussex, in both which counties" it had taken root.[45]

Now that pipes were accepted, a further controversy about the proper size to use and the distance apart of the drains was bound to arise. Parkes, who had become consulting engineer to the Royal Agricultural Society, wrote an elaborate disquisition in 1845 to prove his claim that the one-inch diameter pipe was all sufficient. He made equally elaborate calculations about the area drained by drains at different depths, but, of course, the trenches had still to be dug out by manual toil. There were already at this time several machines for making tubular pipes. The Beart and the Hatcher were two of them.[46] Beart's, one made by Clayton and one invented by Thomas Scragg of Calveley, Cheshire, were three of the fourteen types exhibited at the Shrewsbury meeting of 1845 to compete for the Society's premium of that year. The award finally went to Thomas Scragg, mainly because his machine was "locomotive," or as we should say, mobile.

The subject had now become of the greatest importance. Landowners and tenants, stimulated by frequent articles on drainage which appeared in the Royal Agricultural Society's *Journal* and every other farming periodical of the day, were only too anxious to drain their land. The gradually improving position of farming helped to encourage innovations that might lead to high yields.

Philip Pusey was active in everything concerned with the development of farming, and in 1840 secured an Act "to enable the owners of settled estates to defray the expenses of drainage by way of mortgage." In 1843 the Yorkshire Land Drainage Company was formed with influential backing, but, owing to legal difficulties, it failed. These were finally overcome by the provision of Government money to the amount of £2,000,000 under the Public Money Drainage Act (9 and 10 Vic. cap. CI). A second loan of the same amount was made available by 13 and 14 Vic. cap. XXXI. None of the whole four million remained unapplied for by the end of 1854, though not quite all of it had been taken up by 1867. This scheme was supplemented by the Private Money Drainage Act, 1849, but as this was not very popular, companies for land drainage were established by private act.[47]

A very great deal of land drainage was done with the help of these loans and the new pipes, but it is to be feared that a large proportion of the work was unsuitably done. A writer in the 1856 volume of the Royal Agricultural Society's *Journal* wondered "at the tenacity with which drainers hold to their favourite systems of deep and shallow draining, as if either system would serve as a fixed rule." And in 1869 Evershed remarked that much of the draining done under Government inspection had not been well carried out. "The principle of a uniform depth of 4 ft. when the fall admits is a bad one." He went on to say that "sometimes the surface stratum passes into an impenetrable subsoil at between 20 and 30 inches. The mole plough is then as effective as pipes and very much cheaper."[48]

The mole plough was not, of course, a new thing in 1869, but this faint praise was a sign that it was coming into its own. Its adoption had perhaps been hindered by so much attention being paid to the perfecting of pipes, so that in 1826 it was only considered to be advantageous in pleasure grounds, particularly those with a favourable slope. If a good team were to hand, it could be used to drain wet turnip lands.[49]

Patents for mole ploughs had been taken out by Harry Watts and Richard Lumbert in 1797 and 1800,[50] and in 1843 it was said that the mole ploughs drawn by twenty horses or by a windlass had been "practised" for one hundred and fifty years in Essex. Pusey was then told by another informant that it had been practised in that county "time out of mind."[51] This was a large claim and cannot, I think, be substantiated, though there is some reason to believe that the mole plough originated in Essex, a county where field drainage had always been necessary and where the farmers had become as expert in this job as any in the whole country.

Essex farmers used all the known methods of draining land in the early years of the nineteenth century. They had certainly used hollow drains filled with straw, brush or stone for a very long time, and the great draining plough was used by Mr. Bridge of Buttsbury. This was along the lines of Clarke's draining plough. Mr. Tweed of Sandon had built a heavy plough that "cut from 10 to 12 inches deep with four to six horses; then dug 15 more at one spit and laid in a rope of twisted straw." Mr. Knight of Thaxted had made some improvements to a mole plough invented some years before (could this have been Harry Watts's?), but it is not clear exactly in what these improvements consisted. It was hauled by fifteen horses, three abreast and conducted by six or eight men and boys, one man holding the handles, one sitting on the seat over the beam, to preserve a uniform pressure, and three going on each side to guide the horses and keep them tight and close to their work. I think the "improvement" must have been putting a wheel at the front of the beam, because Mr. Pattison of Maldon then (1807) had one of the old mole ploughs without wheels which must have been much like the subsoil plough later made by James Smith of Deanston. Knight's mole plough was widely used in the county at that time. Mr. John Vaisey of Halstead had added a gallows with two wheels and this was found very effective.

Another implement was the cast-iron draining wheel which was four feet in diameter and weighed about four hundredweight. It had a cutting edge half an inch thick and increased in thickness toward the nave or centre. It was said to scour out or cut a drain half an inch wide at the bottom and four inches wide at the top at fifteen inches deep. The wheel was placed in a frame and weighted at pleasure. What it really made was a wheel track which could be filled with straw or anything else handy.[52]

Lumbert was not an Essex man, but an inhabitant of Rissington Wick in Gloucestershire. He introduced a manual labour capstan which allowed eight men to do the work of twelve horses in hauling the mole plough. A more ingenious inventor, Rogers of Withington, Gloucestershire, had adapted the capstan to work with one horse in place of the eight men.[53] In 1811 it was used with success on pasture in Cambridgeshire, and was there drawn by twelve or fourteen horses with six men to attend them. There is a contemporary illustration, 1799, of a mole plough said to be "similar to Mr. Watt's patent one." It drained fifteen inches deep and may have been lighter than the then usual design.[54] Another mole plough had been used successfully at about this date at Bradfield Hall, Suffolk;[55] this was drawn by twelve horses. In 1804 one was drawn "by the force of women," and three hundred acres in Suffolk were drained in this way by the Rev. J. Thurlow, the furrows first being cut by a large heavy foot plough, and the moles being put in at the depth of eighteen inches.

Perhaps the mole plough's failure to gain immediate recognition was the preoccupation of the drainers with pipes. Josiah Parkes was encouraged to believe that the heavy labour of digging trenches for the pipes by hand would be superseded on clay soils by the use of the draining plough. This pious hope was the result of the exhibition of Fowler's draining plough at the Royal Show in 1851. This was a mole plough on a somewhat cumbersome frame; a lengthy string of pipes threaded on a wire rope was attached so as to follow the mole into the ground and make the drain permanent. It was hauled by a capstan worked by two horses. "But for the American reapers,"[56] Parkes reported, "Mr. Fowler's draining plough would have been the most remarkable feature of the exhibition. Wonderful to see two horses at work by the side of a field, on a capstan which, by an invisible wire rope, draws toward itself a low framework, leaving but the trace of a narrow slit in the surface. If you pass, however, to the other side of the field, which the framework has quitted, you perceive it has been dragging after it a string of pipes, which, still following the plough's snout, that burrows all the while four feet underground, twists itself like a gigantic red worm into the earth, so that in a few minutes . . . the string is withdrawn from the necklace, and you are assured that a drain has thus been invisibly formed under your feet." This apparatus had been exhibited at the Exeter Show in the previous year when the teeth of the capstan had broken in the trials. The pipes used were wooden ones made by the inventor's pipe-making machine,[57] while the apparatus itself was made by Ransome and May for the inventor, Fowler, who lived at Melksham, Wilts. By 1851 it had been used successfully not only on Fowler's own farm, but on two or three of his neighbour's holdings, at Brentwood, Essex, and Wormwood Scrubs, and by a Mr. Harris of Darlington.

At the Lincoln Show of 1854 a portable engine was used to drive the windlass of Fowler's mole drain and pipe-laying plough, and this apparatus was awarded a silver medal by the Society.[58] It was, apparently, taken over by A. and W. Eddington of Chelmsford, who exhibited it at the Warwick "Royal" of 1859. The Judge's Report states that this was "with very slight alteration, the same implement which effected such surprising work at the Lincoln meeting" (when a competing design submitted by one Dray failed to work) "and the real pioneer of steam cultivation as now achieved. It works more efficiently, not only in depositing a series of pipes by means of its singularly strong rope, but effects a stirring of the soil for several feet on each side of the machine as it passes along, thus opening up crevices for the percolation of the water to the drains." It was awarded a prize of £15.[59]

A clever attempt to abolish the heavy manual work of digging the drains was made by Mr. Paul of Thorpe Abbots, near Scole, Norfolk, who invented a machine for this purpose in the 1850s. It was a wheel slotted into a frame and carrying radial tines at the circumference slightly curved towards the line of advance. It was drawn by a chain and capstan and cut out the soil rather in the manner of a modern rotary cultivator, laying the soil removed at either side of the trench. A lifting apparatus behind the wheel allowed it to be raised or lowered "according to the unevenness of the surface, in order to ensure a perfectly even 'fall' in the bottom of the drain."[60]

Yet another drain plough for horse traction had been invented, according to Morton, by Mr. M'Ewan, a tenant farmer of the Carse of Stirling. This had a flat cutting edge at right angles to the beam, and a mouldboard in the same plane rising behind it, forming a shovel-shaped share, and the edge of the drain was split off by coulters at either side. This was apparently of earlier date, having been "invented" in the beginning of the nineteenth century, and improved upon by Alexander of Taylorston, Stirlingshire, in 1840. Heathcote of Tiverton, Devon, patented plans for hauling such ploughs by steam power in 1832, and actually put the system into practice at Chat Moss, but this was really for land reclamation on a bigger scale than field drainage and will be referred to again later.[61]

I do not know whether Paul's digger was anything like the steam digger said to have been exhibited in 1842, "the invention of a lady,"[62] because the report on the implements shown at Liverpool in that year does not mention it. Whatever it was, it was the precursor of a method of cutting drains that many inventors tried to make practical and economic, both in Great Britain and America, "without," as Dan Pidgeon wrote in 1892, "much visible approach to success." Amongst these was Eddington's machine patented in 1865. It opened the drain, laid pipes and filled in the trench again. A rather similar machine was exhibited by Robson and Hardman at the "Royal" show at Derby in 1881. It looked rather like a dredger on dry land, excavating by an endless chain of buckets, of which there were two sets, the second following and cutting deeper than the first. It was hauled by an ordinary steam ploughing engine. The body of the machine contained the drainpipes which descended through a curved "pipe" conductor into the trench formed by the buckets, where they were left lying in position as the machine advanced. The dug soil was elevated, just as in a dredger, and discharged into shoots, whence it fell back into the trench from which it had originally been removed, covering the drainpipes that had meanwhile been laid in it. This machine was regarded as showing promise by the reporter on the implements, but it was not in a good enough state to admit of a trial, a matter of regret because nothing could have then been of more value "to suffering agriculture" than a really efficient labour- and money-saving drainage tool.[63] A decade later it had "so far, rendered little practical service to agriculture." Its maker was the last of the aspirants for the Gold Medal of the Royal Agricultural Society for a really good draining implement until 1892.[64]

These very heavy types of drainage machinery were, like steam ploughing and steam threshing, very largely contractor's jobs, the capital expenditure being far too much for the average farmer. Perhaps there were farmers of very large areas who bought them, but it is doubtful if any of them were ever widely used. The mole plough for horse and steam traction continued to be manufactured, but the continued depression of farming from the mid-1870s until the middle of the 1890s did not encourage capital expenditure on such elaborate pieces of apparatus. Messrs. Fowler's output of their pipe-laying machine was abandoned very soon, though they continued to make their mole plough for steam haulage. Even in the 1880s, R. Scott Burn, a famous and accepted writer of farming textbooks, did not give any details of any other method of making drains than filling them with stones or using pipes. He went into the controversy about deep and shallow drains in a large way.[65] The ninth edition of another standard textbook, Fream's *Elements of Agriculture*, 1914, deals fully with ditches, and speaks almost as an afterthought of the gripping plough, sometimes used for cutting shallow water-courses, and of the mole plough for horse draught.[66] So late as 1919 C. H. J. Clayton only mentions ditches, tile drains and underdrains.[67]

Great efforts had been made to simplify and ease the labour, and to reduce the cost, of land drainage, but they had not come to very much. The hand tools first depicted by Walter Blith in the seventeenth century were probably of greater antiquity than this. The design of the heavy plough with two or more parallel coulters in the mid-eighteenth century enabled shallow trenches to be cut by horse draught, and these were used until the middle of the nineteenth century, if no later. The mole plough was first made towards the end of the eighteenth century and its modern design is substantially what it was then. At about the same time pipes for land drainage were apparently first made by Mr. Read, and machinery for their production was developed in the 1840s. With the adaptation of steam power to field haulage the two systems of mole plough and pipe laying were elaborately conjoined, and other ingenuities for digging trenches and laying pipes of even greater complexity were produced. But most of these things had fallen out of whatever use they may have enjoyed, a good while before the outbreak of the First World War, though some of the principles employed have been used in more modern drainage machinery. Drainage is always costly whatever means are employed to do it, and I fear that the poor times that hampered farming at the end of the nineteenth century discouraged a great many farmers and landowners from doing all the drainage that was necessary, if they did any at all.

CHAPTER TWO

PREPARING THE SEED BED
(a) Animal Hauled Implements

"PROGRESS," AS WE know it, has been termed "an episode in the history of hunger."[1] To many people's surprise, Western Europe has been forced back to the realization that food production is the basic employment of civilized man. It was obvious to our ancestors before 1800, although farming and civilization had gone a long way from the times when small groups of men worked the land with the digging stick. By the time Fitzherbert's book was published, 1523, the plough drawn by animal traction had been known in Europe for some two thousand years, and had been developed into localized types that suited the particular soils and needs of fairly limited neighbourhoods. Yet one type, and that an ancient one, continued to be used until 1850,[2] and possibly might have been found even later in remote districts. It is the type figured in Strutt's *Saxon Rarities of the Eighth Century* as a Saxon wheel plough, and not unlike the Norman wheel plough shown in his *Complete View of the Manners of England*. It was "a simple wedge hauled by means of a beam or pole fastened to its heel."[2]

The development of this big plough took place in that part of Europe north of the Alps, and was a result of the demands of the soil and methods of work there. Its origin is uncertain,[3] and it has been generally accepted that the normal team used was eight oxen. This cumbersome implement had to be forced through the soil; but, in fact, the teams ranged from one to six yoke (twelve beasts) in particularly difficult land, the usual number being two yoke. The formal team of eight oxen was not normally used even in the Middle Ages, the common number being four.[4] Horses were then beginning to be used for traction, and in the twelfth century a mixed team of one yoke of oxen and a horse in front of them was recommended.[5] At Bocking in Essex, an acre a day could be ploughed if four oxen and two horses were used.[6] Such mixed teams were still to be found in the late eighteenth or early nineteenth century.

Later this plough was better known as the Hertfordshire wheel plough which became general in the Midlands. It continued to be used there, possibly with slight and local improvements in detail, because, as Passmore argues, it represented "the highest achievement in plough design which was possible along the old orthodox lines."

The earliest specific description of this plough by its local name is found in Walter Blith's *English Improver Improved*, where it is called the wheel plough. ". . . and is of most constant use in *Hertfordshire* and many up-Countries [for heavy stiff soils] and very necessary for all great Corn-masters to have one of them for strength, so that he may not force his other plows which are made on purpose for other lands in a Tillable condition." It was usually drawn by horses or oxen "geared double two a breast," although Blith thought a single line of animals would be better on wet land. It was a very heavy and cumbersome implement, and a century and a half later the share alone was known to have weighed as much as seventy or eighty pound.[7] It required at least four horses to draw it. The development of this plough was very slight, and in 1809 Lord Somerville was able to reproduce Blith's illustration of ploughs and remark, "how little originality of invention or improvement has been manifested in the greater part of the swing and wheel ploughs constructed within the last hundred and fifty years."[8]

He was rather less than right, of course, as all the makers of generalizations are. Of the many kinds of plough that had been in use for at least three hundred years, some had been greatly improved, and some had been well suited to their job all the time.

Fitzherbert, with the authority of a wide experience of his subject, could then say that various types of ploughs designed to suit different soils were already in use. "In Somersetshire, about Zalcester, the shar beame . . . is foure or fyve foote longe, and it is brode and thynne . . . In Kent . . . somme goo with whels, as they do in many other places and some wyll tourne the sheld bredith at every landes ende, and plowe all one way. In Buckynghamshyre are plowes made of another maner . . . generally good and likely to serve in many places . . . In Leycestershire, Lankeshyre, Yorkshyre, Lincoln, Norfolke, Cambridgeshyre, and many other countreyes, the plows be of divers makinges . . . But howsoever they be made yf they be well tempered, and goo well, they maye be the better suffered."[9] The whole of this passage was reprinted, and much more of the book, by Joseph Blagrave, and presented as a contemporary farming textbook some one hundred and fifty years later.[10]

One of these many ploughs was a light two-wheel type that was capable of being hauled by two horses and controlled by one man without the help of a lad to lead the animals. It is first specifically mentioned by Barnaby Googe, a gentleman of Lincolnshire, who reports that it was used in Gelderland and about Coleyne (Cologne) and "the like with us in Norfolk and Lincolnshire."[11] But this plough, like other types, was confined to a strictly limited area, and was noticed with surprise by a tourist in the reign of Charles II.[12] It was again discovered by Arthur Young a century later; he never tired of recommending it for use in all soils and on all contours, in and out of season, and often without any great reason.

All seed bed preparation is a matter of soil comminution. When Henry VIII was king, it was a simple matter of breaking up the soil as much as possible by ploughing the fallow or the ley three, or at most four, times in the year before the crop was sown. The first ploughing was done in the autumn, the twi-fallow or second ploughing in the spring, and the thry-fallow or third ploughing in the late summer before the winter crop was sown. Peradventure a fourth ploughing might be done if the summer ploughing had been a little on the early side, or if the harvest was late.[13] In some places the clods left behind the plough were smashed with a clodding or clotting beetle, an implement that was little more than a heavy maul. Fitzherbert mentions harrows made with a wooden frame through which iron tines were set, a large one used for a first harrowing and a smaller for a second.

In the neighbourhood of Ripon (and probably elsewhere) a wood-tined harrow was used because of the stony ground, the tines being made of ash. It was not advisable to use oxen for harrowing because of the uneven motion.[14]

Fitzherbert names the parts of the plough and describes them, but Gervase Markham goes one better by providing drawings of the "several parts and members of an ordinarie plough and the ioyning of them together" in order to instruct every husbandman how a well-shaped plough was made. The parts he names are the plough-beam, the skeath, the principal hale, the plough head, the shelboard, the coulter, the share and the foot.

In general Markham advises that the plough should be made sloping towards the earth so that it tends to dig deep; then the plough-man could adjust it by bearing on the hales. If made in any other way, he could not keep it in the ground, and must carry an "akerstaffe," a pole shod with iron, with which to clear the plough if it choked.

This foot plough was evidently Markham's idea of a normal plough, but for ploughing white sand the small plough could be used. I think he means a plough with only one handle and only five feet long, but provided with a little pair of round wheels. As for red sand the irons must be steeled or hardened, and the plough head reinforced by an iron strip covering it. The shelboard, too, should be protected by iron clouts nailed to it. The plough with one hale was used for grey or white clay, the share having a rising wing to protect the shelboard from the stones, and a coulter very curved, "like a bent bow." Markham mentions a great roller for barley, used for breaking up the clods, as well as wooden harrows for peas and beans, and an iron-tined harrow with ten tines in each of the four sides of the wooden framework. This harrow was drawn diagonally, being hitched at one corner.[15]

The early Stuart blacksmiths, doubtless guided by the local demand, made both ploughshare and coulter of different shapes to meet the exigencies of soil variations through the countryside. For stiff clay the coulter was made long, strong and straight; for mixed soil and sand it was long, thin and bending directly in front of the share, which in some parts was very broad with a large wing, in others narrow with a small wing, while in yet others it was round and long like a spindle. Some set the point of the share before the point of the coulter; others set it with the point behind the point of the coulter, the set of the latter being controlled by wooden wedges adjusted where it was fixed in the beam.[16]

This was a statement of things as they were, and Markham did not theorize or express any wish for theory. A few years later, Samuel Hartlib, who was one of the intellectuals of his day, was emphatic on the necessity for some study of the mechanics of the plough. "I wonder," he wrote, "that so many excellent *Mechanicks* who have beaten their brains about the perpetual motion and other curiosities, that they might find the best way to ease all Motions, should never so much as honour the *Plough* (which is the most necessary Instrument in the world) by their labour and studies. I suppose all know, that it would be an extraordinary benefit to this *Country*, if that 1 or 2 horses could plough and draw as much as 4 or 6 and further also that there is no small difference in *ploughs* and *waggons*, when there is scarce any sure rule for making them; and every *Country*, yea, almost every County, differs not only in the Ploughs, but even in every part. Some with wheels, some without; some turning the Rest (as they call it) as in Kent, Picardy and Normandy, others not; some having Coulters of one fashion, others of another; others as the *Dutch*, having an Iron wheel or circle for that purpose; some having their Shears broad at the point; some not; some being round as in Kent, others flat . . . some plough with 2 horses onely, as in Norfolk, and beyond seas . . . and one onely to hold and to drive, but in Kent I have seen 4, 6, yea even 12 horses and oxen; which variety showeth, that the Husband-man, who is ordinarrily ignorant in Mechanicks, is even at his wits end in this Instrument, which he must necessarily use continually. Surely he would deserve well of this *Nation* and be much honoured by all, that would set down exact rules for the making of this most necessary but contemned *Instrument*, and so for every part thereof; for without question there are exact Rules to be laid down for this, as for Shipping and for other things."[17]

Hartlib's complaint that there was too great a variety of ploughs in use, is one that has been made again in the twentieth century, and is as true now as it was in his day, despite the change in production from village smith and carpenter to the large factory of modern times. His plea for the scientific study of the plough, so that it might be made to conform with the principles underlying its use, is one that has been recurrent for two centuries at least. Capt. Thomas Williamson complained in 1810 that the mathematical principles of plough design remained unknown, "in fact, we still remain in doubt as to the precise form even of the mouldboard."[18] But by that time the subject had been widely discussed, although no conclusion had been reached. Hartlib's foresight here is characteristic, but some of his ideas were fantastic. He learned somewhere that the Chinese had experimented with carriages propelled by sails, and that thirty people had been carried sixty miles in four hours in something of this kind in Holland. He therefore suggests that a plough propelled by sails might be designed! What did come from Holland was the iron wheel or circle used as a coulter, which was later to play a large part in the development of plough design.

Besides these things, Hartlib mentions a double-furrow plough, but it is not clear whether he had seen it in use or not. Another novelty of the day was a one-horse plough made by Col. Blount at Greenwich. It may have stimulated Hartlib to press for the study of the theory of the plough. Blount was evidently an inventor of some ingenuity. His plough "that with one horse and a boy, will perform as much in a day, as his neighbours, only with the partition of a hedge between them, upon the same sort of ground, can dispatch with four or five horses and two men besides." But, of course, his neighbours would not use his plough. Farmers' stubborn opposition to novelties is a complaint which permeates the literature produced by those who had novelties to offer. This complaint was heartily subscribed to in the next century by no less famous and sympathetic a man than Arthur Young.

Blount's was the one-wheel plough described by Blith in some detail. He had apparently devised a three-wheel cart as well as his one-horse plough, and a chariot in which he travelled eighty miles in two days with one horse, but no description of these two articles is supplied by the enthusiastic Hartlib who records them.[19]

The theory of the plough that Hartlib wished for was attempted by Walter Blith.[20] He did not subscribe to the current belief that a heavy soil made a heavy plough with a long share beam necessary, nor that it was necessary to have it wide at the heel, turning a wide furrow. This was the design that contented the farmers of his time. It was a clumsy implement of heavy draught, but despite its defects in the eyes of a modern critic, it was "the highest achievement possible along the old orthodox lines,"[21] and was widely used.

Blith laid down four general propositions as elementary to good plough design. "First, that whatever moveth upon the Land, or that worketh in the Land, and carrieth the least earth or weight upon it, must needs move or work easiest. A wheel the lesser ground it stands upon, the easier it turns, and the lesser the wheel the easier still; so the Plough, the more earth or weight it carries with it, the more strength must be required. The naturall furrow it must carry, but the lesser compass both in height and length it bears upon the Plough, the easier the Plough must go.

"Secondly, the more naturally anything moves, the more easily, and the more Artificially, the more difficulty.

"Thirdly, the sharper and thinner is any tool, the easier it pierceth, and the less strength is required; so contrary, the thicker or duller any tool is the more strength must work it, and;

"Fourthly, that which is the plainest and truest to the Rules and admits of least multiplication of work, must needs be the easiest."

He provides a drawing of the ploughs then in use, and complains that most plough irons made by the blacksmith, and fitted to bodies made by the carpenter, are likely to be deficient because neither of these men was in the habit of using a plough themselves. The share, coulter, and "breast plate" all ought to be made according to the natural cast of the furrow, so that the earth does not stick on the plough and the irons wear bright and clean. If a wing or fin was fitted to the share it ought to be welded on, or at least made with a clean and tight join with "its true, whelming, hollow, cross-winding compass, just answering the turn or cast of the Furrow." This, in Blith's opinion, was reasonably well done in many parts of Hertfordshire, and in some parts of Northampton, Bedford, and elsewhere, although the wing was not broad enough.

He thought the best pattern was the one on the Bastard Dutch ploughs which covered all the nose of the breast board, as used in Holland and other parts of Lincoln, in Norfolk, Suffolk and Essex. But in point of fact this was made specially for soft, boggy land, and was difficult to make and maintain. This apparently was made so that it was in one piece with the plate of iron that covered the mould-board. Blith did not think it could be used in ordinary land, nor did he think that the breast plate and share need be made in one piece provided that no gap was left in which grass, roots or weeds would be caught and clog the plough. The shiner, as he calls it, "would do best to be continued all along the Breast-board one solid plate compassed and cross-winding from the middle; the over end foreward looking foreward one way towards the Land, and the other end backward towards the furrow." It should be as high as the earth worked upon the plough. In work it would brighten, and the earth would slip off easily, making the draught lighter.

He did not approve of the Dutch wheel coulter for use "on strong, gravelly, flinty, broomy, gorsey or rooty ground," but it would do very well on turf or pure mould. It should be an inch thick at the centre and thin down to a knife edge at the circumference.

It is not necessary to follow Blith in his detailed description of contemporary ploughs, for they are shown in the illustration. The beam of the Hertfordshire wheeled plough was six feet long and the wheels eighteen or twenty inches in diameter. The Kentish turnwrist plough is not shown, but a modern example, which cannot be very different from that used in the seventeenth century, is illustrated.

Most ploughs then in use had common faults that Blith greatly disliked. They were made too big and heavy in both the wood and iron parts; they were particularly thick in the breast which made it "carry a great furrow with it, yet it goes very sore." The otherwise excellent ploughs of Holland, Lincs, very often embodied this grave defect. Many plough handles were too short and did not give good control. Upright handles were bad and gave no control at all. The straight mouldboard was the most usual serious defect. Placing the rest even with the mouldboard was another. The rest should be good and broad, and six or seven inches shorter than the mouldboard. Dull irons, and either no clouting, or clouting so roughly as to cause more friction than plain wood, were other faults.

The Norfolk and Suffolk light plough with two wheels would, with two horses and one man, plough as much as two acres a day in sandy soil, and so much as three had occasionally been done, though this last was certainly unusual.

Blith claimed to have tried out all these ploughs, and come to the conclusion that "the shorter and lesser any plough is made, having its true pitch, with its true cast on the Shield-board and Short Wrest and sharp irons, the far easier" would it go. He provided a specification of the ideal plough, but I do not gather, as Passmore did,[22] that he actually invented such a plough. He then proceeds to the double-furrow plough, to a plough with a harrow behind it as used in Norfolk, and to a plough having a seed-drill or dropper behind it and a harrow behind that again. The last was only a suggestion, but Blith hoped with the help of "a Gentleman of Art," with whom he was acquainted, to make it and try it on his own lands. There is nothing to show that he was successful in this endeavour; indeed, Worlidge thought these combined instruments "of no great advantage to the Husbandman, only invented to satisfy the minds of some scrutinists," and so he did not bother to go into any detail about them.[23]

I have given his ideas at some length because he was the first man who, as he himself hoped, "in some good measure supplied that deficiency in Husbandry Mr *Hartlib's* Legacy chargeth us withall. . . ." This he had done, and, although he did not know it, he laid a foundation on which future plough theorists built and other writers plagiarized.

Invention was rife in the seventeenth century, but the inventors were so cautious that they provide little more than a name for the novelties, the great advantages of which they proclaim in their pamphlets. Amongst these was a manuring roller, the design of which remains a mystery. Its inventor says that "of all inventions for the easie and speedy manuring of all sorts of Ground, There is none better or more useful than the *Manuring Rowler*, being rightly and seasonably used; The best season for using thereof is the Autumn and Winter, when the ground is wet and not dry and hard frozen." It was filled with dung and drawn up and down the field until the supply of manure was exhausted, and the result was estimated to be three or four times better than that of manure spread upon the ground. Other pamphlets of the day referred to a "manuring plow" and a "manuring waggon" used in tilling and sowing.[24] The latter may have been a forerunner of the modern farmyard manure distributor, though that is admittedly pure surmise.

Another addition to the plough was made by a Mr. Fernyhough of Frodswell. This was "an Instrument of Iron . . . set through the *plow beam* behind the *Coulter*, and through the *plowhead*, steeled with an edge forward, of excellent use in plowing *new stock't grounds*, it cutting roots asunder as bigg as one's arm without prejudice to the *plough*; . . ." The specification is not very exact, but it sounds as if it may have been along the lines that later developed into the heavy grubbers and similar devices, e.g. the Uley cultivator of the nineteenth century. One Mr.

Ashman of Tamworth constructed for the same purpose a plough with two sharp iron wings made fast to the ploughshare and following the coulter, and this must have looked something like the nineteenth-century gripping plough.[25]

But aside from these ingenious and questionably practical devices, no one added anything to Blith's theory of a plough for a century after he died. Most writers of farming textbooks, or theoretical treatises (and some quite fantastic views were set forth), were content to use what may be called the standard classification of ploughs, remarking that many of the rather trivial variations to be found in restricted neighbourhoods were much more a matter of local idiosyncracy than of any practical application.

Edward Lisle found that imported Danish iron was being used in Leicestershire at the turn of the century for all plough tackle except the share and the coulter, because it was considered more durable and tougher than the brittle English iron.[26] Before Lisle, Worlidge had been content to repeat what earlier writers including Blith had said about ploughs.[27] John Mortimer,[28] Stephen Switzer,[29] John Lawrence,[30] and William Ellis[31] at different times in the first half of the eighteenth century also copied from their predecessors.

There were, of course, novelties to be seen here and there by the discerning eye and by the local patriot. Mortimer, like so many epicures of the countryside and rural life, bought an estate in Essex before he wrote his farming book. At Colchester he found a fine light wheel plough "that with two horses they Plough up two acres a day." This was the East Anglian plough that had been mentioned by Barnaby Googe more than a century before; possibly it was even older. Mortimer noticed something new—that it was "very peculiar for its Earth-board being made of Iron, by which means they make it rounding; which helps to turn the Earth or Turf, much better than any other sort of Plough." This suggests that some enterprising ploughwright had taken Blith's hint that an iron mouldboard could be more readily formed into the proper shape than the normal wooden one. This is the earliest reference to an iron mouldboard I have so far found. He shared the general opinion that the Sussex one-wheel plough was "of a very Clouterly sort."[32]

An enterprising cleric, the Rev. R. G. of Barking, near Walfleet, Essex, used what was probably the ordinary light two-wheel plough of East Anglia for making the first tilt, but he used a double mould-board plough with wheels for the second, and for the third tilt, a similar plough with the double mouldboards four feet long, or twice as long as those first used. This, he reckoned, was most effective in making a seed bed as well as making more rapid work, and enabling him to do from four to ten or twelve acres a day, a maximum which, to put it modestly, is rather unlikely. The seed was broadcast under furrow and the ridges split with the same plough to cover it, much as is now done with potatoes.[33]

Early in the eighteenth century the first definite step towards modern factory plough production was made when the Rotherham plough was introduced. There is a good deal of mystery about this step. It has been said that the plough was designed by Joseph Foljambe at Rotherham under the direction of Walter Blith, and that a patent was obtained for it in 1730.[34] Ellis makes one of his oblique offers to supply particulars of a new plough invented in January 1732 that may relate to the same implement;[35] but if Blith actually directed the work done by Foljambe, he must have been at least a hundred years old when he did so, or else the work must have been done at a much earlier date. There can, I think, be little doubt that his praise of the Dutch plough had some bearing on the new Rotherham plough, though the latter is also said to have been brought direct from Holland.

A romantic story is told by William Amos in 1810, and repeated by later writers. It is that someone by the name of Lummis first attempted, sixty or seventy years before this date, to establish the con-struction of the plough upon mathematical principles which he had learned in Holland; but after securing a patent, Lummis decided to keep his principles secret. But an unprincipled fellow, Pashley, plough-wright to Sir Charles Turner of Kirkleatham, discovered the secret and made a vast number of ploughs. His son, more enterprising still, established a factory for making this kind of plough at Rotherham, and so the plough came to be called the Rotherham plough; in Scotland it was called the patent, or Dutch plough. The Americans learned of these ploughs either from England or Holland and claimed priority of invention. Then Jefferson presented the principles of mouldboard construction first to France and next to the British Board of Agriculture as a wonderful discovery in mathematics.[36]

The Earl of Stair is given the credit for having brought a plough from Holland in 1730. A patent was secured for it in Scotland under the name of the Dutch plough and it "was soon much appreciated and largely sold."[37] But there is no doubt that Foljambe took out a patent in 1730 for improvements to a similar plough that was made at Rotherham.[38] Foljambe lived at Eastwood, and in another and clearer account it is said that he sold his patent to Staniforth of Firbeck, who at first charged 2s. 6d. a plough for licenses to make under the patent. Later he tried to raise this charge to 7s. or 7s. 6d., but this was deemed so unreasonable that the patent was set aside on the grounds that the plough was not an invention, but only an improvement upon existing implements. It was introduced to Scotland by Mr. Lomax or Lummis, who was patronized by the Society of Scottish Improvers, and was afterwards made by Mr. Dalziel of New Liston, West Lothian. Dalziel had been sent by the Earl of Stair to England, where he was taught the best and most improved way of making implements at the Earl's expense. This story, like the others, bears some impress of truth,[38a] although it was told long after the event. Whatever its origin, the Rotherham plough, with the coulter and share made of iron, and the breast covered with an iron plate, enjoyed a wide popularity for several decades, both in England and Scotland. Its design was not absolutely stable, and many notions were incorporated in it by the numerous individuals who made ploughs of this type. Nearly forty years after it was patented, it was still considered the lightest for draught and cheapest for general use of any then made.[39]

Jefferson's claim to have originated the mathematical theory of the plough, demonstrates that there must have been competition for priority in having discussed the subject. During the eighteenth century a good deal of theorizing about construction and its effect upon draught, the proper shape of the mouldboard and the set of the plough was published. This was what Blith had asked for a century before; but the seventeenth-century spirit of enquiry into first principles passed by such a rude implement as the plough—although a great deal of attention was then being paid to other forms of mechanical design.

"The truth is," wrote James Small, "that it has been neglected by those persons who have turned their attention to machines, as a rude tool, unworthy of their attention. Such persons imagined that anything could do for the clumsy operation of turning up the ground, and that there could be no nicety in a work which was successfully performed by the ignorant peasants." This was not wholly true, because a good many writers on farming had discussed the various kinds of plough in use and their relative merits. These writers had commonly advised that a plough used in one locality and in one type of soil might be carried to another part of the country and used there with a corresponding advantage, but this was difficult to carry into effect. Not only were many of the farmers themselves antagonistic to changes, but even when they had been convinced of the advantages of the "foreign" plough, their men often made bad work on purpose to show that the new implement was inferior to that customarily used. This is not, of course, quite the same thing as discussing the mechanical principles of the plough; but some theorizing about draught and other factors was made by these writers, in addition to their comparisons between the working of the wheel, foot and other ploughs.

Increasing interest in farming was being taken by all sorts of people as the eighteenth century progressed. The food supply was only just meeting the needs of a population growing more rapidly than it had ever done, and this caused the trend of enquiry to be directed more immediately to farming problems, in particular to those relating to the implements used. Agricultural theorists began to enquire, as Blith had hoped they would, into the principles upon which the most efficient type of plough should be constructed—a problem that would never be entirely solved, and certainly not by any one type of design alone. Amongst those who first tried to solve it there is a curious unanimity.

In 1774 a writer who preserves his anonymity, but discloses the cast of his mind in the signature, "A Practiser of both the Old and the New Husbandry," spoke deferentially of the two-wheel plough, but could not conceal his preference for the swing plough, an engraving of which he reproduces from *The Complete English Farmer*, 1776. This he recommends, especially when a semi-circular section is cut out of the bottom of the mouldboard and two small wheels fitted at either end of this section to reduce friction. This is rather fantastic, but it is one of the earliest attempts to modify the design of the mouldboard for that purpose.[40]

Three years later James Black[41] endeavoured to discover the real mechanical principles which underlie the work of the plough. He condemns wheels. They are not necessary if the proper angles are maintained between the line of draught and the point of entry into

D

the earth when the plough will practically guide itself. This is much the same as our anonymous farmer said, though he added, "a plough is a moving wedge to divide and overturn; it should therefore be constructed according to the laws of moving bodies . . ." These he set out and proposed to follow in the design of the implement.

In the same year as James Small's famous *Treatise of Ploughs and Wheel Carriages* appeared, a pamphlet was written by an Essex Farmer.[42] He was enthusiastic about the improved foot plough that did the work so much more easily than the ploughs of forty years before, and described the breast: "It is 3 ft. long, 1 ft. deep and straight at bottom, but convex or rounding outwards behind as it rises; if a proper degree of strength be give to it, it cannot be too thin. Its form ought nearly to resemble a wedge upon an easy slope before, that it might follow the share, and pass under the earth as easily as possible." With this intention it should be narrow before, approaching close to the share, and open behind. It was of wood covered with a thin iron plate.

Matthew Peters claimed to have originated some of these improvements, and to have gained a silver medal from the Royal Society of Arts, who had acquired one of his ploughs. It had a short beam and an acute breast which carried its line nearly the length of a light earthboard, giving an easy resistance against the quiescent earth. This arrangement turned the furrow more easily. A vertical wheel in the chamber of the plough took off the friction from the bottom of the plough, and a sharp "paring" iron placed close to the wheel behind, dislodged any earth that might adhere to the wheel. This is rather over-elaborate. A circular steel coulter welded on to the land side of the share was provided, and prevented choking—shades of Blith and the Dutch coulter.[43] In an earlier book Peters had recommended the use of cast iron for the share, earth boards and sides and lining pieces of the improved plough,[44] but beyond reducing the size and weight of the swing plough, he, like so many other writers of the day, adds nothing to theory.

It remained for James Small to initiate this, and he has achieved undying fame, despite later critics, as the first ploughwright who tried to lay down the principles of plough design in as scientific a manner as the mechanical knowledge of his day allowed. In common with other great innovators, Small owed a great deal to his predecessors and to his contemporaries who were so vigorously discussing this question. He concentrated and clarified what other men had been thinking in a muddled and indefinite manner, and his work remained the classic of the subject for nearly fifty years; but, naturally, his claim to be the first improver of the old Scotch plough is disputed. "One of the first valuable alterations in ploughs on the old construction, was made long before Small's time, by Lady Stewart of Goodtrees, grandmother to the Right Hon. the Earl of Buchan. She lived . . . in the Burgh of Rutherglen" and, amongst the other agricultural implements, invented the Rutherglen plough, an instrument well known, and much used, in the West of Scotland, although the only county report that mentions it is that on Clydesdale.[44a]

Of the mouldboard, which Small thought had been very much neglected, he said the construction "is of a very nice and complete nature, and requires considerable skill to make it in such a manner as to perform its work to the wish of the ploughman and with as little labour as possible to the cattle. . . .

"It must keep the plough in a proper hold on the ground; it must remove the earth to the furrow side, and it must turn it over."

By earlier ploughs than his, the furrow slice was turned over, only because the straight mouldboard was so long that the slice, which is balanced up on an untouched ridge of earth, must needs topple over; but always there is this untouched ridge below each furrow slice. "Accordingly mouldboards have long been made with a curve or twist" and have differed very much in shape with the varying taste of the individual ploughman. He believed that there must be a universal type of mouldboard that would do the required job. The principle upon which this mouldboard should be built was that "the back of the sock and the mouldboard should make one continued fair surface, without any interruption or sudden change. The twist, therefor, must begin from nothing at the point of the sock, and the sock and the mouldboard must be formed by the very same rule." He proceeded to construct his mouldboard of wood and attempted to set out a mathematical method of discovering the exact shape, so that the natural twist of the earth, in being lifted up by passing over the mouldboard, should be reproduced in the board. He produced a scale showing the width and curve of the board when required to cut a certain depth and width of furrow. In his experiments he used a plank to represent the furrow slice and carefully watched its action in passing over the mouldboard.

Although Small's ploughs were a great improvement on the early

Rotherham, they were not invariably successful. He may have learned the construction of the Rotherham plough when "an operative mechanic" in the factory there, but previously to his alterations this plough "was so clumsy in its construction and so difficult to draw that he has been regarded more as the inventor than as the improver of the swing plough." Small's plough came rapidly into use in all parts of Scotland, but it was opposed in some parts of Lanarkshire, "owing, it is supposed, to the over concavity of the mouldboard—a form not well adapted to the peculiar type of land where the trials were made."[45]

Eleven years after Small's *Treatise* was published, tables akin to his were issued by James Bailey.[46] His idea was essentially that of Small. The curve of the breast should follow the natural twist of the furrow slice in being turned over. He used various soils in his experiments. A slice of fifty-four inches in length was twisted over as in ploughing, and he worked out the angles at every three inches of length, thus providing himself with data on which to design his plough breast. The curve must be continuous, and he is careful to deal with the line of draught and the point of entry into the earth, so as to secure that the draught animals should not be driving the point into the ground and pulling against themselves, a fault that was sometimes very apparent with the wheel plough as well as the swing plough if not correctly set.

In 1808 Small's theories were once more repeated, almost in his own words, by Andrew Gray.[47] For instance, "Although the plough is of vast importance to man, yet it has long been very much neglected" is very reminiscent of Small's comment, indeed of Blith's, Hartlib's and many others in the interval. Gray admitted that Small was the first mechanic in Scotland who published rules for the construction of the plough, but that is hardly a sufficient reason for copying him almost verbatim, and detailing his method of obtaining his data as if it were Gray's own.

But Small's fame is not likely to be injured by Gray any more than by his other contemporary critics. Amos, for example, considered that the theory of the plough was still very deficient, although his criticism was mainly aimed at Jefferson. Amos himself had theories. He had thought of coupling two or more swing ploughs together to form a double-furrow plough, and had made some advance by using a spring steelyard as a dynamometer to measure the resistance of different types of ploughs.[48] He was not the first to do this.

A more vigorous attack was made upon Small, because he was not academic, by Thomas Williamson, a writer who has long since been forgotten.[49] There was some justice in the claim that Small was not a trained mathematician, but this does not impugn his originality. Williamson thought that the beam should be straight because the lines of draught are direct lines from the muzzle to the foot, and should be parallel with the sole or chep. All the land side parts must be in an even plane, and the left side of the foot exactly in line with the coulter and sheath. The head and the share should be made of cast iron. The first mathematicians were "peremptoralily at variance" about the proper sweep of the mouldboard, but the path was plain enough if they would only follow it. Where the cast-iron mouldboard could be obtained the difficulty vanished, but a wooden one could be formed in the proper shape if a matrix of pasteboard was made first. Most mouldboards had too great a swell in the breast. The upper part should have a sort of spiral concavity so that the furrow slice is raised so high as to turn it over to lie at 45°. Many mouldboards were too high.

Small's good name persisted, and a writer in the *Quarterly Journal of Agriculture* for 1828[50] declared farmers to be foolish in not adopting Small's plough, of which a detailed description is provided, or the Rotherham. Either of these required less labour and draught cattle than the locally-made unscientific and old-fashioned ploughs. This writer was in no doubt about Small's merits, remarking that "the forming of the mouldboard of cast-iron, instead of wood covered with plates of iron, as it anciently was, is a great improvement . . . because when a mouldboard is once formed on correct principles, any number can be cast and sent to every part of a county." The form of the mould-board continued to be controversial, and J. Allen Ransome did not think that any precise rule for it had appeared by 1843, or at least none of which he could speak with entire confidence. He had examined the principles laid down by these writers, but no contemporary plough maker adhered to them because different soils, light sand and heavy clay, required mouldboards almost the opposite of one another. The Norfolk mouldboard, for instance, was short, with rather a hollow or concave surface, whilst that used in the hundreds of Essex was long and convex.[51] Matter for endless argument was bound to exist here.

All this controversial theorizing about the mathematical principles

of plough design was a reflection of the passion for agricultural improvement that grew during the eighteenth century until nearly every
landowner and farmer was imbued with it. The progress of enclosure
at once stimulated, and was stimulated by, the movement. Besides
trying to enunciate the theory of plough design, men like Small set
themselves to devise new and improved implements, and of course
each was convinced of the paramount merit of his own design. The
competition between them was intensified by the offer of premiums
by Societies like the Society of Arts, which was founded in 1754. In
1767 this Society distributed three premiums of £50 for plough inventions,[52]—one was for Mr. Duckett's skim coulter plough that
earned the approbation of Lord John Somerville himself.

Many of the modifications introduced had long been anticipated.
Lord John Somerville, writing in the early years of the nineteenth
century, stated that little originality of invention or improvement had
been manifested in the best part of the swing and wheel ploughs constructed since the time of Blith, and reproduced a modified version of
Blith's seventeenth-century drawings to prove his point. He would only
admit that two or three improvements "have really borne the test of
practice with credit and success."[53] Doubtless this statement contained a
modicum of truth, but there was a great interchange of ideas and con-
scious efforts towards improvements. There were "numberless fancied
improvements," but the general level of plough design had been greatly
raised. Besides the Rotherham plough there was an abundance of
types that might suggest improvements.

The aim was quite clearly recognized to be better cultivation and
a reduction of expense, and the means were seen to be better implements and greater skill in using them. The problem could not be
better stated than it was by Arthur Young in 1797. His immediate
subject is a ploughing match at Petworth, but his statement of the
case was intended to have general application, and is as true today
as one-and-a-half centuries ago :—[54]

"There are distinct species of merit which demand to be appreciated :

    1. The skill of the ploughman.
    2. The goodness of the plough.
    3. The furrow ploughed.
    4. The power of the team.

"The first of these objects is seen in the knowledge with which the ploughman adaptes the work to the crop in question, to lay the furrows in such a manner as shall encourage all weeds and grass to vegetate, if (as in fallowing) that is requisite; or, on the contrary, to exclude them from the air as much as possible, as in turning a clover ley for wheat; as well as to vary his depth and breadth of furrow to the object of the farmer. His skill is also seen in the straightness and evenness of his work; in setting his plough to the nature of the soil, and even to the season, whether moist or dry. All these, and several other points give an opportunity to a ploughman to show his skill even with a bad plough; and with the best, a bad ploughman will contrive to make wretched work. . . .

"The goodness of the plough is a most essential point; for there are such as no ploughman can make good work with; and some so heavy . . . that there must be four horses to draw it. . . . The Kentish turnwrist will . . . lay the furrows well; but having a chisel point, of only two, three or four inches wide, and a heel nine or ten, must in various operations drive over roots and weeds without cutting them. The little Suffolk swing plough is a handy tool for three or four inches of depth, but very difficient for a right staple depth. . . . Instances might be multiplied; but the fact is obvious, that furrows may be well turned to the eye but yet bad work is made.

"Another circumstance of equal importance . . . is, to consider how well the construction of a plough is adapted to the peculiar soil or crop, which is the object of the experiment. . . . By consequence . . . the merits of a plough will not be appreciated, if such variations be not in contemplation; and that plough considered as the best which is adapted to the most uses. . . .

"The team does not seem to carry much difficulty in the way of a fair decision; the expense of keeping horses and oxen, or asses or mules, should be carefully calculated, the interest of their first cost estimated, their duration and liability to disease included, and the expense thus deduced of performing a given portion of work, as merit here is all included in cheapness. But in ascertaining what this portion really is in any trial; that is, the quantum of power exerted; there are great difficulties, if the furrow turned by every plough be not very nearly of the same dimensions; a circumstance that clearly appeared in the trials of ploughs by the Society of Arts, in which the draught was ascertained by means of a coiled spring, with an index of the hundred weights applied in drawing. Probably this difficulty will render it advisable, in such trials, that the furrow to be opened be previously specified; allowing a breadth sufficiently proportioned to the depth required."

A full account of the trials carried out by the Society of Arts had appeared in the first volume of the *Annals of Agriculture*,[55] under the title, "Experiments to ascertain the force necessary to draw various ploughs." The instrument used was a spring dynamometer such as is still employed for measurements of no great refinement. It was invented by Mr. Samuel More, the Secretary to the Society, with a view to determining the merits of an iron plough that had been submitted by Mr. John Brand for a bounty. Six ploughs in all were tried: the Rotherham plough; two ploughs of Mr. Arbuthnot's, described merely as "red" and "blue"; Mr. Duckett's trenching plough; the common Surrey plough; and the new iron plough. Twenty tests were carried out, with furrows of different depths, and with weights added to certain of the ploughs to bring them up to the weights of others. The draught was registered in fractions of cwt. Mr. Brand was given a bounty, but Mr. Arbuthnot's plough was "beyond all doubt the best."

The conclusions drawn by the Committee, as Arthur Young said, "Deserve no slight attention":—

"It appears that the weight of the plough is of little consequence very contrary to common ideas; that heaviness is even an advantage oftener than the contrary; and that in some instances to a surprising degree. The weight of the plough is the least part of the horses labour; the great object is the resistance met with in the cohesion of the earth; lightness does nothing to overcome this; it is effected by just proportions only. If a plough is not made on true principles the lightness is prejudicial by adding to the unsteadiness of ill-made ploughs.

"It also appears very decidedly that the share should be nearly, if not quite, as broad in the fin, as the plough is wide in the heel, in order that all the furrow may be cut, and not turn up by force."

Arthur Young, who was present all day at these trials, came to the conclusion that Mr. Arbuthnot's plough "was, beyond all doubt, the best that was tried, and plainly owed its superiority to the share rising in an inclined plane and melting gradually into the admirable sweep of its long mouldboard." He was so convinced of this, that he

17. Kentish Turnwrist Plough. From John Boys, *General View of the Agriculture of Kent*, 1796.

18. The old Devonshire Plough or Sull.   From Charles Vancouver, *General View of the Agriculture of Devon*, 1808.

15 In.

A The Spill of Iron which passes through the brain & supports the front wheel has a number of Iron rings on it by which the depth of stirring is regulated

B Length of Beam 6'9¼ C Breadth of the Earth piece 3'7'¼

D D Large Wheel 3'6 dia E Small Wheel 10 ½

Pieces of Wood of which the Frame is made 4 ¼ square

19. Tormentor. From Charles Vancouver, *General View of the Agriculture of Devon*, 1808.

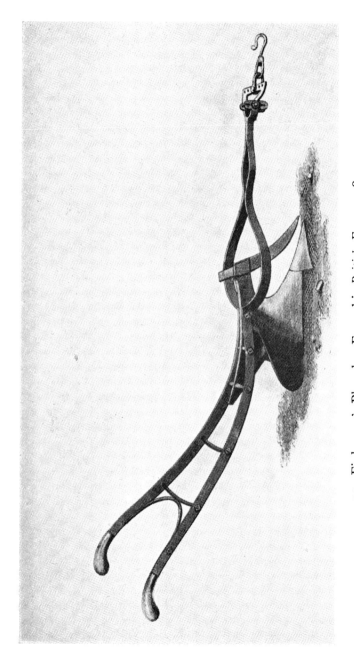

20. Finlayson's Plough. From his *British Farmer*, 1825.

21. Finlayson's Harrow. From his *British Farmer*, 1825.

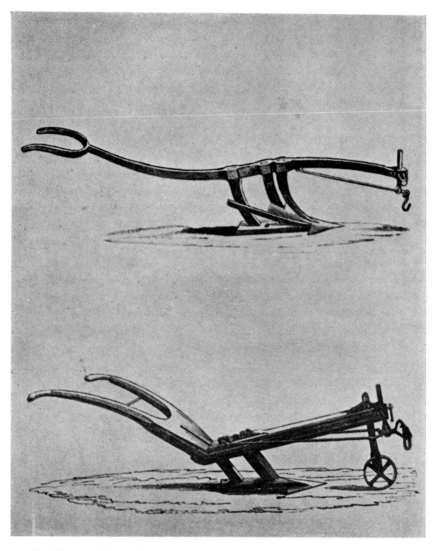

22. Smith's and Rackheath Subsoil Plough. From J. Allen Ransome,
Implements of Agriculture, 1843.

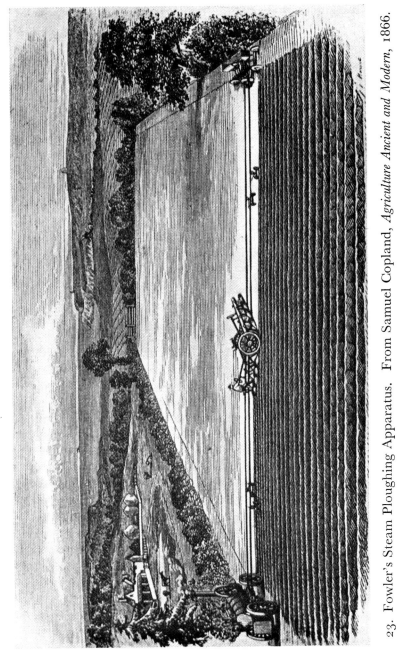

23. Fowler's Steam Ploughing Apparatus. From Samuel Copland, *Agriculture Ancient and Modern*, 1866.

24. Howard's Steam Ploughing Apparatus. From Copland, *Agriculture Ancient and Modern*, 1866.

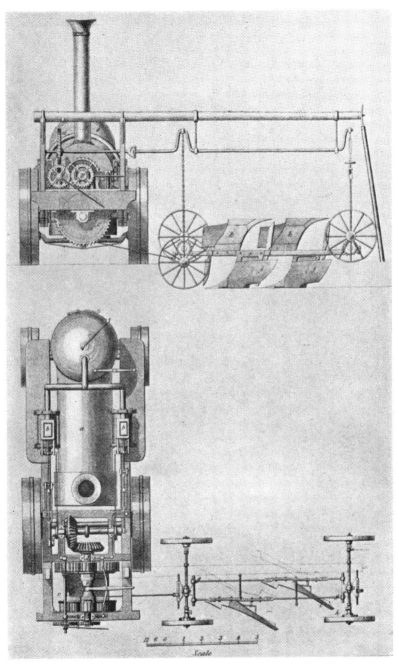

25. Tweedale Steam Plough.   From Slight and Burn, *Book of Farm
Implements and Machines*, 1858.

26. Smith's Steam Cultivator, made by Howard. From John Donaldson, *British Agriculture*, 1860.

27. Garrett's System of Steam Ploughing. From *Rural Life, c.* 1860.

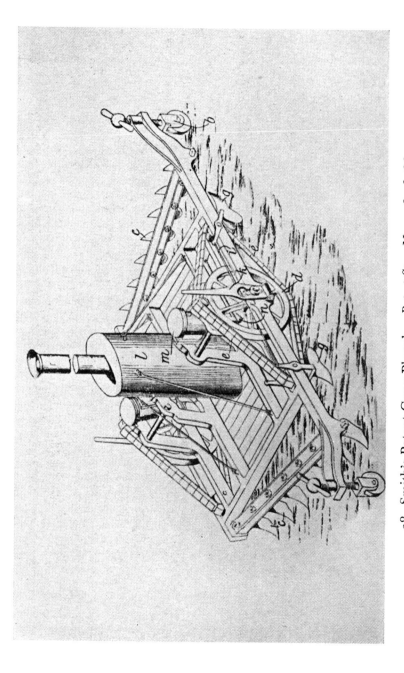

28. Smith's Patent Gang Plough. *Patent Spec.* No. 958 of 1861.

29. Halkett's Guideway System.   From *Quarterly Jour. of Agric.*, 1861.

30. Rickett's Cultivator. From *Jour. R.A.S.E.*, 1858.

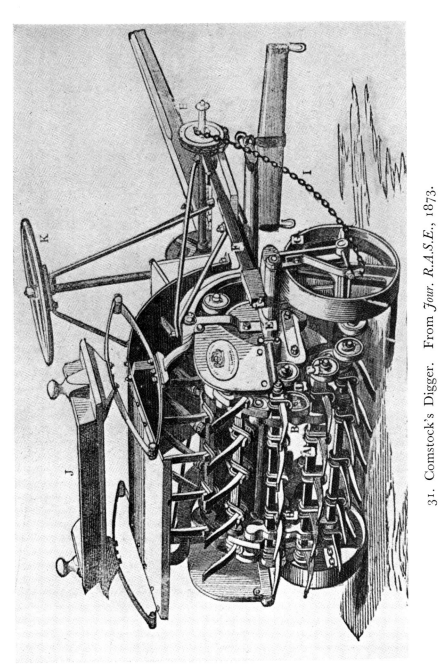

31. Comstock's Digger. From *Jour. R.A.S.E.*, 1873.

32. Darby's Steam Digger. From *Jour. R.A.S.E.*, 1880.

decided to add those parts of it to a plough of Mr. Brand's construction, i.e. the cat-head and the method of fastening the coulter, both of which had greatly impressed the Committee, and were, in fact, a new departure. After some failures, Young was able to consummate this marriage of ideas. He made a plough nearer to perfection, in his judgment, than any he had yet seen. Though it was a swing plough it practically guided itself without holding, and from this Young deduced that it moved with the greatest possible ease.[56]

The invention of the dynamometer made comparisons of draught in the same soil conditions more precise, but it was not very often used in the ploughing matches which sprang up at about the same time. By a coincidence the first certain reference so far found to a ploughing match is one organized by the Odiham Agricultural Society, Hampshire, in 1784, though it is quite likely that unrecorded matches may have been held before that date, if a boast made by Farmer Sandford in the previous year can be accepted. He declaimed, in the role of *laudator temporis acti*, "When I was a boy, farmers did not lie droning in bed as they do now till six or seven; my father, I believe, was as good a judge of business as any in the neighbourhood, and turned as straight a furrow as any ploughman in the county of Devon, that silver cup, which I intend to have the honour of drinking your health out of today at dinner, that very cup was won by him at the great ploughing match near Axminster."[57] Since Thomas Day could refer to ploughing matches in a book issued in 1783 it is fairly clear that the Odiham Society's match in 1784 was not the first, but it is certainly an early example.

At a competition on the Tuesday of Whitsun week, 1784, a prize of three guineas was awarded to the "ploughman that ploughed the best within a given time to be determined by the stewards." Other prizes were given to the boy driving the horses, and to the two next ploughmen and to the boys employed with them.[58] Similar matches then became not infrequent. Arthur Young knew little of them, but in 1797 he anticipated great results "of such annual meetings, were they to take place in various other districts of the kingdom, as well as in Sussex."[59]

It was not to be expected that all societies would have Arthur Young's wide vision or insist upon the number of factors for which allowance should be made in comparing ploughs and ploughing.

Good work, as judged by conventional standards, was a thing easily to be understood, as was also the reduction in the strength of the team (a rough and ready indication of draught), and the possibility of dispensing with the driver. All these points were clearly of importance, while none but powerful and wealthy societies could be expected to concern themselves with scientific refinements.

The evidence of contemporary witnesses is overwhelming that ploughing matches had an immense effect in raising the skill of the ploughman and reducing working expenses.

"These ploughing matches," said Francis Erskine, "raise such emulation amongst the youth, that a gentleman has assured me, that, when travelling along the road, he has seen a young lad (who was ploughing without any person in the field with him), as soon as he came to the end of a furrow, stop, and look back upon his work; and on his perceiving part not done to his mind, that he immediately turned, took his plough to the spot, and endeavoured to rectify the error with great earnestness." [60]

"The ploughmen of Clackmannanshire," it was said, "from being notorious for their want of skill in tillage, are now reckoned among the very best in Scotland." This was a direct result of ploughing matches. "The fields of the good farmers, indeed, appear cultivated like gardens." There was, however, a serpent in this Eden; in some counties the farmers alleged that the matches tended "to make successful ploughmen saucy and self-conceited, and ready to seek higher wages." [61]

Sometimes the rules were directed to reducing the number of draught animals and men employed; in the matches instituted by Lord Egremont at Petworth the prizes were awarded for an acre ploughed "in the best manner, with the least assistance, and with the fewest oxen." [62] Even when the rules were not so definite and the quality of the ploughing alone determined the prizes, the contrast with competing teams could not fail in its effect. At the first match at Alloa, for example:

"One of the members of the club had a good servant, who was, however, prepossessed in favour of three horses in the plough with a driver. The master sent him to make the trial, in hopes of convincing him, and his other servants of their inferiority; and it succeeded; the whole of them being so ashamed of this man's work as to make them ever since reject and give up asking for a third horse or a driver."[63]

There was a danger that too definite conclusions should be drawn from performances under match conditions. Arthur Young suggested to the Bath and West Society that experiments conducted over a period were of more value than competitions in the general use of drills, ploughs or horse hoes.[64] Lord John Somerville stated some years later that he was "not disposed to draw absolute conclusions from ploughing matches, because much may depend upon accident; besides that exertions might be made for three hours, without much apparent distress, which, nevertheless, could not be maintained for three weeks, and so the public becomes misled."[65]

Besides open ploughing matches, trials were arranged for the purpose of determining the superiority of particular types of plough or to decide a wager. One of the most interesting of these semi-private trials was that held on the Norfolk Farm in Windsor Great Park in 1798 in order to test the qualities of Lord John Somerville's improvement of the West of England double-furrow plough against two Norfolk ploughs and one Rotherham plough as ordinarily used on the King's Farm.[66] The result of this trial was quite a definite indication that the improvements designed by the President of the Board of Agriculture enabled more work to be done under given conditions in a day than could be effected by the use of the single ploughs. About a week later, Lord John Somerville's plough was entered in the Petworth ploughing match, but did not obtain a prize owing to the fact that it had been damaged during the journey from Windsor.[67]

Another interesting competition, the basis of which was a wager regarding the relative merits of the single- and double-furrow ploughs, took place in Essex in June 1802. The local farmers had been very much opposed to the latter type of plough, but its backer won the wager, and the farmers were converted.[68]

Scientific or quasi-scientific tests tended to be overshadowed by contests which matched man against man and team against team. The enquiring spirit and the infinite patience that will make the infinite number of measurements—the method of science—emerged only at long intervals. About the year 1800 the names of many more societies engaged in promoting ploughing matches appear in the periodicals,[69] but records of careful tests and trials are infrequent.[70]

In 1842 the Royal Agricultural Society of England allotted 300 guineas to be awarded as prizes for implements exhibited at their annual show, and in the following year "a great number of ploughs were put to work on Mr. White's farm at Rough Heanor and inspected by the judges."[71] It became the practice of the Society to reserve the right to try in the field any implement exhibited,[72] and the Bath and West of England Society later adopted a rule which permitted exhibitors to show their implements actually at work.[73] There was, however, no sustained effort to follow on the experimental work inaugurated by the Society of Arts in 1784. Doubtless various forms of tests were carried out by manufacturers as they adopted new designs, but public trials became practically limited to ploughing matches. Of the number held at different times or at any one time in the nineteenth century no estimate appears to have been made.

The experiments carried out by the Society of Arts were directed to test a new thing, a plough wholly made of iron by Mr. John Brand of Lawford, near Manningtree in Essex. Arthur Young thought very highly of the implement, and had grafted upon it a mouldboard of Arbuthnot's design tried and approved in the same series of experiments. Young is not very explicit about this iron plough, though he reported that it was "an iron swing plough for two horses" which much exceeds "any plough he had yet seen for cutting a regular furrow and preferable to all in strength and duration." Besides this swing plough, Brand invented other iron ploughs for ploughing one or two feet deep with four or six horses. The Suffolk iron plough, as Brand's invention came to be known, had only one handle, "To oblige the ploughman to walk upright and to carry his own weight."[74] This was most probably the iron plough illustrated in Bailey's *Advancement of Arts*, 1773.

Arbuthnot, who was a competitor of Brand in these improvements, had invented a swing plough for a pair of horses to plough six inches deep, and a much larger plough with a pair of wheels for deep ploughing, as well as various other implements. His plough was awarded first place, and he expounded his theories to Arthur Young at some length. He was aware of the difficulty often met with by ploughmen, that the plough was inclined to dig itself in and required the man's whole strength to bring it to a level again. Arbuthnot laid down the rule "that a line drawn from the tug at the horse's shoulder to the point of the share should intersect the notch in the copse immediately below the end of the beam . . ."[75] This plough was fitted with a broadshare besides the sweeping mouldboard already commented upon.

Duckett, of Esher in Surrey, whose trenching plough was also tried at these experiments, developed it into a skim coulter plough which was very effective for cleaning. It was considered particularly valuable in thin sandy soils. It turned the sward in under the furrow and so buried it. The skim "requires a perpendicular direction and the coulter hole to be further removed from the throat and share; because in the common position it would choke at work."[76] This plough, which was one of the plough improvements that in Somerville's opinion had "really borne the test of practice with credit and success," was not much used in 1825. Another improved plough was Mr. Tugwell's Beverstone single-wheel plough. It had been "much countenanced by the Bath and West Society," and though "expensive in iron work" was most effective. The point of draught was "perpendicularly above the point of action, namely, the throat or breast, where the share fits on." This was behind the point that Arbuthnot considered proper. But the Beverstone plough did not enjoy a long popularity, and by 1825 it was no longer extensively used.[77]

Lord Somerville himself made an improvement to the mouldboard by having it in three parts that could be adjusted to modify the shape; he also patented an improved double furrow plough in 1802. This was nothing new. A double-furrow plough is included in Blith's drawing of ploughs (c. 1650), and a double furrow was discussed in many of the textbooks published between these dates. Williamson[78] attributed its invention to "a common wright" in Leicestershire, but he was no more its inventor than Somerville, for it was in use in the south-western counties before then. A premium of three guineas was offered in 1792 by the Devon Society for the Encouragement of Agriculture and Industry to the person who, in proportion to the quantity of his arable land, should plough the greatest number of acres with the double-furrow plough.[79] Again, it was called the Vale of Taunton two-furrow swing plough by Nathaniel Kent in his comments upon its trials on the Royal Farms in Windsor Great Park and at Petworth in 1798.[80] Somerville improved it, and it was used by Billingsley on his farm at Ashwick Grove near Shepton Mallet,

Somerset, though he did not mention it in his *General View of the Agriculture of Somerset*, 1795.

Tweed, of Sandon in Essex, also used the double-furrow plough, and made his men accept it by putting them in competition with it. He told Somerville about this in a letter, saying, "I put my first plough to work, with three horses and one man against two of my own and four horses, held by two remarkably good ploughmen, who were very much averse to any new implements; after exerting themselves to the utmost every day for a month, upon clover leys, bean and pea etches, for wheat, they allowed, very much against their inclinations, that it performed the work best, which is entirely owing to the superior form of the breast, and the great advantage derived from the moveable plates."[81] Ransome made this plough and about 1812 supplied one to Sir William Middleton of Shrubland Hall. It was said to have worked for forty years with a team of two oxen and to have ploughed one and three-quarter acres a day. Ransome continued to make the double-furrow plough, although there was an opinion that it worked well only in tolerably level land, and where the ground had been previously broken up. Billingsley, however, declared that it had always gained the prize at the Bath and West Society's competitions.[82]

The fact that Ransome was making Somerville's double-furrow plough indicates that the factory production of farm implements had already made progress by the second decade of the nineteenth century, both in England and Scotland. Ransome had played no inconsiderable part in this development. Robert Ransome (1753–1830), the founder of the firm, was the son of a schoolmaster at Wells, Norfolk. In 1755 he took out a patent for tempering cast-iron plough-shares, and in April of that year he issued an advertisement in the *Norwich Mercury* stating that these shares could be bought of all the ironmongers in Norwich, and some fifty agents scattered throughout Norfolk and Suffolk. Four years later he moved to Ipswich and on a capital of £200 set up a foundry where he employed one workman. The firm was successful, and a further improvement was made and patented in 1803. It was the chilled share which was so hardened that it remained sharp in use, the friction of wear rubbing down the softer iron, so that the case-hardened edge retained its cutting properties. Other patents taken out by Ransome from time to time included one, in 1808, for making plough bodies so that they could easily be taken to pieces in the field, and fresh parts put in place of any that had been damaged. Ransome's Patent Plough won the second prize at the Bath Society's trial at Deptford Farm between Salisbury and Warminster in 1811.[83] Ransome's improved share of 1785 was referred to in somewhat tepid terms by William Marshall a couple of years after it had been patented. "Cast iron shares," he wrote, "have lately been invented, and a patent procured for them by a person of Norwich. For the Norfolk plow in the Norfolk soil they appear, from the specimens I have seen of them, to be a valuable invention. If they can be made firm enough to stand in a strong soil, and hard enough to retain a sufficient edge in a gravel, they must prove, to agriculture in general, a most valuable acquisition." For some time already the mouldboard of the Norfolk plough had been made of wrought or cast iron, "being a separate strong plate, twisted into a form resembling the mouldboard of the modern little plow of Yorkshire and other districts."[84]

Ransome's was not the only factory turning out iron parts for the plough. In Scotland the mouldboard, sheath and head were being made of cast iron at the foundry of Cooper and Barker in forms approved by the Dalkeith Farming Society; and a mouldboard acclaimed the best by a partisan was being turned out by Messrs. Walker's at Rotherham marked TR.[85] The Carron Ironworks also made one. Joseph Handford and William Davenport of Hathern, near Loughborough, had set up a factory for making farm implements by 1808 and produced three types of ordinary plough, two trenching ploughs and a hoe plough for earthing up cabbage, potatoes, etc., four harrows, and various scufflers, rakes and so on.[86] There were, no doubt, other factories at this time, amongst which was probably one for making Wilkie's improvement on Small's plough, and another for making Plenty's friction wheel plough patented in 1800. The latter was used in Hampshire, although it could not compete satisfactorily in strong stony land with the old Hampshire two-wheel plough.[87]

There were at this date at least four shops in London where agricultural implements could be bought. They were Cooke and Fisher's Agricultural Repository—off the Pantheon, Oxford St;[88] W. Lester (himself an author) of Holborn; M'Dougall of Oxford St.; and Langhorn's Repository in Barbican.[89] The firm of Wedlake may have set

up the City Agricultural Repository for Improved Agricultural
Implements, if a statement in an advertisement by Mrs. Mary Wedlake, who was running the firm in 1849, is correct.[90] The earliest shop
of this kind may have been that of J. Sharp, Leadenhall St. It was
in existence about 1773.[91]

In spite of all this activity amongst inventors and manufacturers,
the use of the new implements did not at once spread all over the
country. For various reasons, many of them good, though most of
them were condemned, the farmers continued to use the implements
to which they were accustomed. A general view of existing practice is
supplied by the surveys made under the instructions of the Board of
Agriculture at this time. Each county was surveyed and a report
prepared according to a standard plan. The reports were circulated
to prominent farmers and others for criticism and suggestions, and a
revised report prepared from the results, and perhaps from a new
survey by a new surveyor. These reports were published under the
title "A general review of the agriculture of the county of . . ." and
though some were compiled hastily and not all were done by the
most suitable persons, they were for long accepted as authoritative.
Indeed, several writers of the first fifty years of the nineteenth century
were content to produce synopses of these reports as descriptions of
current farming. On such matters of fact as the implements used,
they can be accepted.

Of course, those counties most distant from London and the
places where the new implements were made and talked about, were
the last to adopt these improvements. The light two-wheel plough and
the iron swing plough of Norfolk and Suffolk have already been commented upon. These types were used in Essex; in Cambridge, Lincoln
and Nottingham the "Dutch" swing plough was used; while in the
last county a two-wheel plough made at Moor Green, near Nottingham, another early factory, was also used. This was probably like
Handford's of Leicester. In Hunts and Rutland a double-furrow
plough, said to have been introduced from Salop, but then obtained
from the neighbourhood of Northampton, was one type; the common
swing and Leicester wheel plough were others.

In some of the Midland Counties a double-furrow plough capable
of being adjusted so that the width of the furrow could be regulated,
was made by "one Bush, a wheelwright of Hurley in the north of

Warwickshire" about 1770. This was an improvement on the common Worcestershire double-furrow plough that, like Duckett's, was not adjustable. Bush did not patent his design, and though he was still the leading maker in 1786, all the principal ploughwrights of the district were also making it and every farmer "who had the strength," was using it.[92]

Throughout the north the Rotherham (of no very stable pattern, but varying in accordance with the idiosyncrasies of local "carpenters") was common, one oddity being a mouldboard half of cast iron half of wood found in the West Riding. Double-furrow ploughs were also to be seen in that county. Gripping ploughs for cutting shallow open drains, or cleaning them, were found in the north and the turnwrist plough had been brought into the hills of Westmorland so long before as 1724. Besides the Rotherham, Duckett's trench plough and the Miner were used in Lancashire, and were supplemented by a double-furrow plough, a "guttering" plough, in Cheshire. Stafford used a variety of implements, single and double ploughs with and without wheels; and a one wheel which was very good that required no holder. It had lately been much improved by an iron mouldboard formerly screwed to the coulter, called a "flay," for ploughing turf. Joseph Cornforth, a machine maker, is mentioned, perhaps the owner of another early factory. Throughout the Midlands variety reigned. Derby used a double-furrow, and two- and one-wheel ploughs. The old high gallows two-wheel plough was found from Salop to Berks and Bucks, though some Rotherham and Kentish turnwrist ploughs were used in South Bucks. A long swing or foot plough was used on the stony land or breaking ley in Oxford, the wheel plough being reserved for fallows. In Hertford the presumptive home of the two-wheel plough, a very simple plough (no very clear description) with the share and heel in one piece of wrought iron was used. It may have been a wheel plough. Middlesex, curiously enough, stuck to the common wooden swing plough, and the Hertfordshire two wheel for fallowing. The "Rev. Mr. James Cooke of Red Lion Square, London," who was rather more of an inventor than a clergyman, and who may have had a small factory there, expounds his theories of plough design at some length in the Middlesex report. He had come to the conclusion that the mechanical principle was not that of a wedge but of the inclined plane.

E

In Kent and Sussex and on the hills of Surrey the turnwrist plough was the standby, especially in the heavy land of the Weald, but a foot plough was used in Sheppey. This plough was generally admitted to be admirably suited to perform its job of ploughing hillsides and dealing with very tenacious soils. William Marshall's comments upon it are illuminating. "It has a pair of wheels, fully as large as the fore wheels of a moorland waggon; and behind there is dragged a long thick log of wood, which slides upon the ground, as the hob or shoe of a sledge; with a beam rising high above it, which a small farmer of the North would be glad of as a gate post; comprising, in its various parts, as much timber and other materials as would build a highland cart.

"This magnificent implement is called the Kentish Turn Wrest Plow; the large truncheon or wrest—provincially 'rive'—which forces open the furrow, being turned or changed from side to side, at each turning of the team; which, in ploughing with this implement, begins on one side or end of the field, or piece to be plowed, and proceeds, without a break or open furrow, to the other." Even he had to admit that it was obviously and admirably adapted to its job, and he had recommended its use in the Central Highlands of Scotland and the Cotswolds. When fitted with a broadshare three or four inches broad, eighteen or twenty inches long, it formed an excellent skim or sub-plough, the most effective Marshall had seen.[93] It required large teams of oxen to haul it. By some people this is thought to be the Anglo-Saxon plough with little alteration as shown at the Lewes Museum. It turned a broken back furrow very similar to the digging breast of later date. Its deadweight was great, but, through the small friction everywhere except on the slade which did not exceed that of the common plough, the draught was not excessive as compared with that implement.[93]

Hampshire used several ploughs including Plenty's patent already mentioned, and Spark's patent iron plough. Wiltshire used the two wheel with the draught chain on the hill farms. The chain was supposed to strengthen the beam and lighten the draught. A lighter plough was used in the north-west of the county. A single-wheel plough was also worked in Wiltshire, similar to that used in the Cotswolds. There, Tugwell's Beverstone was still popular with its single wheel and bastard coulter, a compact, light and symmetrical implement which had made a good impression at the Bath Society's trials in 1808 by its rapidity and ease of working when hauled by two horses.[94] In Gloucestershire a double mouldboard plough was employed for making water furrows. The neighbouring county of Hereford used the light Shropshire plough in the north, but the "long heavy one of the district" elsewhere. This must have been the same as the "long straight heavy plough" of the Vale of Evesham in Worcester. Worcester farmers used a double-furrow plough on light lands, and in the Cotswolds a one wheel with a swing share, much like that used in Devon and other Western counties. Other types were the hammock plough and the string plough. The Somerset double-furrow and other ploughs have already been commented upon.

There were a few Norfolk ploughs in Dorset, but the "Sull," long, heavy and large, which was common to the South-west, was prevalent here. It was a swing plough with a beam about seven feet long, nearly parallel to the head and heel of the plough, and with a straight wooden mouldboard, so made as to enter the land obliquely. For such a rude instrument it did surprisingly good work, and, made by a hedgerow carpenter, seldom cost, irons included, more than 15s. Different patterns of shares were used in this plough for different jobs. A so-called light Dorset swing plough with a well-curved iron breast was also worked. The Cornish ploughs, dismissed as awkward and inconvenient, were of the "Sull" type and were drawn by large teams of oxen. Although he considered this plough so primitive as to be "heraldic" in appearance, Marshall noted "three notable peculiarities of construction." It had no wrest, the mouldboard standing some inches above the level of the chip, head, soal or heel of the plough. This was sometimes an advantage in turning whole ground, but in fallow rather made a rut than a furrow, half the soil perhaps remaining unstirred. The sheath or breast was not fixed in the beam but was made longer or shorter, as required, by adjusting a wedge driven into a notch made across the end of the tenon about the beam; and the principal handle was not, as usual, tenoned into the beam, but its foot was crooked, shooting horizontally forward, in a line parallel to the "soal," and fastened to it by two thick wooden pins. This gave great firmness and strength of construction. In Marshall's opinion this was the pattern of the ancient Anglo-Saxon plough. He thought the turnwrist might be useful in the more hilly parts of the South-west.[95] Three patterns of plough, the Hertfordshire two-wheel plough, the Kentish turnwrist and the South-western "Sull," were all considered by different people, at different times, to have been the prototype of the ancient English plough, and this divergence of opinion seems to confirm that even before the Conquest there were local variations in plough construction.

A few Rotherham and Dutch ploughs were used in Wales, at Langharne Marsh in Carmarthen, in Flint and in Montgomery, but on the whole the ploughs there are reported to have been too long and heavy, and the long established and rather crude form had not been altered. Wales was, however, very largely devoted to cattle and sheep breeding. Tillage, except in such places as the vale of Glamorgan and the coast of Pembroke, played a small part in its agricultural economy. The common Welsh plough used in Pembroke was a pattern of that generally used, and was not calculated to cut a furrow, but to tear it open by main force. The share was like a large wedge; the coulter was sometimes set before the share, and sometimes above it. The earth board was a thing never thought of, but a stick, a hedge stick or anything of that kind, was fastened to the right of the heel of the share and extended to the hind part of the plough. This was intended to turn the furrow and sometimes did so, but not very often. After it had been used, the field looked as if a drove of swine had been moiling it. Some Castlemartin farmers had improved it by adding an earthboard and a wing or fin to the share. Nevertheless, surprisingly good work was made by some men who used the more primitive patterns. Horses and oxen together formed the team here.

In spite of the acceptance of Small's plough, Wilkie's improvements upon it, and the foundry-made mouldboard of the late eighteenth century, the old Scots plough continued to be used over wide areas of Scotland. Only in one county, Kinross, is there any mention of the Rutherglen plough that was invented before Small's time. The Rotherham plough and Small's type of plough had been introduced to Ayr, Berwick, Clydesdale, Dumfries, Elgin, Fife, Forfar, Galloway, Kincardine, Kinross, the Lothians, Nairn, Perth, Renfrew, Roxburgh, Selkirk, Stirling, Tweeddale and some parts of the northern counties, but in what proportion it is difficult to determine.[96] The more remote parts of Scotland continued, as in Wales, to use the heavy, strong and clumsy old Scots plough which was so inefficient that in the Hebrides, for example, it had to be preceded by a turf-cutting implement called a "ristle" when breaking up old grassland or ley. This system, formerly general, was condemned by Sir John Sinclair. Two horses drew the ristle, "a piece of sharp iron shaped like a coulter, but bent farther forward, and like it fixed to a beam. It had two handles and required two men to manage it, though intended merely for cutting the rough sward before the plough, which followed in the same line drawn by five horses, and attended by two men." It was also used to facilitate digging with spades.[97] The Western Islands, too, were the home of the caschrom (the crooked spade) and the cas diriach (the straight spade)[98] which have been regarded, by some authorities, with the rather different so-called breast plough or push plough, as being of earlier origin than the hauled plough, a conclusion to which I do not altogether subscribe.[99]

This large system of detailed reports on each county in the kingdom has never been repeated in the same way, and no such complete information about the patterns of implements used is to hand for any later period. The reports, of course, deal with other implements as well as with ploughs.

By about 1800 the clodding mell or beetle had been superseded by the roller, although the mell is mentioned in one report. Rollers were made of wood, stone or iron, and weighted in different ways to increase their pressure on the land, often by a box filled with stones on the top of the framework. The actual roller itself was made in various patterns. One predecessor of the ring roller was made of iron and wooden "wheels" fixed alternately, an arrangement that certainly must have made for the maximum wear on the wood. Some rollers were solid and some were in two or more parts. Cuthbert Clarke claimed to have invented a spiky roller. His claim was disputed, but he answered his antagonist in characteristic vein, "Let who will be the father or grandfather of this valuable instrument of husbandry. I had reason to be extremely pleased at my lucky hit, in constructing it from Mr. Ellis' barely mentioning a spiky roller; though with his usual giddiness he gave his readers no more than the name." Ellis's statement was, however, quite categorical and his description precise. The roller should be of elm, seven feet long and eighteen inches in diameter. Iron spikes seven inches long should be driven three inches deep into the wood at two inches asunder throughout the whole length.[100] Some of Ellis's contemporaries gave Randall the credit for this invention.[101] Perhaps Ellis's hint did suggest it to him, but something of the sort was used in

Essex fifty years before Randall wrote his article. It was a "rowl fitted with Oaken pins" three inches long and four inches apart in rows twelve inches asunder.[102] Marshall, who saw a spiky roller used in Norfolk for "indenting the surface of a clover ley once plowed for wheat," did not think it was ever in common use; it was strongly re-commended nevertheless, and was ingeniously arranged by William Amos in conjunction with a plain roller so that either the one or the other was in contact with the ground as required.[103] The more ordinary rollers of wood, stone or iron were longer or shorter, thicker or thinner, heavier or lighter at the choice of the user, and the variety of harrows was largely determined by the same personal taste.

There were large harrows fitted with iron teeth in substantial wooden frameworks, and lighter ones of the same kind. These harrows were square, triangular, or rhomboidal. The number of teeth was widely different. Some harrows were used in sets of two drawn squarely behind the horses; other were harnessed to one corner so that more complete tearing of the ground was accomplished; and there were innumerable patterns of scufflers, drags, breaks and so on. Even the ancient harrow made of a thorn bush weighted by a log had not been entirely aban-doned. The "tormenter" of Devon and the South-west was an example of a new type that received some approbation, but these things were always subsidiary to the plough, though they became more important during the nineteenth century.

Though in 1822 the semi-official Board of Agriculture died of inanition, caused mainly by the difficulties of the post-war de-pression that followed the victory of Waterloo, the factory manu-facturing of agricultural implements was firmly established, and new firms were being set up. Many of these were in East Anglia and Scot-land; they had the most humble beginnings in the local blacksmith's shop, like Wilders at Reading in 1818, Nicholson and Sons of Newark in 1825, and Kell and Co., of Barton Foundry, Gloucester, in 1828. Many others, particularly in Scotland, were established in other centres of the farming industry.

It was in Scotland that the next developments took place. The first was the production of Finlayson's Patent Rid or Self-cleaning Plough, and later his self-cleaning harrows, and the second was Smith of Deanston's subsoil plough. Both these men also designed turnwrist ploughs.

Finlayson[104] was very interested in the reclamation of moss and heath lands, a job his father had begun in 1788 on his farm, Kairn's. He found that in breaking up this type of land the ordinary plough was apt to get clogged with the vegetation, and had continually to be stopped to clear it, which made for a great waste of time and labour of the animals. By curving the beam and coulter, as shown in the illustration, he was able to overcome the difficulty, and although I do not think his plough was ever widely used, his self-cleaning harrows became nationally known and were worked for several generations.

Smith of Deanston's many projects are well known, and his subsoil plough was, with his system of thorough drainage, his great contribution to the art of farming. It was designed to break up the pan under-lying the normal depth of ploughed soil without bringing the sterile earth to the surface, and was extremely successful in doing this. It very soon found imitators, the best known of which is perhaps Sir Edward Strachey's Rackheath sub-soil plough. The process was largely discussed in the agricultural periodicals of the day, and more especially in the early volumes of the *Journal of the Royal Agricultural Society*, in which numerous descriptions of ploughs of this kind can be found.

It was in Scotland, too, that one of the earliest agricultural museums was established, though one had been in existence in Hanover Square, London, in the early years of the nineteenth century, about which very little can be discovered. Messrs. W. Drummond and Sons of Stirling set up an agricultural museum in 1831, and exhibited farm imple-ments as well as curious plants. This lasted for some years[105] and was approved by the Highland and Agricultural Society, by Sir John Sinclair and other eminent agriculturists. It was promptly copied by Messrs. Lawson of Edinburgh, and Dickson and Turnbull of Perth. All three firms, I think, were nurserymen and florists and showed specimens of the various productions of the field, and the forest, with models and improved implements of husbandry, no doubt with the idea of promoting sales.

By 1844 the Highland and Agricultural Society had set up a museum of its own, which displayed models of agricultural implements and machinery made largely by Messrs. James Slight and Co., Agricultural Engineers, of Leith Walk, Edinburgh. These included swing ploughs, subsoil ploughs, a turnwrist and a double mouldboard plough, a paring plough and various other designs, as well as harrows and grubbers of various shapes and sizes.[106] This Society, too, had begun to issue, in 1828, the *Quarterly Journal of Agriculture*, a magazine that contained authoritative articles on all branches of farming by writers from all over the kingdom.

As might be expected the list of ploughs exhibited in the Highland and Agricultural Society's Museum was not widely different from the list set out in contemporary encyclopaedias of farming. Loudon in 1831 catalogued Small's plough, the chain laid aside as a useless encumbrance; that used in Northumberland and Berwick which was very like Small's; Wilkie's, the best iron swing plough in Scotland; Finlayson's iron plough that was rather like Wilkie's but intended for moss cutting, his Kentish self-cleaning plough intended to be a substitute for the Kentish pattern, and his line plough with a rod from sheath to muzzle intended to facilitate depth control; Somerville's swing plough with a long narrow mouldboard, and his double-furrow plough; Gray's turnwrist swing plough; Wetherby's movable stilt plough; a ribbing plough that was on a smaller scale; Duckett's skim coulter plough; the Agyllshire swing plough without a coulter, designed by the Rev. Alexander Campbell, but having a fin or knife on the left side of the share; Clymer's iron plough; Stotherd's plough with a perforated mouldboard; Gladstone's water furrowing plough and the double-mouldboard plough. In addition to these there were the Beverstone wheel plough; the Kentish and Hereford wheel ploughs that were heavy and clumsy; the Norfolk wheel plough that looked clumsy but did its work well; Wither's friction wheel plough and the paring wheel plough, besides various draining ploughs; so already the list of types was very long and this is probably not complete.

The anonymous author of *British Husbandry*, 1837, adds to these the great Hereford wheel plough of which the faults were numerous; Ransome's patent swing plough; their double-furrow plough; a three-furrow plough invented by Dr. Cartwright; a ribbing plough made at Dr. Morton's manufactory of implements at Leith, which was introduced to the East Riding by Mr. Charles Howard. Wheel ploughs are also listed by this writer, and various types of harrows, etc. He suggests that two types, one with a long, slowly curving breast, the other shorter and more sharply twisted, would be sufficient for all general purposes in England, a sentiment that was repeated by J. Allen Ransome half a dozen years later.

None of this looks much like finality in design, although Martin Doyle, in the same year as the English Agricultural Society, afterwards the Royal Agricultural Society of England, was founded, expressed himself as satisfied that the true formation of the plough, and the correct adjustment of the several compound parts, was then perfectly understood by the scientific mechanic,[107] an opinion that was not shared by other contemporary writers. For example, the Rev. W. L. Rham at almost the same date contributed a long article to the *Penny Encyclopaedia* on plough design, most of which he included in his *Dictionary of the Farm*. He claimed that his theory was the basis of Ransome's design.[108] Rham adds Ransome's Rutland plough and the Bedford wheel plough to the growing list of types. The latter was an iron-framed plough with two wheels and had a draught rod rather like Small's skim. Passmore thought it typical of the best ploughs manufactured about 1825.[109]

Though great progress had been made, and despite Doyle's dictum, the best construction of plough was still, in 1839, a matter of controversy. The harrow was confessedly most imperfect, though Finlayson's harrow, little enough used in the south, or the scarifier, could occasionally be used to take the place of a plough.[110] As I have said, J. Allen Ransome was of the same opinion, when he wrote his *Implements of Agriculture*, 1843, that the best form of the mouldboard had not yet been decided. He does agree substantially with Rham and this lends some colour to the latter's claims.

Naturally when this subject was still so controversial it was largely ventilated in the early volumes of the *Journal of the Royal Agricultural Society*, and both the Society and individual members carried out trials to determine the effectiveness of different ploughs. For example, "Trials on the draught of ploughs" were organized by Trelawney Freeman of Haverfordwest, Pembroke, and reported in the 1841 volume. He altered the mouldboard of Hart's plough and found it better than Ransome's or the common Welsh plough in local conditions. In the previous volume, Henry Handley discussed the insoluble question of the relative advantage of wheel and swing ploughs. Philip Pusey discussed his "Experimental enquiry on Draught in Ploughing," in which he tried ten different ploughs on two kinds of soil. Six trials in all were made, but the figures obtained were an insufficient guide to the proper shape of the plough breast. Pusey suggested that when a standard plough was obtainable it might be possible to "employ the draught gauge in the classification of soils to register their different degrees of tenacity." Henry J. Hannam went even further in 1842 when he suggested that all farmers should make dynamometer tests of their ploughs in the various soils on their farms and while doing different jobs. They should also keep careful records in order to accumulate a large body of evidence. Some experiments on the draught of ploughs were carried out at the Society's show, and at Bristol, 1842, when Howard's two-wheel Bedford plough carried off the palm. This confirmed the report of the Judges of Implements at Liverpool, where wheel ploughs had been found the lightest in draught; but was only conclusive about the conditions under which the trials were conducted. Illustrations could be multiplied. Annual essays on the county where the show was held became a normal feature of the Society's journal, and in these essays there is an infinity of evidence about the types of plough used in the different counties. But this did not make any one kind of plough general, and Wedlake's, a firm of agricultural merchants, were prepared to sell no less than forty different kinds of plough at their City Repository in 1847.[111]

A plough that was used on the hills in the South-west was double ended. This was improved, and the improvements patented by Lowcock in 1843. It was intended to cast the furrows all the same way, like the Kentish and other turnwrist ploughs; but it had the two plough bodies attached to the same beam, placed heel to heel on the same side of the beam, one being right handed and one left. It could be hauled from either end, and it was arranged so that, when the horses turned on the headland, the draught chain could slide from one end of the beam to the other. There was an early plough of this kind with a wooden sheath and beam in the Torquay Museum, probably dating from the late eighteenth or early nineteenth century. Passmore[112] suggests that this type originated in Devon. Lowcock lived at Marldon, in that county, in 1843. His patent covered several improvements on the early type that made for easier working, and Ransome's took up its manufacture. With some further improvements, notably that of Murison in 1876, which made for strength and ease in working, this type of plough continued to be used until the end of the nineteenth century, though it had the competition of the balance plough.

The multiplicity of ploughs, their merits and demerits, continued to be described by the writers of textbooks and the contributors to farming periodicals all through the second half of the nineteenth century.[113] Doubtless some of the exceedingly numerous patents that were taken out made for greater ease of working, lighter draught, easy manipulation in breakdowns and so on, but at the turn of the half-century inventors began to give most of their attention to the latest thing, the application of steam power to farming operations. Indeed it was possible for a writer in the *Encyclopaedia Britannica*, 11th edition, 1911, to say that in the later part of the nineteenth century there were numerous improvements but no fundamental alterations in the construction of the ordinary plough. George Bourne found that the demand for wooden beams and stilts (which his father had used with ploughshares, turn-furrows, and other castings obtained from the Reading Ironworks), disappeared a few years after he had taken over the business. Their place had been taken by "cast iron ploughs, painted a pale bright blue." He added that the history of harrows and drags was much the same. The coming of the iron harrow was slightly earlier.[114]

I have already commented upon the new rollers and extirpators, etc., that came upon the market in the nineteenth century. A few names that come to mind are Biddell's extirpator, Ducie grubber, Parmenter harrows, the chain link and expanding harrows, Crosskill's clod crusher, the Cambridge roller, but these implements were legion.

The iron age had descended upon farming as upon other industries, and the second half of the nineteenth century saw the first of those gargantuan engines and machines, the steam ploughs and cultivators. Then no one would have thought that their reign was to be only of three-quarters of a century's duration.

(b) Steam Cultivation[1]

The first man to use a digging stick in the dim ages of pre-history began farming. There was no farming in any real sense of the word before the digging stick was used.

The first step towards mechanizing farm operations in Britain was the seed-drill made by Jethro Tull in the late seventeenth or early eighteenth century. This drill comprised, in its own structure, working parts set in motion when it was drawn along the ground. The second step was the making of a successful reaper by the Rev. Patrick Bell in the early nineteenth century. This again was a machine in the sense that it embodied working parts set in motion by gearing from the ground wheels. Incidentally, neither of these men was the originator of the idea of their respective machines.

Although these devices were machines, the use of steam power for traction is properly the first phase of farm mechanization; the internal combustion engine tractor is the second. The possibility of using a steam engine for this purpose was recognized by an ambitious patentee some three centuries ago, if the vague terms in which all early specifications are couched can be so interpreted. David Ramsey in 1630 entered a patent for "Making the earth more fertile," which seems to have suggested that steam power could be applied to land transport, and by analogy, to the haulage of cultivating implements. Some hundred and forty years later, in 1767, Francis Moore, who patented "a fire engine to supplant horses," not only for the cultivation of the land, but the dragging of carriages, told his friends that horses were doomed and about to be superseded by steam as a motive power. His certainty was so assured that he sold his horses, and induced some of his friends to do the same in order to escape the inevitable slump in horse prices that would follow on the introduction of steam traction.[2] This belief was still not shared by a great farmer writing just after the "Ivel" agricultural motor had first been demonstrated in 1904, and after steam ploughing had been a practical reality for over half a century. He only went so far as to admit that as an auxiliary in wet seasons, or in scarcity of labour, or on foul land, or to backwardness of preparation, the aid of steam might be invaluable.

But few farmers, he believed, would afford both horse power and steam power. They certainly could not do without horses. It was possible that the time might be at hand when agriculturists might find it not only invaluable but indispensable to rely upon an arm that never slackens, never tires and never strikes, and the Ivel agricultural motor might be the forerunner of further developments.[3] This hesitating prophecy has been more than amply fulfilled.

Following closely upon the heels of the sanguine Moore, Richard Lovell Edgeworth, the father of the novelist Maria Edgeworth, patented in 1770 a "sort of endless railway" for the haulage of land cultivating implements, a precursor of Boydell's 1846 patent, which was along the same lines, and which, unlike Edgeworth's, was actually tried out in the field. Even James Watt himself thought it necessary, in 1784, to protect some ideas he had, but did not go beyond a notice. These activities were followed by a standstill for thirty years so far as published patents are concerned, but the idea was still simmering. An elaborate specification was patented by a Major Pratt in 1810. This may have been the inspiration of Wren Hoskyns' eulogy of rotary cultivation.[4]

Pratt's claim was "Cultivation of land is performed in several ways—(1) A series of ploughs revolve in a horizontal axis, the ploughs being raised over the ploughed land; (2) Harrows are worked in a similar manner; (3) Land is cultivated by means of chains having tines or grubbers fixed in them, working longitudinally over two vertical pulleys, one at each end of the machine; and (4) By means of an endless chain passing over horizontal pulleys or carriages placed along the field, one pulley being on each carriage. To one side of the endless chain a plough is attached, and works alternately between two carriages, the carriages being moved forward as the work proceeds. Thus a carriage on four wheels, one at each end or side of the field, and a locomotive or portable engine in the centre with endless chain and two ploughs, would form the details of the project for ploughing a field of land." There is no evidence that these ideas were ever tried out in the field, but they may have inspired later inventors to produce the apparatus of similar design that came into common use about fifty years later.

A number of other patents were taken out between Major Pratt's and 1832, amongst which two are worth mention because they were in principle much the same as successful equipment of later date. In 1812 Messrs. Chapman took out a patent for "a steam carriage with a rigger working on a stretched chain or rope, secured at both ends with anchors." This principle of "rigger" traction for hauling ploughs was adopted with numerous modifications by many inventors, and by 1857 had met with practical success. Twenty years after Chapman's patent, Joseph Saxton, in 1832, patented a system of "differential pulleys." Part of this was applicable to the working of ploughs, an endless rope being used to give motion to a windlass to which the ploughs, etc., were attached. Again I can find no evidence to show whether these written descriptions of machines ever generated full-sized apparatus that worked in the field, either experimentally or practically. Indeed, all the systems invented until 1832 have been described as abortions—although it was conceded that some of them in the hands of a Fowler or a Howard "might have been rendered available."

In that year a practical machine was designed. It was used in 1836, the year before Queen Victoria's Accession. It was the patent of John Heathcote, M.P., a lace manufacturer of Tiverton, Devon, and gave traction by a direct pull from a stationary engine. "One end of a drag-rope is fixed on to a long drum situated longitudinally over the boiler, and in length equal to the length of the field coiled upon it. The rope then passes to the opposite headland round a large pulley there of an auxiliary carriage, which serves for an anchor. The rope then returns and is fixed to the opposite end of the long drum. To one side of this rope the plough carriage is fixed. The drum is then set in motion when it coils up one end of the rope as it gives off the other, the engine and auxiliary carriage moving along opposite headlands as the work of ploughing advances." Heathcote was assisted in his enterprise by Josiah Parkes, and brought out his engine in 1834, when he drove it over a mile and a half of unreclaimed bog on its primitive "caterpillar" track.

A plough made by Parkes "performed admirably, laying the furrow slice as straight as an arrow, being the first time known at present (1866) of land having been ploughed by steam." It was intended for use in bog reclamation, and was tried out on Chat Moss, Lancashire, where Sir John Forbes, amongst others, saw it at work. Forbes remarked thirty years later that the method of hauling the plough between the engine and an anchor was still in use. One plough went back and fore and turned a good furrow slice, but turning over the surface of a peat bog is a special job, and was too limited to arouse general interest. The projectors were afraid to tackle ordinary cultivation, though Howard (I think the reference must be to a member of the Bedford firm) is said to have thought that if Heathcote and Parkes had adapted their invention to ordinary cultivation they would probably have been successful. A prerequisite was the wire rope not yet invented, so that the projectors failed and lost the £12,000 spent in bringing out their invention.

The Highland and Agricultural Society had offered a prize of £500 for the first successful application of steam power to soil cultivation, and they awarded Heathcote £100 towards defraying the expenses of exhibiting his machine at Dumfries in 1837, but this did not go very far towards meeting his deficit.[5] I seem to remember reading that the engine was left out on a bog one night and when its owners went to work in the morning it had sunk out of sight.

The Highland Society withdrew its offer of a prize for this type of machinery in 1843, whether from an opinion that steam could not be applied to hauling agricultural implements or not is difficult to decide. Be that as it may, this opinion was strongly held by many eminent men, including no less an authority than J. Allen Ransome, whose *Implements of Agriculture* appeared in that year. "The mode of drawing ploughs by locomotive engines, on the same plan that railway engines are drawn," he wrote, "does not offer a prospect of success . . . we believe it to be the wisest way not to attempt a matter beset with difficulties of greater magnitude than road haulage by loco." He thought it might be possible to do something on the lines of the Heathcote invention and that "the time is perhaps not very far distant when a steam engine will be one of the matters to be thought of on every well conducted farm with 300 or 400 acres of arable land." He was then thinking of a stationary steam engine which could be used for barn work and for boiling food for animals.[6] When in 1849 Robert Ritchie produced his *Farm Engineer*, a book that dealt with the types of steam engines available for farm work, but mainly for use in driving threshing machines, he also categorically stated his conviction that ploughing by steam power was a chimera.[7]

Mr. Hannam gave him the lie the very next year. He was "a well-known agriculturist of Burcote, near Abingdon in Berkshire," and his idea was carried out by Messrs. Barrett and Exall of Reading. This was to haul ploughs on a wire rope moved by an ordinary portable engine either at the corner of a field or outside it. It was the original "roundabout system," afterwards adopted in Smith's and Fowler's systems. Wire ropes were used, and coiled and uncoiled by a windlass with two drums or winding barrels. This apparatus ploughed sixty acres at the rate of five acres a day, and then the rope broke and this, with other difficulties, caused the projectors to abandon their system. If they had had the advantage of steel wire rope and had possessed more perseverance there is little doubt that they would have made a successful issue of their idea.

Two years later Lord Willoughby d'Eresby exhibited a set of steam ploughing tackle at the Great Exhibition of 1851. This had all the elements of success. It was a double engine set, and two furrow ploughs on Lowcock's turnwrist principle were carried on a frame, the whole of which regulated the depth of the furrow. Two engines stood on the headlands at opposite sides of the field, and each alternately hauled the plough towards it by means of a chain, the other engine idling. This apparatus proved capable of ploughing four acres a day, but the chain haulage was declared "the fatal cause of a want of success." The system was widely adopted later, wire ropes being used in the place of chains.

The Marquis of Tweeddale followed with a similar system, but thought it necessary, before steam ploughing, to subsoil by horse traction and to clear the land from boulders. He invented a subsoil plough for this purpose, and modified the mouldboard of the plough, making it shorter and rising more acutely than was usual. At first he tried steam ploughing with a single-furrow plough, but found that it was easily possible to use a double-furrow plough of the balance type. Slight and Burn thought that the part played by this nobleman in developing the steam plough had not received the recognition it deserved. The apparatus was made by Tullock.

Messrs. Fisken of Newcastle took out a patent for a very similar apparatus in 1855 (Specn. No. 1629), and Forbes states that it was exhibited at the "English Society's Show" of that year. The Report on Implements at the "Royal" show at Carlisle makes no reference to it, and indeed makes a specific disclaimer of any successful attempt at Carlisle "to carry out the much sought for application of steam power to the cultivation of the soil." It was evident that "the minds of mechanicians have been extensively turned to that subject." Fisken's apparatus was demonstrated on a small farm in Perthshire and won a small money prize from the Highland Society.

Fowlers had shown a steam draining plough at the "Royal" show at Lincoln in 1854. The judges made the obvious comment that the same arrangement could surely be applied to other operations. This hint was so well taken that, at the "Royal" show at Chester in 1858, they were obliged to award the long offered prize of £500 to John Fowler, Jun., of 28, Cornhill, London, for his steam plough manufactured by Robert Stephenson and Co. of Newcastle-upon-Tyne and Ransome and Sims of Ipswich. This outfit won several other prizes in the same year.

The hint given to Fowler's was taken, too, by William Smith, an owner-occupier of a farm at Woolston, near Aylesbury, Bucks, who bought an engine and windlass, invented his "cultivator," and at once began work with these things on his own farm. This was said by Forbes to have been "for some time the only working steam plough in the country." It was worked on the "roundabout" system, either with the engine and windlass at one corner of the field and three anchors at each other corner, or with the engine and windlass in the middle of one side of the field and four anchors appropriately placed. It was considered necessary to use the cultivator first to tear up the ground to a depth of six or seven inches and then to use a heavier implement of the same kind travelling the opposite way to shift any portion not moved by the first. The soil was left with a rough irregular surface that must have been painful to those contemporaries who adored the straight, clean-laid furrow, but was probably very like the seedbed prepared by some modern implements. The machinery was made by Howard's of Bedford.[8] This system of haulage by steel wire rope on a stationary engine became the prototype of successful steam cultivation, and finally came to be the pair of traction engines of the common practice of the late nineteenth and early twentieth centuries.

Meanwhile a good deal of ingenuity, money and time was wasted in the production of steam diggers or rotatory implements. These formed so definite a break with accepted methods that they had an inevitable attraction for original minds. Dan Pidgeon writing in the *Royal Agricultural Society's Journal* for 1890 went so far as to say that "the introduction of steam ploughing was long retarded by the firm hold which the idea of rotary cultivation had taken upon the public mind, thanks in a great measure, to the clever writings of Mr. Wren Hoskyns, and large sums of money were spent in demonstrating the impracticability of the plan before agricultural enquiries settled down to the conviction that they must seek the solution of the steam tillage problem in Haulage." But jocular and cynical as Hoskyn's presentation of the case for rotary cultivation was, he was by no means the originator of the idea. Possibly if may have been the Major Pratt, whose patent of 1810 has already been mentioned, although that is not certain. Robert's Patent Rotary Digging Machine was protected in January 1822, the action of which was described as similar to Morgan's Feathering Paddle Wheel. It was provided with tines set in discs that curved towards the line of advance of the machine, which must have notably increased the draught, and these tines could be raised or lowered in or out of work by a worm.[9]

F

This machine must, I think, have been designed for animal traction, though there is a possibility that it was intended for mechanical haulage.

One of the most sanguine of the admirers of the rotary principle was John Algernon Clarke, whose report on the subject fills many pages of the *Royal Agricultural Society's Journal* for 1859.[10] His conclusion was that "with so much evidence in its favour and so much mechanical and agricultural intellect at work upon it, the revolving steam digger has every prospect of vanquishing all obstacles and entering on a career of success." Forbes, who had a good deal to do with Usher's invention, which was of this type and proved impracticable, was able to say only a few years later (1866) that Clarke's prophecy had "entirely misgiven." The system, however, played an integral part in the development of steam ploughing, and must be described not only for this reason, but for the interest of some of the more peculiar pieces of mechanism proposed and even constructed.

A necessary result of Clarke's enthusiasm for the rotary principle was that his report was very detailed and must be very briefly summarized here. Not all the rotary cultivators and digging machines were designed specifically for steam power. For instance, in 1846 Messrs. Bonser and Pettit patented a tiller formed of a cylindrical shaft with a number of radial cutters, prongs or tines, straight or curved, attached at right angles and arranged round it spiral wise like a screw. It was set in the back of the machine, its axis at right angles to the line of travel, and revolved rapidly by toothed gearing in the same direction as the wheels of the carriage so that the cutters entered the soil downwards, tossing the crumbled earth backwards, and tended to propel the machine forwards. This was designed for horse traction, but the inventors contemplated using steam power. Clarke comments that an engine mounted on the platform and driving the travelling wheels would have made it like some subsequent inventions. One of these was Romaine's invention patented in 1853. At first it carried an engine to drive the cultivator but was hauled by horses, a sufficiently incongruous job. It was afterwards fitted with gearing to make it self-propelled.

Other similar horse-drawn rotary implements were patented. One was by a certain Paul in 1847. This was a revolving drain cutter and a revolving subsoiler hauled by a horsepower windlass. Another was by Sir John Scott Lillie. He invented a tillage apparatus, driven either by gearing from one of the travelling wheels, if horse drawn, or more directly from a steam engine placed upon the machine, the carriage itself being propelled by the engine winding along a fixed rope. A further curiosity was patented by a Mr. Bethell in 1852. It was a rotary digger attached to an agricultural steam engine. "The machine was drawn forward by horses and the steam driven digger cut away the earth and threw it backwards." In 1857 Bethell abandoned the anomaly and patented "the attaching of a revolving forker behind a locomotive engine, having the Boydell rails upon its wheels." These Boydell rails, originally patented in 1846, consisted of "moveable detachable parts of a railway (fitted) to the wheels of the carriages, whereby each part is successively placed by its wheel on the road or land over which the carriage travelled, each part of the portable railway, when down, allowing its wheel to roll over it, the wheel depositing and lifting the parts of the railway in succession."[10]

This crude forerunner of the track-laying vehicle enabled a heavy steam loco to travel over the land without unduly compressing it. It could therefore haul a rotary cultivator, a plough, or any other cultivating implement, or a trailer carrying produce or manure, so that horses could be dispensed with, or so the inventor was convinced. Though not successful on the land, the Boydell system was apparently used for the transport of heavy loads on the roads.

Clarke was particularly enthusiastic about Usher's invention patented in 1849, although Forbes, who played an important part in its development, considered it a failure some years after Clarke's report had been issued. Clarke's description is "A portable steam engine is mounted upon a framework mainly supported by a pair of broad felloed wheels or a wide roller, and also by a front pair of wheels turning in a transom for steerage. A lever frame at the back of the carriage supports a horizontal transverse shaft, which may be raised or lowered at pleasure, and both this shaft and the main bearing wheels are driven by toothed gearing from the engine crank shaft, the wheels rotating so as to give a slow progressive motion to the machine, the shaft revolving at greater though moderate speed. On this shaft are fixed four or more discs or plates, each carrying three ploughs of a curved form, so arranged that no two shares strike the ground at the same instant. These ploughs penetrate the ground in the opposite direction to that in which the machine is advancing, thus propelling

it, the spur wheel on the carriage wheel regulating the rate of advance."
This was supposed to allow all the engine power to be applied to the
digging shaft, the forward movement being aided by the thrust of the
diggers. It was a part of the controversy whether more power was used
in hauling rope-drawn implements, or moving the engine itself over
the land with the implements attached. Forbes's conclusion was that the
amount of power required to carry the whole machine over uneven
ground rendered it quite unmanageable, a fatal objection to the system.
The first of these machines was made by Mr. Slight of Leith Walk,
Edinburgh, and tried in the autumn of 1851 and spring of 1852, at
Niddry Mains near Edinburgh.

Wren Hoskyns, whose pungent criticism of the proposal to haul
ploughs by steam had perhaps been responsible for the direction of
men's thoughts towards rotary cultivation, himself patented an idea in
1853 but did not build a machine. His proposal was to have a series of
cutters mounted on an axle placed just in front of the driving wheels
and adjusted for depth of work. The cutters (or tines as we should say)
were to be fixed diametrically opposite to one another, two on each
ring but staggered as regards the rings on the shaft so that they were
self-cleaning. The shaft was to be driven by a chain gear from the
engine driving shaft. It could be worked while the engine was stationary.
The process flocculated the soil rather than ploughed it, and so was
similar to the modern gyrotiller.

In 1853 the then famous razor-maker farmer, Alderman John
Joseph Mechi of Tiptree Hall Farm, Essex, introduced to the Society
of Arts a steam cultivator patented by Robert Romaine of Peter-
borough, Canada. This was a sort of cart on large broad tyred wheels,
carrying an upright boiler engine. A lever frame extended behind and
was raised or lowered by an adjusting screw. It supported the digging
cylinder, which carried a number of bars armed with picks, knives or
teeth, and was driven at high velocity. Mechi thought so much of this
machine—his opinion was that it was about to introduce a new
economy into British Agriculture—that he provided the capital to
patent and manufacture it. But the engine did not provide traction, and
it had to be hauled by horses. This was an anomaly speedily realized by
the inventor, who later modified it by using a horizontal engine to
supply driving power for the machine as well as the digging cylinder.
This improvement was made in Montreal in 1855 and shown at the

Paris Exhibition. One or two were afterwards built by Mr. Alfred Crosskill at the Beverley Iron Works, Yorkshire, but its weight was against it, for it was apt to sink in soft ground however wide the tyres.

From this time onwards the Patent Specifications are full of all sorts of steam ploughing apparatus, improvements to ploughs and so on, some of it quite Heath Robinson in appearance. A fair specimen is W. Smith's steam gang plough (Pat. Spec. 958 of 1858).

About the most ambitious of all the inventors who dealt in direct haulage was Lieut. Halkett, R.N., the inventor of the "Guideway Steam Agriculture."[11] The prime necessity of this system was to lay down permanent rails (or guideways) across the land at intervals of fifty feet on which to run a locomotive cultivator driven by two engines, one on each of a pair of rails. The cultivator was carried on a sort of suspension bridge fifty feet long spanning the distance between the rails. To the underside of this bridge cultivator or other implements were attached. On the headlands were other rails and a shunting engine for transferring the cultivator from one set of rails to another. All the ordinary implements could be used by this system, and it was claimed that the work was cheaply and efficiently done.[12] Ploughing, harrowing, scarifying, hoeing, drilling or dibbling seed, reaping (cutting and delivery) as well as setting cabbage and watering them, rather like the modern robot transplanter, could all be done at a few pence an acre after the necessary capital outlay for rails, amounting to £10 an acre for timber, and £20 an acre for brick and iron, apart from the cost of the machines.[13] A special rotary cultivator could also be used. It was like a long-toothed Norwegian harrow or spiky roller, was carried forward endwise, in the same direction as its length, and was driven at high velocity by shafts and bevel gearing. This made a very fine seedbed and was known as the "comminator." It was certainly ingenious.

A Mr. Grafton, who had worked with Halkett, modified the latter's system of rails. He had only a permanent rail on the headland with an endless railway of vulcanized rubber on which the propelling wheels, eight on each side, would run. The line of road must be kept perfectly smooth, free of obstructions and be perfectly straight. The endless railway was a continuous belt of vulcanized indiarubber combined with flax threads. To this belt wooden shoes about twelve inches by eighteen, faced with iron, were fastened by a staple across the centre of each shoe, at right angles to the belt. It passed round drums placed before and behind each series of wheels and through the side girders under the engines. This rail was said to be quite noiseless and a limited amount of steering was possible. It carried a spade plough in front to clear the road of obstructions.[14] It is not known whether anyone ever tried it out.

Yet another oddity was the rotary tiller patented by Thomas Rickett of the Castle Foundry, Buckingham, in 1857. It had a curious form and revolved in the opposite direction to the traction wheels, "thus tending to retard the progress of the machine and involving greater expenditure of power."

There were many other inventions of the same general type as a cursory examination of the Patent Specification discloses, and attempts to design rotary cultivators for use with steam went on sporadically until the 1880's. None, however, was ever widely used and all of them have been dubbed by Sir James Scott Watson "revivals of hope in rotary tillers and steam diggers."[15] Dan Pidgeon was even more emphatic. Like many other things, rotary tillage had to await the internal combustion engine, and the crawler track, before it became really possible.

Meantime rope haulage of tillage implements actuated by steam power had proved more practical than rotary cultivation. Perhaps the simplest form was that produced by John Fowler who won the R.A.S.E. £500 prize. The equipment consisted of a combined engine and haulage drum at one end of the field, and a self-propelling perpetual anchor and pulley at the other, both slowly moving along the headland so as to be always opposite the work. The plough, or other implement, was hauled up and down the land between them by an endless wire rope. Instead of coiling on a barrel, the rope was gripped by passing round grooves in a drum placed on a vertical axis underneath the boiler. A balance plough, cultivator, subsoil plough, harrows, etc., were designed for use with this set, and the engine could be driven under its own power from field to field or upon the road; but it had to have one or two horses in the shafts to steer it. By 1859 ten sets of this machinery had been supplied to farmers in widely scattered parts of the country. Wiltshire had one, Oxford two, Norfolk one, Essex one, Stafford one, Surrey two, Kent one, Scotland one; and twenty-five other sets had been ordered for delivery by August of that year.

Another system of rope haulage was that patented by Mr. Williams of Baydon, Wiltshire, a landowner-farmer who made some of the earliest experiments in steam cultivation. His method was to use a portable windlass, attached when required to a portable engine, both shifting together along the headland opposite to the ploughing. Another of his patents was a pitch chain wheel and pinion for making engines self-propelling. The engines used were those originally purchased for driving a threshing drum.

Mr. William Smith, of Woolstone, Fenny Stratford, Bucks, patented a combined double-breasted trench plough and subsoiler in 1855.[16] It was made by J. and F. Howard of Bedford. It consisted of an engine, separate windlass on travelling wheels, anchors, snatch blocks, ropes, rollers, cultivators and, of course, the combined trench plough and subsoiler. This outfit was used on what was known as the rectangular method, the ropes passing round two fixed and two movable snatch blocks, arranged so as to cut off one corner of the plot. The windlass was driven by a belt from any common portable engine of at least 7 h.p. Even more of this apparatus than of Fowler's had been sold by 1859. It was distributed in the following counties; Bedford took two, Berks two, Bucks ten, Cambridge one, Gloucester one, Herts one, Hunts two, Lincoln two, Northants four, Norfolk four, Oxford one, Stafford two, Warwick one, Wilts three, Yorkshire two, Ireland one and Scotland one.

Different arrangements for driving the windlass and for the disposition of the rope over anchors and rope porters were devised by other nimble brains. Messrs. Chandler and Oliver of Hatfield hung winding drums on an extended hind axle tree of a portable engine, one on each side of the boiler, driving the drums by toothed gearing from the engine crankshaft. This admittedly made the engine a heavy and cumbersome piece of machinery. Moreover, it was not placed in a corner of the field like Smith's rectangular system but half-way down one side, which obviously made the handling of the ropes more complicated.

Another windlass was designed by Hayes of Stony Stratford somewhere near Smith's farm. The two drums were driven from riggers (pulleys?) placed on the frame between them by a belt from the engine, and thrown in or out of gear by shifting the belt from one rigger to the other. A slack or dead rigger (loose pulley?) carried the belt when the drums were not working.

Mr. Massey of Newport, Salop, added a guide to the windlass for adjusting the coils of rope which traversed to and fro by means of a double screw like "the Scandinavian printing press." Howard's of Bedford also made a self-winding windlass, the motion "being ingeniously adopted from the endless rack of Baker's patent mangle."

The development of the portable steam engine and of the traction engine are well known. Already in 1849 the subject had occupied most of Robert Ritchie's *Farm Engineer*, which has been referred to above, and Robert Scott Burn contributed a series of detailed articles on "The steam engine and its application to agriculture" to the *Journal of Agriculture* in 1855, dealing almost entirely with the design and construction of different types. By then the stage was set for the practical application of steam power to tillage operations.

Clarke estimated that there were eight thousand portable steam threshing engines in use by the year of the Great Exhibition. This was only ten years after a portable engine was first exhibited at the "Royal" show at Liverpool in 1841. Five years after this innovation there was still only one steam engine shown at Newcastle in 1846, but at Worcester in 1863 there were one hundred and thirty-five. One of the exhibitors who had made a single steam engine in 1845 averaged an output of four hundred and eighty-eight engines in the four years 1859-62 and three hundred and seventy-three steam threshing machines per annum. Five thousand were then said to have been sold by one maker between 1852 and 1864. But these engines were mainly used for driving either portable or stationary threshing sets, or barn machinery for grinding, chaffing, pulping and slicing various kinds of feed for livestock.[17] Small farms and little fields were still an obstacle to the general adoption of steam cultivation.

Naturally the literature of the subject of steam tillage increased apace. P. H. Frere contributed an essay *On the present aspect of steam culture* to the 1860 volume of the "Royal" *Journal*, and referred largely to J. C. Morton's paper read to the Society of Arts and Wells's lecture to the Farmers's Club on the *Use of steam power in Agriculture* in the same year. Frere discussed, with quite inadequate data, an average day's work, the volume of work done in a season, the cost of labour and water cart, removals (in the field), the cost of steam power, and the cost of horse-power. He supplied the names of the farmers on whose views his

33. Babylonian Drill. Reproduced by courtesy of Dr. Anderson, *Thirty-nine Centuries* . . ., Agric. Hist., Oct. 1936.

A
NEW INSTVCTION
OF PLOWING AND SET-
TING OF CORNE, HANDLED
IN MANNER OF A DIALOGVE
betweene a Ploughman and a
Scholler.

Wherein is proued plainely that Plowing and
Setting, is much more profitable and leſſe
chargeable, than Plowing and
Sowing.

By EDVVARD MAXEY. Gent.

He that withdraweth the Corne, the people will curſe him: but bleſſing
ſhall be vpon the head of him that ſelleth Corne. Prou.11.26.

Imprinted at London by *Felix Kyngſton*, dwelling in Pater
noſter Rowe, ouer againſt the ſigne of the
Checker. 1601.

34. Setting Board. Title page of Edward Maxey, *New Instruction of Plowing*, 1601.

35. Worlidge's Drill. From his *Systema Agriculturae*, 1669.

36. Worlidge's Drill made by Mr. M. M. Averill, Severn Bank, Shrawley, Worcs.

37. Models of early Drills constructed at Chicago. From Anderson, *Thirty-nine Centuries* . . ., Agric. Hist., Oct. 1936.

38. Tull's Drill reconstructed, From Anderson, *Thirty-nine Centuries* . . ., Agric. Hist., Oct. 1936.

This four Wheel Drill Plow, with a Seed and a Manure Hopper was first Invented in the Year 1745. and is now in Use with W.m Ellis at Little Gaddesden near Hempstead in Herfordshire, where any person may View the same. It is so light that a Man may Draw it, but Generally drawn by a pony or little Horse—

39. Ellis's Drill. From William Ellis, *The Farmer's Instructor*, 2nd. ed., 1750.

A Drill Plough for single Dropping

40. Sharp's Seed Drill. From *Farmer's Magazine*, 1772.

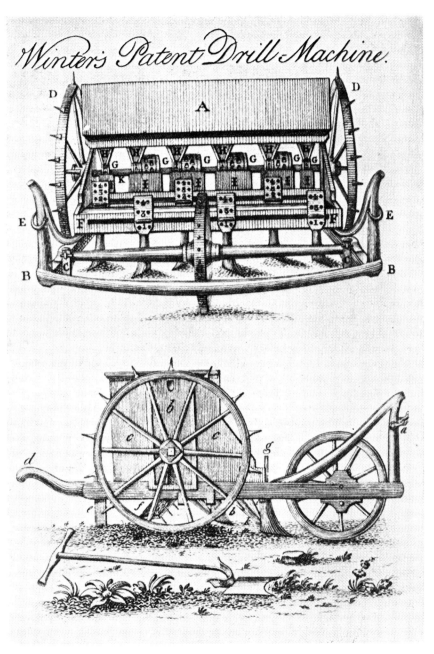

41. Winter's Drill. From George Winter, *A New and Compendious System of Husbandry*, 1787.

42. Cooke's, Morton's and Garrett's Drills. From John M. Wilson, *Rural Cyclopaedia*, 1849.

43. Northumberland and other Drills. From R. W. Dickson, *Practical Agriculture*, 1805.

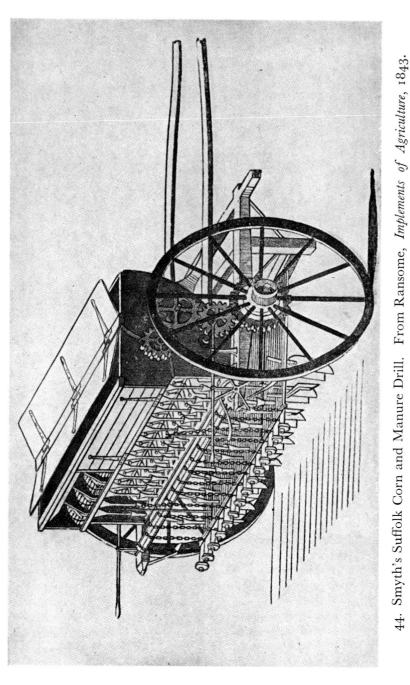

44. Smyth's Suffolk Corn and Manure Drill. From Ransome, *Implements of Agriculture*, 1843.

LORD WESTERN'S PATENT DRILL.

45. Lord Western's Drill. From Ransome, *Implements of Agriculture*, 1843.

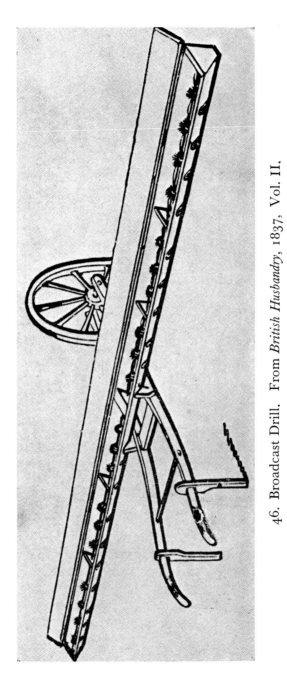

46. Broadcast Drill. From *British Husbandry*, 1837, Vol. II.

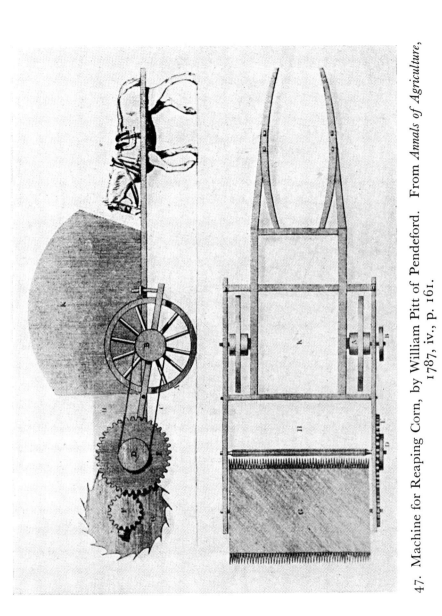

47. Machine for Reaping Corn, by William Pitt of Pendeford. From *Annals of Agriculture*, 1787, iv., p. 161.

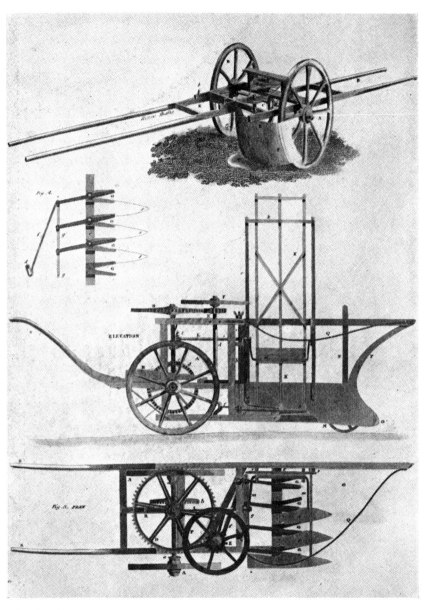

48. Plucknet's and Salmon's Reaping Machines.   From *Encyclopaedia Britannica*, 1797

conclusions were based. W. J. Moscrop described in the same *Journal* for 1863, three years working of a Fowler set on a farm at Buscot, Faringdon, Berks, and Clarke in the same year contributed an essay on *Five year's progress in steam cultivation.*

The Royal Show was held at Worcester in 1863 and thirteen different manufacturers' sets appear in the catalogue for that year. Some of these sets were entered for the Society's field trials. Clarke provided some useful figures. He extracted reports from the *Agricultural Gazette,* and tabulated them, covering the performances of eight of Fowler's sets, five of Howard's and twelve of Smith's sets in the previous year. He does not supply the addresses of the farmers so the distribution of these sets is not known. He does, however, give the place of working of some other sets discussed although some of them may already have been included in his calculations. For what it is worth the distribution was as follows:

Fowler's		*Howard's*		*Smith's*	
Berks	2	Berks	2	Bedford	4
Bucks	1	Essex	1	Berks	1
Essex	2	Hants	1	Bucks	3
Gloucester	2	Hunts	2	Hunts	1
Northants	2	Kent	1	Lincoln	3
Oxford	3	Oxford	2	Oxford	1
Somerset	1	Sussex	3	Somerset	1
Wilts	5	Warwick	3	Surrey	1
Worcester	2		—	Warwick	1
Yorks	1		15	Wilts	1
	—			Worcester	1
	21			Not Stated	1
	—				—
					19
					—

Four years later the "Royal" instituted a large scale enquiry into steam cultivation and issued reports from three committees in its *Journal* for 1867. The number of farms visited by members of the committees was one hundred and twenty-five and in addition eight contracting persons or companies were interviewed. The number of farms is nearly double that dealt with by Clarke in 1863, and their geographical distribution is wider, but a comparison of the two sets of figures shows that the one hundred and twenty-five is not complete because Clarke reported a larger number of sets in some counties than the committees reported. The committees' figures are as follows:

Bedford	6	Hunts	7	Stafford	2
Berkshire	3	Kent	1	Suffolk	4
Bucks	2	Lancs	2	Surrey	1
Cambs	2	Leics	3	Sussex	5
Cumber-		Lincoln	9 and 2 con-	Warwick	2
land	3		tractors	Westmor-	
Derby	2	Norfolk	3	land	1
Dorset	2	Northants	6	Wilts	5
Durham	2	Northumb	4	Worcester	3
Essex	6	Notts	8	Yorks E.R.	2 and 1 con-
Glos	4	Oxford	7		tractor
Hants	2	Somerset	1	Yorks N.R.	3
Hereford	2 contract-	Shropshire	4 and 2 con-	Yorks W.R.	2 and 1 con-
	ing com-		tracting		tractor
	panies		companies	North	
Hertford	3			Wales	2

The detailed reports on each undertaking give elaborate data of cost of working, effect on crops, economy in horsepower effected, etc. These data, however, although they could be assembled in tabular form would not be strictly comparable because the form of the reports is not absolutely standardized; so only the conclusions of the committees will be presented here.

No. 1 committee thought that many "steam" farmers did not reap the full advantage to be derived from the use of the new power. It was to the character of the farmer rather than the apparatus that the advantageous results were mainly due, but experience was yet too limited to enable a precise measure of the use of steam cultivation to be made. On medium and heavy soils the benefits obtained were undeniable. Deeper culture was obtained at cheaper rates than horsepower could have given, and nearly always with resulting higher yields. It was, however, easier to estimate the costs than yields. More work was possible in a given time and it was less arduous for the farm worker who also made better wages. With their growing experience of the use of the steam engine in the barn and in the field the agricultural population was being trained for the coming age of machinery in farming. The light land farmers did not think steam cultivation was useful, but deep stirring of the soil was beneficial even on such land. Unfortunately the implements available had been designed for heavy land, and special types were necessary before the system could be extensively adopted on lighter soils. It was thought that double-engine sets with bigger implements should be used. Some Fowler's had been worked in Norfolk with six-furrow ploughs and ninety-inch cultivators by contractors on six farms.

Sport was a definite impediment to the progress of steam tillage. Straggling hedgerows provided cover for hares, and stubbles were left late for cover for partridges. Committee No. 2 heartily agreed with this conclusion, adding that the clay lanes along which the tackle had to travel to farms should be made into roads, that mile after mile of straggling hedges and primeval copse and spinneys should be closely trimmed, and where tenants were forbidden to use a reaping machine and limited to stubble of a certain number of inches height, the proprietors should take a more serious view of their responsibilities, and do their part in preparing their estates for the steam plough. Committee No. 1 added that a better system of tenant right and less stringent lease covenants would help. The four course system, they commented, while calculated to raise an unproductive district to a fair state, is not suitable for places where £12 to £14 and even £20 an acre is invested in land by tenants.

Estimates of the minimum acreage on which it would be economic to use steam-driven apparatus varied between three hundred and fifty acres heavy land, five hundred of lighter soil plus two hundred and fifty acres of strong land, and three hundred and fifty to four hundred acres of light land, but the engine would still have to earn most of its keep at other work as well. The Supplementary Committee which made the second estimate stated that as the time worked is increased so the profits are increased. It was an exaggerated claim in 1867 to say that the steam ploughing engine was so far perfected and settled in form and details, that it might be classed among old established, standard farm machinery, and no longer among the novelties of the day. But it was doubtless true that, in the main, it answered well, the failures being easily explicable by the bad management of some sets, the neglect of repairs and leaving the machines exposed to the weather.

These reports covered some sixty-six thousand acres of farm land which was estimated to be one-third of the whole steam-tilled area in the kingdom. This was a sufficient advance in the comparatively few years that steam tillage had been established, but was certainly not a major part of the total area under tillage, which can then have been no less than twelve million acres. It was certainly not sufficient to justify Forbes's enthusiastic prophecy that "years may yet elapse before the consummation of the process, but the 'jocund' team is doomed. Changes must be made, fields squared, companies formed, implements improved, but the silent march of events will most surely bring the new power into general use."[18]

Unfortunately the "Royal" did not conduct any later enquiry into the progress of steam tillage, although in discussing these Reports the then President, H. S. Thompson, said that of one hundred and seventy-eight owners only one had operated more than ten years and only thirty-three more than five years, so that insufficient experience had yet been acquired to lay down hard and fast rules on the subject. One thing was clear. In the early days there was a great number of inventors and makers, but the effluxion of time had weeded them out so that the farmer was now able to make a suitable choice from the comparatively small number of types offered, always supposing he could afford to invest the necessary £800 to £1,500.

Progress continued, but the general types had become stable, although it is doubtful whether more than a small proportion of the arable acreage was ever tilled by steam ploughing sets. Steam ploughing was mainly done by contractors, and Russell M. Garnier was over-credulous in 1893 when he said "the evolution of machinery, the application of steam power to all the more important farming operations has gone far to settle the question in favour of the large holding. The steam plough has obliterated the necessity for small fields, and utilised the ground formerly occupied by the fences between them."[19]

A more exact estimate of the progress made is that recently presented by J. H. Clapham[20] who speaks of the brand new system of steam cultivation. "The agricultural literature of the sixties is full of it—the various methods; the costs; the soils and surfaces fitted for it; the size of farm which could carry its own tackle; the difficulties of hiring tackle. Actual progress was slow . . ." The "Royal" Committee maintained that its extension required, apart from mechanical improvements in the tackle and less folly in the handling of it, the introduction of a normal thirty to forty acre field, greater freedom of cropping, the establishment of tenant right, and more co-operation between landlord and tenant in getting rid of the hedgerows.

Progress thereafter there was, but not so rapid as it might have been; for the committees' conditions were very imperfectly fulfilled. Soil and surface limited steam cultivation in Britain, but the human limitations were more decisive.

The knell of steam ploughing sounded during the war of 1914–18, when large numbers of farm tractors driven by internal combustion engines were imported in order to speed up food production. Although the heavy old equipment was still to be seen on farms and in contractors' yards a few years ago, it is now quite definitely superseded. The first phase of farm mechanization in England may be said to have ended in the early years of the current century.

CHAPTER THREE

SOWING THE SEED

MODERN TECHNICAL LANGUAGE cannot describe the crop prospects of a farmer who sows his seed broadcast in poorly tilled land, better than the simple words of the parable of the sower.

"Behold a sower went forth to sow; and when he sowed, some seeds fell by the wayside, and the fowls came and devoured them up; some fell upon stony places, where they had not much earth; and forthwith they sprang up because they had no deepness of earth; and when the sun was up, they were scorched; and because they had no root they withered away. And some fell among thorns; and the thorns sprang up and choked them; but others fell into good ground, and brought forth fruit, some a hundred fold, some sixty fold, some thirty fold."

And in all the centuries of corn-growing before the seventeenth, no other method of sowing corn had been proposed except the broadcast, a system which continued well into the nineteenth century. Millet's painting "The Sower" reminds us of it. But in the seventeenth century men attempted the seemingly impossible task of overcoming the farming difficulties hitherto regarded as natural, inevitable and unchangeable.

It was not until some two centuries later that the practice of seed-drilling had been fully discussed; even then it was by no means the general practice it is today. The uncertainty of the results of hand broadcast sowing, combined with the heavy burden of manual labour, gave birth to the idea that some other method might be adopted.[1]

The name of Jethro Tull is inseparable from our conception of the origin of the seed-drill. He has become the eponymous hero of the seed-drill, just as Townshend has of the turnip. All our farming historians have said proudly at one time or another that he was the first man to construct a practical apparatus for sowing seed instead of broadcasting it by hand. I have even said so myself, though I have been careful to point out that such a machine had been thought of in our country at least one hundred years before Tull's time (*c.* 1700). Less than forty years after Tull had published his book, Arthur Young wrote dubiously, "It is so many years since the first notion of sowing corn, etc., in rows was first started, that writers do not even pretend to decide who was the inventor; but certain it is that the use of the drill plough never made any progress worth mentioning, till Mr. Tull, perhaps *originally* (though not very likely in a man of his reading) *again* invented it."[2]

The seed-drill is only one of the very many inventions which have been lost sight of by neglect, or for some other reason, and re-invented as something quite new and original centuries later. Many countries claim to have been the birthplace of the inventor of the seed-drill. Italy[3] is, of course, amongst them, but even the antiquity of Roman civilization does not make that claim good. An engraving of an antique object, once in the possession of John Canton of the Academy in Spital Square, is adduced to prove that Rome invented the seed-drill, but the interpretation is a little generous.[4]

A month before the Italian claim appeared, the U.S. Department of Agriculture, Bureau of Agricultural Engineering, issued a summary of our knowledge of the history of the seed-drill, and demonstrated that it was certainly used in civilizations much more ancient and long precedent to the wolf that suckled Romulus and Remus. History, this summary stated, fails to reveal who invented the first seeding machine or even where it was made; yet the records show that a rude kind of drill has been used from a very remote period, and the husbandmen of China, Japan, Arabia, and the Carnatic have drilled and dibbled their seed from time immemorial.

China, where the first mention of a machine for seeding or drilling grain occurs about 2,800 B.C., is given precedence by another authority.[5] The Chinese machine was one of the wheelbarrow form, having a hopper to hold the seed, with three spouts carrying the grain through crude furrowing devices to the soil. Breasted, in his *Ancient Civilizations*, gives a reproduction of a drawing of a type of drill used in ancient Sumeria. It was a box placed on the plough beam behind the share; from it the seed dropped into the furrow immediately it was turned. A model has been constructed in the Museum of Science and Industry, Chicago.

In modern Europe the Italians can claim priority of date, and this Anderson concedes. The first patent was granted to Camillo Torello in 1566 by the Venetian Senate, but details of the machine, if one was used in this system of sowing grain, are lacking. Torello was followed by Tadeo Cavalini (or Cavellina) of Bologna whose drill was described by Canon Battista Segni in 1602 as wonderfully useful for flat country. "By means of it the corn is planted rather than sown, and there is a great saving of grain on the sowing. Its construction resembles that of a flower sieve carried on a small, simple carriage, with two wheels and a pole. Part of the body holds the grain to be sown and part is constructed under the sieve and is perforated, and to every hole there is fitted an iron tube directed toward the ground and terminating in an anterior knife-blade of sufficient length to make a furrow into which the sifted grain at once passes through the tube and where it is so completely buried that none of it is damaged. It is then immediately covered, by means of another iron implement, with the earth that has been excavated in the making of the furrow." Cavalini had solved the problem of the seed-drill or perhaps re-solved it. Segni is not sufficiently explicit about the seed-dropper, but all the elements of the modern seed-drill were embodied in this device.

Actually English inventors were working on the same project at about the same date, and probably people of other nations as well. The first English patent for a seeding machine was granted to Alexander Hamilton in November 1623, but the machine is not described in the specifications, and as no plate is printed, no idea of its practical character can be formed. Judging by the claims made for it by the inventor, it is unlikely to have been a practical implement, although, of course, it may have been able to do all that its inventor claimed for it. Another attempt to build a seed-drill that came to nothing was made by Daniel Ramsey in 1634. A patent was granted to him and another to Gabriel Plattes in 1639.[6]

By the end of the sixteenth century the English literature of farming was some seventy-five years old. General treatises had appeared and been supplemented by books on special subjects like hops, poultry and so on, but it was not till 1600 that proposals for "setting" corn were made.

The occasion, we are told, arose in this way. "Happily," wrote Sir Hugh Plat, "some sillie wench, having a fewe cornes of wheate, mixed with some other seed, and being carlesse of the worke shee had in hand, might now and then instead of a Raddish or Carret seede, let falle a wheate corne into the ground which after branding itselfe into manie eares and yeelding so great encrease, gave just occasion of some farther triall."[7]

The further trial must have been on a very small experimental plot, because Sir Hugh says, "to my remembrance, the first man that ever attempted the setting of corne, made the first holes with his finger." It is not surprising to learn that "this course being afterwards found to be very long and tedious, an instrument was devised, having many teeth or pinnes, like a rake, with a staffe fastened in the middest of the backside thereof, which being thrust into the ground, did at one instant make twelve or twenty holes more or lesse, according to the number of teeth or pinnes therein. Afterwards this toole was also disliked as not making sufficient riddance of the ground."[8]

The instrument, which was to make the work more speedy, does not seem a great advance upon doing it by hand. It was a setting board, three feet long by ten or twelve inches wide, punched at regular intervals with holes through which a dibber could be pushed to make setting holes in the earth. The dibber had a shoulder three inches from its end to prevent it going any further through the board, thus ensuring an even depth of sowing. The line of sowing was kept by a gardener's line. This must have been a more laborious method than the rake-like tool, because the man had to kneel on the board to use his dibble.

Platt hesitated to recommend the depth and distance apart of the sowing; he had only heard it said that three inches deep and three inches apart had resulted in a yield of thirty bushels an acre, or about twice the existing average.[9]

Exaggeration of scientific results is not solely a modern vice. Another

G

writer, Maxey, did not hesitate to promise more certain and adequate results to those who would adopt the new system. He supported his statements by an interesting set of imaginary accounts. The charges recorded are nevertheless probably an accurate reflection of the costs usually incurred in producing wheat at the time. In making a comparison of the results of the two methods of sowing, he says:

"The land according to the use of the common fields, doth lie sommer fallow the first yeare, and beareth corne the other, and so the Farmer payeth two yeares rent before hee hath his crop, which rent cometh to thirtie shillings."[10]

For three acres ploughing and sowing		*One acre plough and set*	
Rent	30s.	Rent	10s.
Ploughing four times at 2s. an		Five ploughings ..	10s.
acre	24s.	40 loads dung	20s.
Dunging at 12-14 loads an acre,		½ bushel seed	2s.
6d. a load	20s.	Setting:—	
Seed 2½ bushels wheat or rye an		1 man at 8d. a day;	
acre at 4s. a bushel ..	30s.	4 people at 4d. for 6 days	12s.
Weeding, reaping and other		Seeding, etc. .. .. 3s. 4d.	
charges for 2 years	10s.	Total 57s. 4d.	
Total	114s.	Seven or eight qrs. pro-	
Usual increase 2 qrs. an acre,		duce at 4s. a bushel =	
but he allows 2½ at 4s. 32s. a		£12 16s.	256s.
qr. = £12	240s.	Balance .. .. £9 18s.	
Profit £6 6s.	126s.	or 5 qrs. at 4s. = Balance	
Per acre	42s.	£5 2s. (to give a lower estimate).	

How far the farmers were convinced of the veracity of this new gospel, or how many tried it or even heard of it, it is now impossible to say. The subject dropped out of the literature of the day and did not reappear for about thirty years. Then a patent was granted to Otwell Worsley in 1637 for a method of setting carrots,[11] and other patents for instruments for mechanical sowing to Ramsey and Plattes.

Fortunately Plattes was articulate, and has supplied a more detailed account of his machine than is usually found in the vague patent specifications of that date. Unfortunately he was a little too articulate, and his descriptive matter is too verbose for full quotation. It was his desire to remedy the cost and inconvenience of the operation of setting.

In his opinion, as was perhaps natural, there was no way of doing this but by his "two new Inventions or Engines; the first remedieth the great charge and labour of workmen; for by this invention two men or boys, may set an acre upon a day; whereas before fourtie persons were little enough to do it.

"And the other Engine doth afterwards lay the land in little furrows or ridges, just upon the top of the rowes of corne; so that all other inconveniences are remedied."[12] It is not sufficient to dismiss this machine as one designed "to punch holes in the ground as it went along."[13] It was much more than that, as the inventor's own description shows. It was intended to feed the seed as it went along, and for that purpose had a hopper "ledged about with large ledges to keep the corne from spilling."

It is unlikely that this idea ever materialized. Hartlib, depreciating the extravagant yields promised by such theorists, said that Plattes offered a hundred to one increase. With some show of reason Hartlib did not think this possible, but his mind was not clearly made up about the proposed seed-drill. On the one hand he said that he could not recommend "M. Gabriel Platte's setting Instrument, for I know there are many difficulties in it, which he himselfe could never wade through." In fact he thought setting too much trouble for too little profit.[13a] In the same year he published a book entitled *The Reformed Husbandman*. It contained information that he had received some years before from a correspondent who had invented a sowing machine that sowed manure as well as seed, and planted at regular intervals and at regular depth. No details are supplied, but its inventor promised very profitable returns if it were used. Indeed, it would lead to the immediate recovery of the nation from the distress consequent upon the Civil War.

There was, too, *An Invention of Engines of Motion lately brought to perfection whereby may be dispatched without wind, water or horses any work now done in England or elsewhere*, 1651. This anonymous pamphlet hints at modern methods, but the invention is not described. Instead it makes a claim "To save or rather to set a plant in a way so much superior and more advantageous than the common way is hard to believe. The land thus sowed, set or planted, to manage the Crop when above ground got more to a double advantage by ways not formerly known or hardly thought on."[14]

A rather naïve proposal was made by another contemporary would-be public benefactor, who addressed *The Humble Petition of Thos. Ducket, Gent, Practitioner in Physick, to Parliament* on May 1, 1646. This was no less than that he should be allowed to publish a book showing his various inventions illustrated by prints, either with official approval, or over the House of Commons imprint. He asked, too, for powers to make a general survey of the kingdom, and that his book should be distributed to each parish throughout the country. Amongst his projects farming improvements played a large part.

Besides Hartlib, another well-known contemporary held the same opinion, a very just one, about Plattes. He admitted that "Mr. Gabriel Plattes' discovery of Hidden Treasure is very ingenious, and could'st thou but fathome his corne-setting Engine and cleare it to thine own and other apprehensions, it would be of excellent use without question."[15]

Blith also mentions a book entitled *New Inventions for the Improving Lands*, 1646. This is now very rare, the only copy of which I know being in the possession of Mr. Robert Boutflour, Principal of the Royal Agricultural College, Cirencester. It describes various implements, apparently newly invented, amongst which was a seed barrow. This Blith "thought might be of some good use, because certainly setting corne, could it be done with speed and at a certaine depth and well covered, would be worth discovering, but of this I have as little hope and as low an esteeme as of his other aforesaid Instruments."[16] This seed barrow was only intended to set one row; Blith thought hand setting would be quicker.

Another book that Blith commented on is a part of *Briefe Discoveries of Divers Excellent wayes and meanes for the Improving and Manuring of Land*. Imprinted at London for J.S., 1646. The author was almost certainly J. Sha, whose book was reprinted with a slightly different title in 1657. He told the reader that he had formulated certain instructions in husbandry that had not yet been practised by anyone, but that he could not describe the instruments to be used because words "for new *Inventions* must have new nominations, both the things themselves, and also of the particulars thereof," a truism of which modern times is only too well aware.

The instruments were a seed barrow, a manuring plough, a manuring waggon and a manuring roller. The seed barrow was a combined seed and manure drill with three funnels in the middle for seed and two side ones for manure. The manure to be used, both in this and in the manuring waggon, which was of much the same construction, was to be fine mellow dung in the form of dessicated powder, or marl, chalk or any other fat soil that could be beaten up to a powder for use in the machine. The waggon funnels were to be fixed so as "to goe as deepe in the earth as it is possible for the Cattle to draw the same." The ground must be prepared for them by ploughing "very slender and deepe, and breake the clods with a heavie Oxe-harrow or Horse rakes." The advantages of these new implements were that the three operations were done at one and the same time, and that seeding was regular and the dung directly applied to the seed. This sounds very much like the classical implement of des Carrières, and the idea may have derived from classical reading, a commonplace of every educated man's experience in those days. Further advantages claimed were that the manure was sown so as not to be leached out; the seed was covered at once and thus protected from birds; manure, a scarce commodity, was economically used, and the seed was put in at a proper depth, because the machines could be adjusted for that purpose. There is nothing to show that these ideas were any more than ideas. They are, alas, nebulous, although correct in theory.

Hartlib's and Blith's criticisms were not supported by John Worlidge either in his first book published in 1669, or in a later work issued in 1716.[17] In the former he gave Plattes's description of his drill verbatim, "lest any mistake might be imputed to the Relater. To ingenious men it is plain enough, but to others, this and everything else besides the plain Dunstable-road is intricate." This is repeated in the later work; but of course, Worlidge was a special pleader because he had himself invented a drill. After quoting the normal practice of setting peas, and exclaiming that he has himself set peas "as beans in a double row 'at a good distance, with admirable success . . . the same method is used at this day about Godalming in Surrey," he goes on to say, "I shall give here a plain and perfect description of an easy and feasible Instrument that shall disperse your Corn, Grain or Pulse, of what kind soever, at what distance, and in what proportion you please to design, and that with very great Expedition, and very little extraordinary charge, expense or Hazard." He was as modern in his ideas as J. Sha and, like him, he suggested that it was also possible to spread manure with his drill at the same time as the seed.

"By the use of this Instrument," Worlidge said, "also may you cover your Grain or Pulse with any rich Compost you may prepare for that purpose, either with pigeon-dung, dry or granulated, or any other Saline or Lixivial Substance, made dispersable, which may drop after the *Corn* and prove an excelent Improvement." This was to be done either by an extra hopper on the same carriage, or by another drill following immediately behind the seed-drill. And the seed could be covered in by "certain *Phines* or pieces of Wood or Iron, made flat at the end, and a little sloping, set on each side such rows of Corn or Grain." His description combined the three elements that are essential to the construction of a successful seed-drill.

But alas for the vanity of human aspirations! Worlidge was able to describe his drill in words, and even to give his readers a drawing of his machine. When, however, Richard Bradley tried, in 1727, to follow these verbal instructions and sketch, he was unsuccessful.[18] The machine he built would not work. Bradley, undoubtedly, was not "an ingenious man" in Worlidge's sense, because models which will work have recently been made by Mr. M. M. Averill, Severn Bank, Shrawley, Worcester, and by the Museum of Science and Industry, Chicago.

Dr. Anderson's description of Worlidge's drill is much simpler than the inventor's. It runs, "Worlidge's drill had a rectangular wooden frame. Behind the iron drill-shoe spread at the bottom was a curved wooden seed pipe leading from the dropper above. This dropper was an important contribution of Worlidge's to drill construction. From this device began the fluted force feeds so commonly used in America. It consisted of projecting strips of leather set in a wooden wheel. These strips, together with the rim of the wheel and the sides of the enclosing case, formed pockets which filled with seeds as the wheel was rotated below the hopper opening by means of a belt to a pulley on the back axle. . . ."[19]

Worlidge's drill was an elementary type of force feed drill. The year after his book appeared an elementary type of spoon feed drill, invented by a German, Locatelli, was introduced to the Royal Society by John Evelyn.[20] The German Emperor had given Locatelli a certificate in 1663. There is some controversy about the origin and demonstration of this drill.[21] It was attached to the Spanish plough, and as such known, I think, as the Sembrador. "The seed box was divided into two parts, the first holding the seed, and the second containing the seed dropper. This device consisted of a wooden axle or drum into which were placed four rows of brass spoons (at first made of tin), which, with the turning of the drum, caught the seeds in the lower part of the box and dropped them into funnels from which they fell to the ground. This drill which was tied closely to the plough, sowed the strip as ploughed. Like the Babylonian drills it had a drill shoe in the form of a plough, but it had no seed pipes to ensure accurate and even spacing of the seed. Its contribution was a seed dropping device which has proved successful. It is the common type of dropper in use in Europe today. . . ."[22]

It is doubtful if any of these devices for seed drilling were ever put into practice. They interested the growing body of scientific and experimental amateurs. They penetrated to the Royal Society, but few, if any, farmers ever heard of them.

There matters rested until the end of the century, when Jethro Tull produced his drill and horse hoe, and, thirty-odd years later, his book, *The Horse Hoeing Husbandry*, 1733, which contained drawings. There has always been a great deal of controversy about Tull, no less amongst his contemporaries than amongst later writers,[23] but there is no doubt that his was an original mind. Although he did not originate the idea of a seed-drill, he certainly did make a machine that worked. No better description of Tull's drills can be set out than Dr. Anderson's: "His first seeding device was built on the frame of a wheelbarrow. He enlarged one of the iron gudgeons to an inch and a half, made cavities around it to receive the seed, and placed it through the seed dropper case which he made in the ear of the wheelbarrow. As the wheel turned the seed was dropped by this device into open furrows and then covered by a light harrow. About 1701 he made his first drill for seeding sainfoin and wheat, describing it as one that made channels, drilled the seed and covered it. He made a number of variations of his drill, but all had the same type of seed dropper, a cylinder with rows of cavities which received the seed from the seed box and dropped them evenly into the furrows.

"The Tull drill for wheat, described and illustrated in the first folio edition of his book *Horse Hoeing Husbandry* (London, 1733), may be considered typical of his machines. This drill, which sowed three rows of seed, was drawn by one horse. The three coulters or hoes were narrow and shaped to enter the soil readily. At the rear of the coulters were passages open behind, which served to guide the seed from the funnels above to the channels in the ground. These coulters, the framework supporting them and the shafts resting upon the ground and not upon the four wheels of the machine. The two large wheels in front carried the seed box and dropper unit which fed the centre coulter on a one and threequarter inch axle. Two smaller wheels at the rear carried the droppers and seed-boxes feeding the two other coulters placed fourteen inches apart and some distance back of the central coulter so there would be no interference between them—an arrangement much used during the last century. The dropper unit consisted of the case at the bottom of the seed-box, and the notched axle which passed through it. The axle, with its notches and cavities in the periphery, turned with the wheels, received the grain from the boxes above, and dropped it into the funnels below. The passage of grain past the notched dropper was controlled by a brass cover and an adjustable spring, patterned after the tongue in the organ mechanism." This mechanism had been Tull's inspiration.

Tull himself declared he had not read any agricultural books before he invented his drill, having only undertaken this task when he was pressed to write for the general information of interested persons, who might not be able to make personal contact with him. His procedure has been rather summarily dismissed by Prof. Marshall[24] because he first evolved his system of husbandry, then invented a scientific theory to explain it, and finally studied the literature of his subject.

Though there was immediately a good deal of controversy about Tull's claims, Arthur Young could write mournfully in 1770 that "the spirit of drilling died with Mr. Tull, and was not again put in motion till within a few years." Young thought the real reason for its slow progress was the overweening claims of the inventors of the machines and the real insufficiency of the machines put forward. He was most probably correct in that assumption. Incidentally, he was so uncertain about drilling that he did not know whether to support the system or not.[25]

Tull's system was, however, taken up with some enthusiasm by two Frenchmen, Chateauvieux and du Hamel du Monceau. Chateauvieux carried out many experiments. They are described in du Monceau's book which was translated into English by John Mills and published as *A Practical Treatise on Husbandry* in 1759. This treatise discusses the history of the drill from Worlidge and Locatelli to Tull and the modifications introduced into Tull's seed dropper by Chateauvieux. The Frenchman's contribution was a single seed box and a cylinder with rows of cavities set close together which must have given a thicker seeding than Tull's drill. Du Monceau's seed dropper was on much the same principle, but sowed only three rows if I understand the text and the diagram correctly.[26] The whole Tullian operation was trenchantly described in 1760.

"The drill husbandry consists in a regular manner of sowing by means of a plough with a box, which delivers the seed as it goes. The plow opens trenches of a regular depth, the seed is dropped into them from the box in a regular manner; and there is a kind of harrow behind which throws in the mould and covers them. By this method the wheat is sown in rows, one, two, three or more together; with such intervals as the farmer pleases. There is the convenience of going to weed, and there is a part of the ground left unoccupied and consequently unexhausted, and fit for receiving the crop next year. A field of drilled wheat has a prettier aspect than one sown in the common way; and it is easier managed. The question remains whether an equal piece of ground produces this way a larger crop."[27] This was a question that could not be answered. The multiplication of inventions and exhortations went on increasing. As it is an impossible task to record them all, a few examples must suffice.

John Randall, a schoolmaster, of Heath, near Wakefield, Yorkshire, the apostle of the spiky roller, also invented a seed-furrow plough.[28] He had bought a drill plough from William Ellis of Little Gaddesden, Herts, built on the lines of Worlidge's at a cost of 4 guineas, but condemned it in the words "tis rather a child's go-cart." It was temperamental, did not always work, sowed one row only, and the seed and manure were from two separate hoppers. Du Monceau had tried to improve on Tull's drill, but the seed delivery of his machine was uncertain and irregular. Chateauvieux's drill, as simplified by de la Leoni, was the best. Randall's own machine was at first difficult to use and expensive. To make it cost £20. One which would set potatoes, beans or any kind of grain, had been used by a gentleman for some years. Randall apologizes for mentioning the despised potatoes—they were to be used as a cleaning crop and for feeding pigs.

None of these drills, according to Hunter, was fit to be put into the hands of ordinary servants, because the drills had neither strength nor simplicity.[29] There were, however, simpler drills in which there does not seem to be much that would go wrong; for example, James Sharp's drill plough for single-row seeding. This was simply a seed box placed between the plough handles which permitted the seed to drop in the centre of a group of tines fixed below the box behind the share to a triangle of wood.[30]

Other examples were produced by W. Winlaw, whose drill plough at £8 was regarded by Arthur Young as having very great merit;[31] by David Young of Perth, who made a drill about four feet broad, which was carried on four wheels and ploughed, drilled four rows and then covered the seed;[32] and by Francis Forbes who advertised a drill plough accurately constructed on the principles improved by the latest experience of the celebrated Mr. Tull. Forbes's drill was made by Joseph Tyler, Cabinet Maker, 54 Wardour St., Soho.[33] Needless to say Forbes was a strong protagonist of what is now called inter-row cultivation for which he, like most others, designed horse hoes.

George Winter of Charlton, Gloucestershire, produced a seed-drill that could be used for all kinds of seeds. It had one rather modern feature. Sharp spikes were fitted at equal intervals round the iron rims of the wheel to give adhesion and to make the machine run steadily. The axle was fitted with four large and two small indented cylinders, the latter two being nearest the wheels; these could be changed for different sizes to suit different seed. From these cylinders the seed dropped into funnels, hollowed in the back of coulters, and at each revolution of the land wheels, one hundred and fourteen grains of wheat, for example, were dropped at one-inch intervals "on the same length of land." The seed was covered by a small harrow set in the lower part of the rear of the machine behind the seeding coulters.[34]

Still more drills were invented, if that word can be properly used to describe productions that were all very similar to one another and based upon the general principles already accepted. Some of the inventors were John Horn,[35] the Rev. James Cooke,[36] William Amos, Erasmus Darwin,[37] and many others, and there was great competition and jealousy. William Amos made no bones about accusing Cooke of having taken advantage of his membership of the Society of Arts to purloin a design, based on Locatelli's Sembrador, that Amos submitted for the Society's premium. This was a machine which fed by "indented cups," and was much the same as Cooke's spoon or cup feed. Amos had also designed a machine with an indented cylinder feed.[38] Such an accusation could easily be made because there was nothing novel in any of the machines so far as the two systems of seeding were concerned. Cooke's drill became a favoured one, and explained Amos's jealousy. The original design of Cooke's drill was patented in 1782 and was used as a basis by later inventors, and its principles were acknowledged by J. Allen Ransome to have been "adopted in the construction of some of the most approved of the present day," (1843).

The men who invented the two greatest improvements to Cooke's drill were Henry Baldwin of Mendham and his bailiff Samuel Wells who was still living at Wymondham in 1841, though he had worked for Baldwin from 1778. These improvements consisted in (1) a sliding axle tree which allowed the wheels to be extended to the width of stetches or lands, and permitted additional cups and coulters to be fitted; (2) self-regulating levers to which the coulters were attached. They worked as separate units so as to accommodate themselves to irregularities in the land and obstructions.[39] It is said that a hundred of these machines were made and sold in the twelve years ending 1804. Many of them were used for doing contract drilling, the machine in those days being regarded as more of a contractors' job than as one for the use of the individual farmer.

This list of makers and inventors is, as I have said, incomplete, but many of the inventions were of little significance and others were made or planned but not patented. The trend of design of seed-drills has been indicated, but it is not easy to get a clear idea of what it all meant in the field. Though inventors of drills were scattered hither and yon over the kingdom, it must not be thought that numerous farmers were using drills by the end of the eighteenth century. How few drills were made can perhaps be gauged by Cooke's output which does not appear to have been more than ten a year. Progress in the adoption of the drill was restricted to a few counties, and limited to the few progressive farmers and landowners. And the controversy whether drilling was superior to dibbling still went on, though both methods were, of course, considered better than hand broadcast sowing.

In the seventeen-nineties Marshall could report "Notwithstanding the high degree of cultivation in which the lands of Norfolk are undoubtedly kept, no county has less variety of implements." And "There is not perhaps a drill, a horse hoe, or scarcely a horse-rake, in East Norfolk," despite all the progress that had been stimulated by "Turnip" Townshend, Coke of Holkham and others. Nor could he find drills in the famous highly farmed Isle of Thanet. What looked like drill sowing in this part of Kent was the result of the use of the "stricking" plough, which made rows into which the seed was hand broadcast and harrowed in, so that it grew in rows.[40] A drill roller or presser did the same work in Norfolk.[41]

In Berkshire some spirited farmers, following perhaps the King's example, had introduced the skim, the drill and the scarifier, while Cooke's drill was "but too partially introduced into Buckinghamshire." Drilling had been tried by two farmers of Halse in Somerset, and Mr. Anderdon of Henlade in that county had drilled all his crops for twenty years before 1794 with Willey's drill plough for sowing double rows, an example of which was then to be seen in the repository of the Society of Arts in London. Anderdon originally drilled two rows about a foot apart on five feet ridges, leaving intervals of four feet for horse hoeing, but changed to single row on three feet ridges. John Billingsley, who reported this, found space for a word of praise for Cooke's drill and horse hoe and was particularly impressed by his skuffler or scarifier. Across country, in Leicestershire, Cooke's was the only drill used, and only by a few people, though it was gaining ground. Mr. Hoyte of Osbornly, Lincolnshire, and a few others in that county also used Cooke's drill, but Mr. Cartwright preferred Amos's improvement, perhaps because Amos was his bailiff. Mr. John Codd of Ranby had used Duckett's drill machines, and other implements very profitably "without their being much sought after by the farmers in his neighbourhood." A one-wheeled drill plough for turnips was made at Moor Green, Nottingham and was thought highly of, but how many farmers used it is not stated. Drilling was moderately introduced in Stafford, and William Pitt knew a dozen farmers who had drill machines. Cooke's cup feed was one of them, and another was a patent of a person in Yorkshire, sold by Mr. Joseph Cornforth, machine maker, Bushbury, near Wolverhampton. The delivery of the seed was by hollows or cavities cut in a cylinder. Both did their work well. A Mr. Shenstone had made an improved Cooke's drill. Several farmers in South Warwick used Cooke's original drill, but John Wedge felt that the drill

system must be left to time and the effect of successful practice to establish it in Warwickshire.

Northumberland and the Lothians were already advancing to the
foremost place in farming in the kingdom. An apparently rather
insufficient turnip drill, made of a hollow tin cylinder with holes for
letting the seed drop, was used in Northumberland. It could not be
relied upon because the holes were apt to clog and leave lengths of land
unsown. The drill with globular cavities on the outside of a solid
cylinder was here preferred to Cooke's drill, but it, too, failed to
regulate the seed sown. In this area a drill was then (1794) being made
which, it was hoped, would remedy this defect. The drill husbandry was
in its infancy in Westmorland, where instruments for drilling or hoeing
were few. The North Riding did not generally use the drill, but some of
Cooke's drills, one made by Perkins, Proud's drill for sowing turnips,
and the Scotch drill were used by a few farmers.

Various drill barrows and horse hoes were used in East Lothian for
sowing peas, beans and turnips. James Clephan, a carpenter at
Neriwar, near Dunbar, had made an expanding horse hoe. It could be
contracted or expanded on one or on both sides at pleasure by means of
a lever at each end of the hoe and a notched bar which could be worked
separately or together. There were many drilling and hoeing instruments in Midlothian, usually of a plain and effective construction. In
West Lothian they were few and simple. More complex machines were
found in Roxburgh. The turnip drill and "one which, by changing a
rut upon the axis, which turns round at the bottom of the hopper,
sows either beans or small grains." These were also one-row drills.
Mr. Craik of Galloway had invented a drill for sowing grain in drills,
but this is all that is told about its design. He only used a third of the
usual quantity of seed and his success during the previous thirty years
had been so great that many of his neighbours had adopted it.[42]

But it was perhaps in Suffolk that the greatest progress was made.
Between the dates of his two reports on the county, Arthur Young,
Secretary to the Board of Agriculture, noticed great changes there.
In 1794 drilling, though practised with great intelligence and marked
success by individuals, had nowhere in the county the least tendency
to become the common practice. Dibbling was well established and
increasing every year, and its expense was being abated by the use
of the Norfolk drill roller which made little channels four and a half

inches asunder across a clover ley after ploughing, the wheat seed then being hand broadcast and brush-harrowed in. A decade later a revolution had taken place on the strong land, for drilling had "become universal" in many parishes except in the southwest corner, but it even promised to spread there.[43]

At the turn of the century a young wheelwright set up in business at Peasenhall, Suffolk. He carried out repairs to the Norfolk drills then being used. All the coulters of this drill were set in a transverse beam and could not be moved independently of one another. James Smyth and his brother Jonathan of Swefling, under the patronage of a Robert Wardley of Grove Farm, Peasenhall, just across the road from the wheelwright's shop, produced their first lever drill. In this machine each coulter was fixed to an independent lever for its ready adjustment to different widths; it also embodied the gear drive of Cooke's drill in place of the belt drive of the earlier patterns. It had an improved manure box fitted with cups for sowing the manure with the grain. Swing steerage enabled the operator to move the coulters to the left or right to keep the line of sowing straight. It was not, of course, the first combined drill.

The immediate market for the drill was amongst the neighbouring farmers, of what was and is a predominantly arable district; but a wider market was necessary if the infant firm was to prosper. Smyths' sent out travellers, expert in the use of the drill, who exhibited the machines in various markets and offered to do contract drilling for 2s. 6d. an acre. This plan was successful, and contract drilling became the practice so far away as Oxfordshire. The firm prospered and there were widely dispersed offshoots. Jonathan Smyth set up at Swefling. One of their employees, William Woolnough, went to Kingston-on-Thames and became a partner in Messrs. Priest and Woolnough. George Smyth began business in Ipswich in 1837. Woodgate Gower, a son-in-law, went to Hook in Hampshire, and his sons later departed to such distant places as Shropshire and Buckingham so that the influence of James Smyth was felt all over the country during the nineteenth century. The firm still flourishes.[44]

Messrs. L. R. Knapp and Co., Ltd., was a Berkshire firm founded in 1745 as wheelwrights and smiths at Clanfield, Oxon. They took up the manufacture of all kinds of drills and established a great reputation.

In 1804, Richard Garrett was a blacksmith and sickle maker at

Leiston, Suffolk. He took his son as partner in 1826 and died in 1837. The firm made drills (to which they had added some improvements under a patent), threshing machines and various types of "cutting machines."[45] They enjoyed great prosperity during the nineteenth century, but no longer operate in Suffolk.

A drill that must have been somewhat similar to those made by Smyth and Garrett was exhibited at the Holkham sheep shearing in 1811. It was Mann's patent drill for sowing wheat in nine-inch rows with pulverized manure. At this exhibition another drill, one for sowing turnip seed and crushed oilcake as manure, was also shown.[46] At about the same time the Bedfordshire drill invented by Robert Salmon, of Woburn, gained a premium offered by the Duke of Bedford at his annual sheep shearing at Woburn. This was an ingenious steerage drill, and was a new departure in drill design. The seed box was hung on two centres so as to remain level when the drill was going up or down hill or over ridges. It was a cup feed drill and activated by a spindle connected with the nave of one of the ground wheels. It was reputed useful for corn, but could not be worked as a combined drill, the weight of a manure box when full pressing the coulters too deeply into the ground.

A rather over-elaborate provision for steerage was a characteristic of Lord Western's patent drill of about the same date, but the use of iron bearings at certain points of strain was more practical.[47]

Contemporary opinion on the value of the different drills obtainable was divided. Mr. Bury's Northumberland force feed with adjustable coulters was improved by John Bailey of Chillingham, who was said to have done much to render drills more perfect by adding a piece of flat iron which could be adjusted to make the slot into the hopper entrance larger or smaller. Later he added a contrivance that enabled all the entrances to be adjusted at once. Cooke's drill, too, continued to be praised. There were various other one-, two- or three-row dropper barrows for sowing turnip seed. One was a rather elaborate arrangement on a double mouldboard plough fitted with a share with two wings, one at each side. A wheel was placed in the V behind the mouldboards and a dropper box fitted there, but some opinion still held that it was better to make the drills with a Rotherham or swing plough and dibble in the seed by hand.[48]

By 1830 the two types of drill were sufficiently determined. They were the cup feed and force feed drills for cereals. Some had a manure box that dropped the fertilizer adjacent to, or with, the seed. There was a variety of forms of turnip and bean drills as well as a machine for sowing clover and small seeds broadcast. Loudon adds Morton's improved grain drill machine to the long list of those already named. This was a three-row force feed and the three coulters could be moved closer together by a nut working on a screw. He also mentions a horse dibbling machine that had been invented but was very little used because it was too complicated.[49]

The discussion of seed-drills in the textbooks and other literature does not mean that seed-drills were as yet generally used. In the areas of advanced farming in East Lothian and the Mearns of Kincardine there were many drills and horse hoeing machines by 1829,[50] as there doubt-less were in Northumberland. It was here, in the Border Counties, in East Anglia and in some parts of the Midland Counties, that the most up-to-date farming was to be found in the 1830s, but progress was also being made farther afield. This was doubtless what encouraged two brothers, S. A. and A. H. Kell, drill makers from Suffolk, to move west and set up in business at Barton Foundry, Gloucester, in 1828.

The broadcast drill was on quite modern lines. It was a fairly wide box, seventeen feet long, containing the seed. Through the whole length of the box ran a spindle rotated by mitred gearing from the ground wheels. The spindle was fitted with radial pinions at intervals, or short brushes, which forced the seed through holes perforated in the seed box. The size of the holes was adjusted to that of the seed by iron slides actuated by a lever at the side of the machine. The seed fell on to a wooden platform and so was broadcast. A disadvantage of this machine was that the holes sometimes clogged and so some ground was left unsown.[51]

Although the horse-drawn dibble mentioned by Loudon came to nothing, another indomitable spirit tried to build one and so far succeeded that he took out a patent in 1840. This was J. W. Newbury of Oxfordshire. The machine "consisted of a shaft having five (later seven) wheels having projecting dibbles and provided with separate feed tubes from the seed box above. The dibbles were divided longitud-inally in halves. As the dibble left the ground one portion of it, which was hollow, slid down, allowing the seed to fall into the hole."[52] Some of these machines were made but they did not become popular, probably because of their complexity.

A new note was struck in 1839 by Grounsell, who produced a drop drill with a spacing mechanism designed to drop the seed and manure at intervals and not in a continuous stream as heretofore. A circular iron ring was fixed to the inside of one of the ground wheels. This iron ring had a series of holes in which studs could be fixed. The studs were a striking mechanism. As the wheel revolved, they opened valves for the delivery of the corn and manure. The valve closed again directly the stud had passed. By this means the seed and manure was spaced at the distance required. The seed and manure boxes were fitted with "projecting arms or shovels" instead of cups to feed the funnels.

A widely different patent drop drill was made in the same year by Richard Hornsby and Sons, a firm set up by the father in 1815. At the Royal Agricultural Society's show of 1844, Garrett's also showed a drop drill which could be adjusted to space the seed and manure, or to drop it in a continuous stream.[53]

By this time the use of the drill was becoming more frequent in southern as well as in northern England, though so slowly that travelling machines were still making yearly journeys from Suffolk (Smyth's of Peasenhall?) to Oxfordshire, as they had been doing for the past few decades, "for the use of those distant farmers by whom their services were required."[54]

It was in 1839 that the English Agricultural Society held its first show at Oxford, and at that show the first of its long series of implement trials. Only nineteen manufacturers exhibited implements. The firm of Ransome was awarded a gold medal for six tons of machinery that had travelled from Ipswich to Oxford in horse drawn waggons. Most of the other firms sent single implements only, amongst which was a combined seed and manure drill for turnips. Although there is no record of it, Garrett's were probably represented, and maybe others. Certainly Garrett's showed a general purpose drill in 1841 as did Smyth of Peasenhall. Hornsby showed both a general purpose and a turnip and manure drill. Grounsell exhibited his drill and Drummond and Son of Stirling a one-row turnip and manure drill, and a drop drill. The following year, Wm. Crosskill of Beverley, showed, like Grounsell, a lime and soot drill, and Thomas Huckwale of Over Mostyn, Oxfordshire, a liquid manure drill. In 1843 the number of

H

this class of implement rose to no less than sixty-one drills, pressers and seed barrows, and four dibbles.[55] The Museum of the Highland and Agricultural Society repeated this wealth of types in its exhibition which contained models of broadcast sowing machines, drills for grain, turnip and beans, a combined turnip and bone-dust drill, and drills for grass seeds as well as a dibble, a soot distributor and so on.[56] A few years after 1843 Mrs. Mary Wedlake showed drills, including the dibbling machine invented by her late husband, Thomas Wedlake, of Hornchurch, Essex,[57] at the City Agricultural Repository for Improved Agricultural Implements.

Though hand broadcasting, dibbling and drilling seeds were all in vogue, probably in that order of importance, drilling was slowly ousting the other methods, so that it could be said that "no class of implements has been more abundantly multiplied in the land within the past few years." Both Smyth and Garrett had by the early 1850s competitors for their drills in every county in the kingdom. No doubt Smyth's sales were many times what they had been a few years before. Garrett's were reported to be selling ten drills a week.

Most types of drill were by this date fitted with flexible feed tubes made of jointed tin tubes held in position by chains and allowed play to meet irregularities. These were not altogether satisfactory, the seed sometimes being caught when they were jerked and thus not delivered with absolute regularity. Hornsby had overcome this difficulty by using indiarubber tubes. Garrett tried to do the same by increasing the depth and overlap of the cups in their telescopic tubes. Other firms adopted rather similar devices. The three systems of feeding the seed to the tubes were firmly established. They were what they had always been, the grooved cylinder in the turnip drill, the brush or pinion, and the cup feed. Of these the cup feed was much the most common form in English sowing machines.[58]

In Scotland the broadcast sowing machine continued to be extensively used. The firm of Scoular and Sons of Haddington had improved it by adding the third wheel and by splitting up the seed box into three sections, the middle one nine feet long and the two ends four and a half feet each. The latter could be folded over on to the middle box in order to allow the machine to pass through a nine foot gateway. The East Lothian drill was a six-row fixed drill. It was said to be best for drilling across the ridges.

A new smaller and simpler lever drill had been made by James Slight on the lines of the English machine. In this the seed was forced into the slots by a ten-toothed pinion wheel, and the funnels were of jointed tin cups within each other strung together by three lines of small chain which allowed enough play to permit the rise and fall of the lever with its coulter. Of turnip drills the variety was too numerous to be detailed even in an encyclopaedic work. John Wightman of Upper Keith, East Lothian, received a Highland and Agricultural Society premium for his turnip drill in 1827, and thirty years later it was very generally used. Geddes of Cargen Bridge in Scotland added spur-wheel gearing to the turnip drill.

In the late 1850s, Sidney Pitcairn of Green, Perth, who had first produced his drop drill soon after Grounsell, was still making the chambered cylinder. In Chandler's machine, made by Reeves of Bratton, Westbury, Wilts, there was a press wheel instead of a coulter. It actuated a recessed cylinder which dropped the seed into a furrow made by the press wheel. Chandler also made a liquid manure drill, and so did Isaac James of the Tivoli Iron Works, Cheltenham. The Sigma Depositor Dibble for manure was made by Charles Powell, of Ticehurst, Sussex.[59] The drills made by James Coultas of Perseverance Iron Works, Grantham, founded in 1863, won many prizes at "Royal" shows in 1861, 1865, 1871, 1874, and 1891. The firm continues to flourish.

In all essentials seed-drills were of modern design by the 1860s, and only minor improvements have been made since. The main firms then making drills were Smyth of Peasenhall, Garrett of Leiston, Hornsby of Grantham, Wedlake of Hornchurch, Coultas of Grantham, and Ransome of Ipswich, all of whom were by now making a drop drill. There were also Kell of Gloucester and one or two Scottish firms, whose number was added to later by the foundation of the Bon Accord Works of Benjamin Reid and Sons in 1876. This list is not, of course, complete and it is now hardly possible to make it complete, so I hope that firms whose names are not mentioned will forgive me. By 1866 there were many manufacturers of corn drills, but all their products were different modifications of the same principle.[60]

This was confirmed fifty years later when a writer in the *Mark Lane Express* remarked that there was not a vast difference in the drill of 1922 and that of fifty years before. The main features were almost identical[61]. The Science Museum confirmed this conclusion by saying that modern corn drills in 1930 were of two types: the Suffolk type, so long a standard, with cup feed, rocking hopper, chain and roller lift, compression hoe coulters and a special arrangement for steerage; and a force feed type, rather more compact, having a lever lift, spring compression and double- or single-lift coulters.[62] These were the two basic types that had shared the attention of designers since the sixteenth century, and though the intervening period had been fruitful in perfecting both types, all the essentials had been provided in a crude form by the earlier inventors. The story of the seed-drill since its invention or re-introduction into Europe in the sixteenth century is one of gradual perfection of an idea as the resources of modern engineering developed.

HARVESTING THE CROPS
(a) Reapers

HARVEST WAS ALWAYS the time of the heaviest work of all the heavy work of the farming year. Men's minds, when not dulled by long and arduous physical work, must often have turned to thoughts of easier ways of harvesting.

Long ago, in classical times, there was a machine of a kind for reaping corn that seems to have been used in Southern France. It is mentioned both by Pliny and Palladius, though the one may, of course, have merely copied the other. The tradition of this machine persisted through the ages. It was, apparently, a cart pushed before the horse into the standing corn, and had in front some sort of cutting or tearing gear for ripping off the heads of the grain and tossing them backwards into the cart.

Crescentius, who compiled the first of the long series of *omnium gatherum* treatises on farming and rural life, does not say that this apparatus was used when he was writing in the thirteenth century, but in his description of it he may have been repeating information drawn from the classical authors.[1]

Barnaby Googe, an English writer of the sixteenth century, thought the machine referred to by Palladius was a contrivance that might be used in level and champion countries, but that in England "it would make but ill-favoured work." In reaping you must go with the wind, he wrote, or mind your eyes.[2] Adam Dickson towards the end of the eighteenth century produced a book about classical farming and referred to this harvesting cart.[3]

A year before Dickson's book appeared, William Pitt of Pendeford, Stafford, who afterwards became one of the reporters to the Board of Agriculture, inspired by Mr. Loft's translations from Pliny and Palladius, actually produced a design to show how this machine could be made. A drawing of Pitt's proposal was published in Arthur Young's *Annals of Agriculture.*[4] It was a toothed cylinder revolving horizontally on its axis before the cart, motion being given to it by gear wheels moved by a belt from a pulley on the ground wheel of the cart, and so arranged that the cylinder revolved at twice the speed of the travelling wheels. Pitt did not attempt to make the machine, but contented himself with recommending it to William Winlaw, who had just designed a threshing mill.

Young made no editorial comment upon Pitt's proposal, but twelve years later, when expressing enthusiasm for the equipment of Mr. Cartwright's farm at Brothertoft, Lincoln, he said that he feared it would be a long time before a practical reaper was designed. This remark was stimulated by Cartwright's unsuccessful efforts to design reaper scythes pushed forward by the horses; he afterward also attempted to draw them laterally but failed.[5]

In spite of Young's opinion the first patent for a reaping machine was issued in the very same year. Joseph Boyce of London, to whom the patent was granted, could not release his mind from the domination of the scythe. His cutting apparatus was a series of scythes or knives projecting from a circular disc, revolving horizontally on a vertical shaft geared to the live axle of the travelling wheels. It was successful in cutting down part of the corn, but did not clear the ground entirely, and there was no provision for collecting the grain. The patent specification does not show how the machine was driven, whether pulled or pushed. As Loudon says it was wheeled over the ground it was presumably pushed manually[6]. The defect of this machine was that it had no means of keeping the corn up to the cutters which could not grip the stalks, the inventor having relied entirely on the effect obtained by a scythe used by hand. It also lacked any method of laying or collecting the corn that it cut.

This was the beginning of a spate of inventions, most of which were not very effective. They did little more than warn later workers what to avoid. The next patent to be issued was for a decidedly impossible machine. It was granted in 1800 to Robert Meares of Frome, Sussex, for a gadget that was simply a large pair of shears on wheels with a simple appliance of wire or rods to make the corn fall in the required direction. It was intended to be pushed forward and worked by one man, but it is doubtful whether it was ever manufactured, though the inventor may have made a sample.[7]

Thomas James Plucknett, implement maker, of Deptford, or London, abandoned the idea of scythes and shears in the machine he patented in 1805. He used a circular steel plate made very sharp at the edge and notched at the upper side like a sickle. It worked parallel to the ground and could be adjusted for height. The plate acted like a fine toothed saw and cut the corn better than scythes. Leaders, fitted with projecting horns, directed the corn to the knife. The cut corn must have fallen right in the path of the man or horse pushing the machine, a fatal objection.

This idea was improved upon by Gladstones of Castle Douglas, Kirkcudbright, who does not seem to have applied for a patent. His machine was drawn by a horse, and there was the same circular cutting wheel to which motion was given by a system of belts and pulleys from the ground wheels. Just above the forward half of the cutting wheel there was a fixed semi-circular plate with teeth projecting forward. It was said by Lawson to be of wood, and by Robert Brown to be of iron.[8] The teeth gathered the corn which was held to them by a couple of small forks revolving on the same axis but more slowly than the cutting wheel. Loudon says that at the rear of the cutter and in contact with it was a fixed, semi-circular plate covered with emery that kept it sharp as it worked. Gladstones apparently only made a model of this machine, but succeeded in interesting the Highland and Agricultural Society, who asked him to make a full-sized machine. For some unknown reason they withdrew their support. Then Sir Edward Croften had one made, but it was defective and did not work. By 1811 the design had been improved, and the Dalkeith Farming Society ordered one from Alexander Scott of Ormiston, according to the principles of a model that had won their premium.

Mr. Salmon of Woburn made a further advance, and in his machine there were indications of a cutter on the clipping principle, though Gladstones' machine also had intimations of that principle. Salmon's went further in that it had an apparatus for collecting and delivering the cut corn "in parcels like sheaves" ready for binding. It was brought out with the "most flattering hopes of success," but did not obtain "the approbation of the class for whom it was intended," and by 1858 it had, like its precursors, been forgotten.

A farmer in Northumberland, Donald Cumming, patented a rather different design in 1811, which foreshadowed some much later and possibly more effective appliances. A triangular platform with the apex in front carried a series of revolving knives actuated by the driving wheels, and a series of holdfasts in front gathered the corn to the knives. The cut corn fell on revolving vanes or drums, and passed on to endless cloths or webs to be deposited at either side. The horses pushed the machine along in the path between the cut corn. The whole machine was guided by a wheel in front, and the operator was placed on a seat above the driving wheels.

Smith of Deanston, too, was busy on his idea of a reaping machine, and his adoption of the rotary principle may have been influenced by his experience in his cotton mill. The cutter was circular and worked horizontally. It was fixed to the bottom of a drum rotating on its axis, the blades projecting some inches beyond the periphery of the lower end of the drum which was a little smaller than that of the top end. In moving forward the cutter, and, of course, the drum, were rapidly revolved by gearing from the ground wheels, and the corn cut fell upon the drum to be thrown off in regular rows. The final form was that pushed by horses. It was the only competitor for the Dalkeith Farming Society's premium in 1812, and was shown again in 1813 when it was awarded a piece of plate valued at fifty guineas, as a solatium for not getting the full award. Shortly afterwards it was examined by the Highland and Agricultural Society, and a further fifty guinea piece of plate awarded. Contemporaries regarded this machine as full of promise, greatly admired Smith's perseverance in designing ingenious yet simple contrivances to overcome defects, and regretted that it was not brought to a practical state, although it had effectively cut beans and other crops. The non-fruition of this idea was attributed to Smith's preoccupation with his cotton mill, and to the insufficient remuneration and encouragement he received for what he had done

49. Gladstones' Reaping Machine. From Robert Brown of
Markle, *Treatise of Rural Affairs*, 1811.

50. Smith of Deanston's Reaper. From J. C. Loudon, *Encyclopaedia of Agriculture*, 1831.

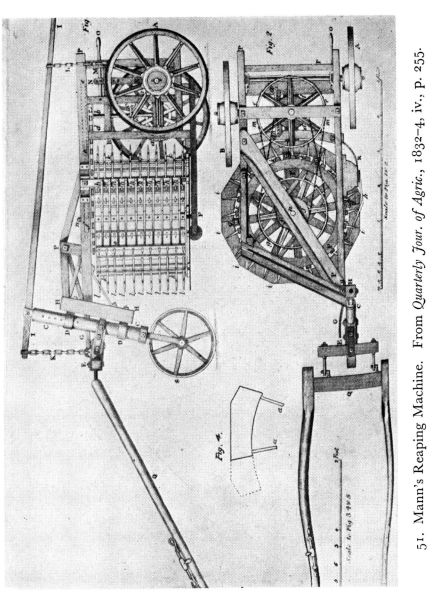

51. Mann's Reaping Machine. From *Quarterly Jour. of Agric.*, 1832–4, iv., p. 255.

52. Bell's Reaping Machine.   From J. C. Loudon, *Encyclopaedia of
Agric.*, 1831.

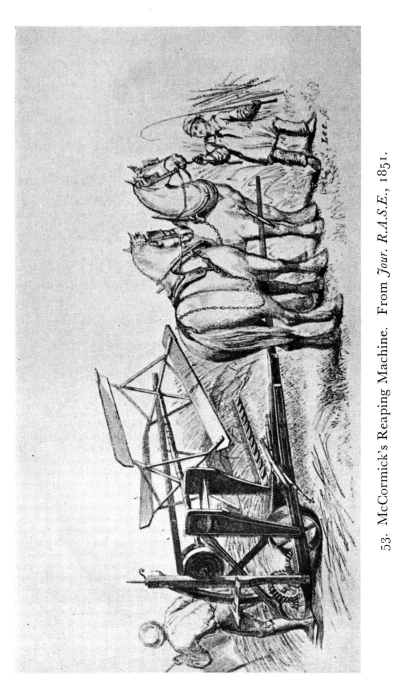

53. McCormick's Reaping Machine. From *Jour. R.A.S.E.*, 1851.

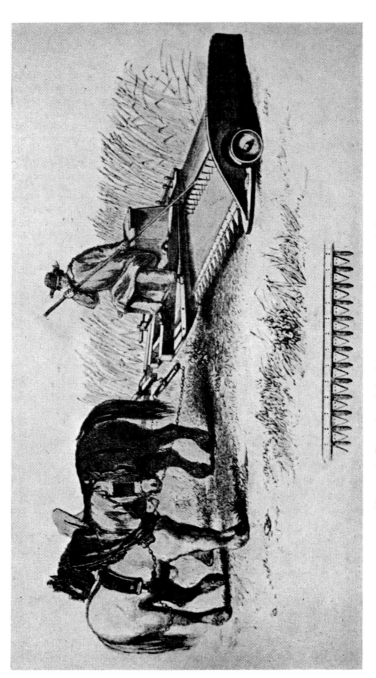

54. Hussey's Reaping Machine. From *Jour. R.A.S.E.*, 1851.

55. Aveling and Porter's Steam Power Reaping Machine. From *Implement and Machinery Review*, Sept. 1876.

56. Johnston Reaper and Sheaf Binder. From *Implement, etc., Review*, July, 1880.

57. Samuelson's New Sheaf Binding Reaper. From *Implement, etc., Review*, Jan. 1881.

58. Bissett's Canvasless Chain Conveyor Binder. *Implement, etc., Review*, July 1892.

59. Ketcher's Bean Stubble Rake. From Arthur Young, *General View of the Agriculture of . . . . Essex*, 1807.

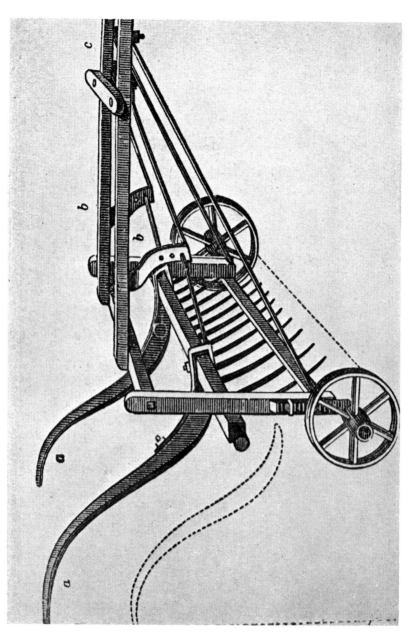

60. Weir's Rake. From Loudon, *Encyclopaedia of Agriculture*, 1831.

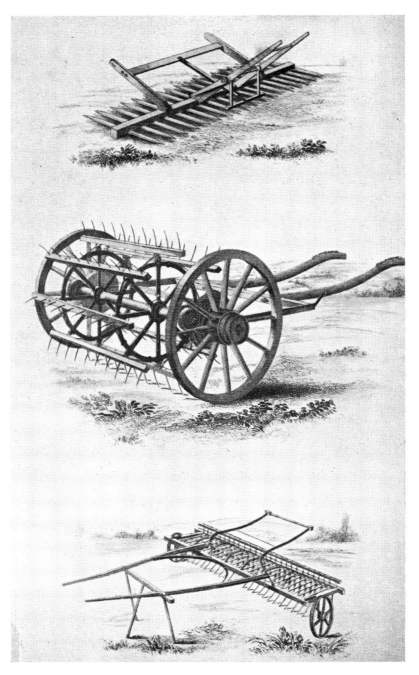

61. American Hayrake, Salmon's Tedder, and Grant's patent lever
Horse Rake. From John M. Wilson, *Rural Cyclopaedia*, 1849.

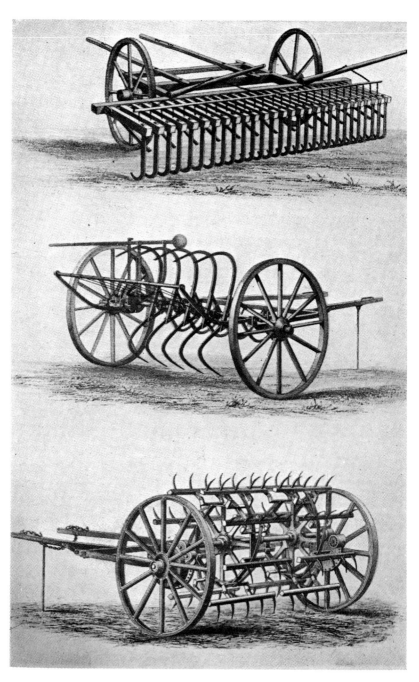

62. Scotch Horse Rake, Ransome's Swath Horse Rake and
Wedlake's Haymaking Machine. From J. C. Morton, *Cyclopaedia
of Agriculture*, 1856.

63. Smith and Ashby's Horse Rake. From J. Donaldson, *British Agriculture*, 1866.

64. Smith and Ashby's Hay Tedding Machine. From Slight and Burn, *Book of Farm Implements*, 1858.

already. Finally the machine was lodged in the Highland and Agricultural Society's Museum, later transferred to the Technological Museum.

Another Scotsman adopted parts of the machines of both Gladstones and Smith. He was Mr. Scott of Ormiston, factor to the Earl of Hopetoun, "an amateur mechanican of no small merit." His machine had a cutter on the revolving principle, though not circular. A wheel carried sixteen small toothed sickles, with projecting prongs in front of them like Gladstones'. Smith's inverted conical drum was copied as a gatherer, but with the addition of twenty-four jointed prongs or fingers acting as collectors or rakes to convey the cut corn to the side. It was also fitted with a brush to keep the cutters free from weeds and stubble "but with all these precautions and auxiliary appendages, it is known that the machine never performed beyond a mere trial."

Then, a Birmingham actor, of all improbable people, designed and patented a reaper and in 1814 demonstrated it, cutting artificially planted crops on the stage. He advertised it by playbills as if it were an ordinary theatrical performance. This machine had a circular cutter with teeth like a common sickle, which could be changed for different crops, e.g. it had fine saw teeth for beans. Its novel feature was that the cutter was worked independently of the ground wheels, and was operated by a hand winch. This was intended to save draught and make the work of the horses lighter. The straw was caught by rough surfaced rollers that revolved over and under the cutter and the grain was delivered into the body of the machine that was shaped like a wheelbarrow.

It is odd that when so many people were thinking about reaping machines, and innumerable machines were designed, tried and abandoned, there was not enough encouragement to stimulate manufacture on a sales basis. This happened not only to Smith of Deanston, but also to Ogle and Brown who designed a machine a few years later. According to Slight and Burn, it was indistinguishable from the McCormick, though these writers admit that the coincidence of two widely separated inventors designing precisely the same piece of apparatus is not unknown to engineering. Ogle of Remington, near Alnwick, Northumberland, and Brown of Alnwick together produced a specimen of their machine in 1822 that was reported to have reaped wheat and barley very well in the field. This design was not patented, but a drawing and a description of it was published in the *Mechanics Magazine*, 1826.

"The framework or body of the machine closely resembled a skeleton of a common cart with its wheels and shafts, to the latter of which the horses were yoked to draw the machine, walking by the side of the standing corn. To the right of the carriage was projected the cutting apparatus—a light frame, whose front bar was of iron, and armed with a row of teeth three inches long, projecting forward; immediately upon the teeth lay the cutter, a straight-edged steel knife, equal in length to, and a little more than the breadth of the corn to be cut at one passage. By a motion from the carriage wheels this knife was made to vibrate rapidly from right and left, as the machine travelled. Above and a little before the cutter, a fan or vane was, from the same source made to revolve, which thus collected and held the corn to be cut by the knife; and on being cut, was by the vane carried backward and laid upon a deal platform immediately behind the cutter; here by the assistance of a man with a rake, it was collected to the extent of a sheaf, and then discharged."

It is a great pity that this machine, which embodied so many of the principles that have yet to be superseded, did not get more support, and that it was not put into production, or that its inventors did not even take the trouble to take out a patent.

Another curiosity of the time was a model reaping machine made by Mr. A. Kerr, of Edinburgh. His cutter and gatherer was precisely the same as Smith of Deanston's. Kerr admitted this but contended that the two machines were designed quite independently. Kerr's machine had two small wheels within the drum to serve as prime mover, but though they helped to support the cutter and drum and thus relieved the horses of some draught, they were inadequate as motive power, and probably were the cause of the failure of the machine.

The experiences of Joseph Mann, of Raby, Cumberland, recall one of Aesop's Fables. He produced a working model of a reaping machine in 1820 that met with the approval of the Abbey Holme Agricultural Society. The Society suggested some alterations, amongst others that the machine should be pushed rather than hauled as the inventor proposed. These alterations turned out rather unsuccessfully when a full-sized machine was shown to the Society two years later, the inventor having tried to satisfy so many opinions that his machine became unduly complicated and impractical. It was laid aside until 1826. Then he went back to his original ideas and spent the leisure of the next four years improving them. At the end of this time he claimed that the machine had the four essentials of a good reaping machine. It preserved the line of draught, though it was hauled from one of its angles in front; it had a polygonal cutter; gathering was by a series of revolving rakes; and there was an arrangement for stripping the rakes so as to lay the cut corn in a regular swathe to the side of the machine.

This machine was shown to the Highland and Agricultural Society at Kelso in 1832. It cut oats in a satisfactory way, but not uphill or across the ridges, and failed therefore to get the premium. The inventor, like so many others, was an amateur, and possessed no capital, so his machine was rather crudely made. The polygonal twelve-sided cutter was an advance on the circle, for the angled sides of the polygon gave a series of cutting strokes to the stalks of the corn, a more certain method of cutting than the continuous smooth action of the circle. The machine was set on a triangular framework. There was a single wheel in front and two at the back irregularly placed. One was about a foot in front of the other, from which the motion of the cutter was derived. A cylinder mounted with twenty-five six-inch four-pronged rakes, and revolving much more slowly than the cutter, gathered the corn. There was an ingenious method of clearing the rakes of straw, but however good it may have been it never worked through a whole harvest. The extent of its work was a few consecutive hours.

Much later, Hussey remarked that there was at about this time half a score or more of inventors in Great Britain whose machines were far from successful, and who, after limited efforts, sank into a Rip Van Winkle slumber from which they never waked.[9] Nevertheless, before Mann's machine was tried at Kelso, the Rev. (then Mr.) Patrick Bell had produced a practical reaper that survived to compete with the American machines brought over for the Great Exhibition of 1851.

The story of the production of Bell's machine is better known than most because he himself has recorded it in detail. In the same year as it was first exhibited, doubts of the possibility of such a machine becoming a practical working job were expressed. "The daughters of Cain," it was said, "or at least of Tubal Cain, probably reaped as much corn in a given time (with the sickle) as the nymphs of Caledonia at the present day." Since there had been no development in the way of doing this work for thousands of years, the production of a practical reaping machine was very desirable. This was particularly true in Scotland, where barley and wheat were being extensively grown in addition to the traditional oats. There was now so much more corn to cut. The acreage in England too had undoubtedly been extended.

The anonymous writer of the article "On the use and advantage of a reaping machine" (it may have been John Slight), regarded Smith's reaper, tried in 1815, as the most valuable tool next to the plough in the annals of husbandry. He said that Bell had designed a machine on a new principle. For himself he thought the matter so important that a premium of £20,000 or £30,000 should be offered and three years allowed in which to perfect a machine.[10] He was rather extravagant in disposing of other people's money, and naturally no one complied with his suggestion. Even in 1837, William Youatt did not "deem it necessary to enter into any detail of the mode of operation of reaping machines" in his book *British Husbandry*.[11]

Bell himself felt that he, in common with other inventors of reaping machines, had been neglected before the arrival of the American machines in 1851. His own words are that "little or no interest was felt ten years before that time either in the agricultural or mechanical world in favour of reaping machines." When he began he had been ignorant of all other machines except Smith's, of which he had seen a print when a boy. The idea of his cutter was suggested to him by garden shears, and the idea of the canvas came to him when he was making a model.

Many of the features of Bell's machine are still to be found in the modern reaper-binder, and some in the combine. The cutters were on the scissors pattern. They were both triangular in shape, point foremost. Each triangular plate, or finger as they are now called, was screwed in its place on a horizontal bar. The upper bar was given a reciprocating motion by gearing from the travelling wheels, and the lower bar was fixed so that cutting was caused by the closure of the upper cutters in a scissors clipping manner. The grain was held, or brought to the cutter, by sails very similar to the modern machine, but the method of laying aside the cut corn in swathe was naturally somewhat different. This was managed by a cylinder of canvas, on to which the cut corn fell, and was laid aside by the revolution of the cylinder whose motion was also supplied through gearing from the travelling wheels.[12]

Bell's invention suffered many vicissitudes. He was very secretive about it in its early stages, and made his first trial in a barn with a crop planted by hand, stalk by stalk. When this proved successful he made a trial by night assisted by his brother in 1828. This was successful and the next year the machine was exhibited at Greystone Farm, Monikie parish. As a result, four or five machines were made, but' the ignorance and incapacity of the workmen were the cause of defective construction, so that the machines were perpetually breaking and after two or three seasons fell into what Bell himself describes as "deserved disuse." For some time after this, mechanics, millwrights, smiths and wheelwrights took to machine making. Some made the reapers exactly like Bell's; others altered his design, but made no improvement. Bell was doubtful whether any of the twelve or eighteen machines constructed worked for more than a few seasons.

Some influential persons, who saw Bell's original machine at Greystones, decided to have a machine exhibited to the Highland and Agricultural Society. The one made by Bell and his wright, David Hill, was too rough and ready for them, so they ordered another to be made at the East Foundry, Dundee, and agreed to pay the cost which they expected to recover from the Society. The machine was made in a hurry, and Bell considered it worthless. However, it was shown to the Society at Glasgow and Bell received a premium of £50 which he promptly paid over to defray part of the cost. Indeed, he was out of pocket on his invention, which he steadfastly refused to patent, believing himself amply compensated by the pleasure he enjoyed in making the first experiments with it. Bell claimed that his invention was published prior to any American machine, but this is now an exceedingly difficult matter to determine, although there is some reason for agreeing with him.[13] Further credence is given to Bell's claim by the statement made in 1876 by Lord Kinnaird of Rossie Priory, Inchture, to the effect that George Bell, who was Patrick's brother, employed Simons, a millwright at Errol, to make these machines, and about ten or twelve were sent to America, "These were in fact the origin of all reaping machines." This statement, however, is palpably incorrect.[14] In point of fact neither Bell nor the successful American inventors "originated" reapers, the idea having been discussed for hundreds of years.

For a few years after its exhibition to the Highland and Agricultural Society, Bell's machine cut a fair acreage of corn without much trouble. The cutters were the only part apt to get out of repair, and had to be kept carefully adjusted. If only one half of a shear blade was out of true, it spoiled the work of the machine. It was essential to keep the cutters accurately adjusted and to sharpen them after every fifty acres had been cut, if no accident had made it necessary to do so before.

According to the records the following acreages were cut in the five years, 1828–32 inclusive.

```
1828 one machine cut   7 acres
1829 two machines  ,,  30  ,,
1830 five          ,,  ,,  87  ,,
1831 seven         ,,  ,, 219  ,,
1832 ten           ,,  ,, 320  ,,
```

Besides these, ten more machines were made, two being sent to Poland and one to Van Diemen's land. "With these plain and unexaggerated statements, we will leave Mr. Bell's reaping machine to work its way for a time into public notice and favour."[15] But this it quite failed to do, because, I imagine, its manufacture was not taken up by one of the then rapidly expanding firms of implement makers.

In the same year as Bell was secretly trying out his machine in his barn and in the field by night, Lawson printed a statement that "A machine for reaping the heads or seed pods of clover when the second growth of that crop is left for seed, has been used in some parts of Norfolk and Suffolk. It consists of a comb, the teeth of which are lance-shaped, very sharp and set close. This comb is fixed horizontally to the fore part of the bottom of an open box or barrow which is drawn by one horse and guided by a man who empties the barrow in regular lines across the field by means of an implement which serves also to cleanse the teeth." This machine is nowhere else mentioned so far as I have been able to discover; it is not described in two exhaustive treatises on each of the counties written a decade or so later.[16]

Though Bell's machine had only a moderate success and probably fell almost into desuetude, I think it is likely that some of his machines may have gone on being used for some time. It is quite certain that the idea of making a reaping machine did not fall out of mind. Patents continued to be granted to successive inventors, but none of their machines came into general use. They did not get so far as to be produced in any number, and it is unlikely that some of them ever got beyond the stage of a paper specification.

At least half a dozen patents were granted between the dates of Bell's demonstration at Glasgow and the showing of the American reapers at the Great Exhibition. Edwin Budding of Stroud, Gloucestershire, patented in 1830 a mowing machine for grass. The cutter was a horizontal drum carrying a series of spiral knives or blades on its periphery. It was more a paring and shaving off machine than a reaper.

John Duncan of London patented a somewhat similar, but more elaborate, machine ten years later. This had a vertical drum, to the under end of which was fixed a plate carrying six small scythes, the points extending beyond the edge of the drum. It was supplied with fingers projecting beyond the scythes with spaces between them, the ends forming part of a circle. They gathered up the corn in close bundles and held it firmly to the cutters. The corn was brought to the fingers by curved pieces attached to one side of the shaft. It was collected on the body of the machine whence it could be taken into the back or bound into sheaves.

Another reaping machine was granted a patent in 1841, but the specification is a little difficult to understand. It was designed by Charles Phillips, an engineer of Chipping Norton, Oxford. Its novelty was apparently in the method of conveying the cut corn. In the front were two ranges of pointed plates, the lower range near the ground and extending beyond the upper. To guide the corn between them, the tips of the lower and under ranges were connected by wires upwards and backwards to meet an endless web which carried the cut corn to a receptacle in the back of the machine. The actual cutter was circular edged like a single-cut file to prevent the straw from slipping. There was a paddle-wheel gatherer which was probably like the modern sails. The machine was pushed by a man or horse on the stubble side of the work. Phillips changed his design in 1843. He then used a reciprocating bar to work a toothed cutter bar; he had also a design (if I am not mistaken) with reciprocating two-bar cutters with tapering teeth and a raking system for the cut corn.

Matthew Gilson of Newcastle-on-Tyne returned in 1846 to the revolving drum. On the under plate he put a series of knives bevelled to form cutting edges which might be serrated for corn. He not only proposed to cut the corn and lay it in swathe but also to rake it into shocks or sheaves as required. The knives could be raised or lowered by the driver, who was provided with a seat.

In the following year Sir John Scott Lillie of Fulham prepared a much more ambitious scheme. He mounted a steam engine on a long narrow framework which travelled broadside on, along a guide rope placed across the field. Broad drums revolved by a band from the driving pulley of the engine, and carried an endless chain to which scythes, at intervals, were attached. As the machine advanced the scythes swept along the grain. It is doubtful whether such a contraption would have worked. It had the further disadvantage that there was no provision for collection, so the wheels would have passed over some of the grain.

This spate of inventions was above the heads of the farmers, and none of the machines designed and produced became popular enough to justify manufacture on a commercial scale. All may be said to have failed, even Bell's, though J. Bell of Inch Michael in the Carse of Gowrie, used a Bell machine for fourteen years. The categorical statement is made by Slight that four of these machines were sent to America in 1834. He adds that six reapers were exhibited at the Great Fair in New York in 1851, all of which were provided with cutting apparatus resembling Bell's. He condemns Hussey's machine as a cheap imitation.[17] The Great Fair in New York was contemporary with the Great Exhibition of 1851 in London at the Crystal Palace in Hyde Park, a year that marks the turning point in reaper history. In that year the McCormick and Hussey reaping machines were exhibited. At last this was the real beginning of the acceptance, by practical farmers in this country, of the reaping machine, though it took a further half-century completely to oust the sickle and the scythe. The reaper was seen for the first time in quite advanced farming districts well within living memory.

In the previous year, both Philip Pusey, writing "On the progress of agricultural knowledge during the past eight years" in the *Journal of the Royal Agricultural Society*, and the Rev. John M. Wilson in his *Rural Cyclopaedia* of 1849, had expressed doubts of the practicality of any reaping machine to be made in the future. This was not because either of them was unaware of what was happening. Wilson wrote a good article on the subject, and when Pusey prepared a report for the Prince Consort, the President of the Commission for the Exhibition, he retold the story of the earlier efforts to make such a machine. He mentioned the award made to Bell but attributed the decline of the reaper after some time both in this country and abroad to its intricacy. Pusey also mentioned that another had then recently been invented in one of the colonies (Australia) which cut off the heads of the corn but left the straw standing, "a fatal defect in an old established country where the growth of corn is forced by the application of dung."[18]

Pusey quotes McCormick's own account of his invention, and it must, I think, be repeated here. It runs:

"My father was a farmer in the county of Rockbridge, state of Virginia, United States. He made an experiment in cutting grain in the year 1816 by a number of cylinders standing perpendicularly. Another experiment of the same kind was made by my father in the harvest of 1831, which satisfied my father to abandon it. Thereupon my attention was directed to the subject and the same harvest I invented and put in operation, in cutting late oats on the farm of John Steele, adjoining my father's, those parts of my present reaper called the platform for receiving the corn, a straight blade taking effect upon the corn, supported by stationary fingers over the edge, and a reel to gather the corn, which last, however, I found had been used before, though not in the same combination. . . .

"No machines were sold until 1840 and . . . were not of much practical value until my second patent, 1845.

"These improvements consist in reversing the angle of the sickle teeth alternately—the improved form of the fingers to hold up the corn, etc.—an iron case to preserve the sickle from clogging—and a better mode of separating the standing corn to be cut."

The teeth on the cutter were fixed and were placed in groups of four at an angle like saw teeth, each alternate group of four looking towards opposite ends of the bar so that whichever way the bar was

I

moving half the teeth were cutting. The claim made by the inventor was that his was the first successful reaper, and that he had combined for the first time the basic principles which have since been found essential in all cutting machines.[19]

Hussey, an American contemporary of McCormick, also claimed to have invented the first practical reaping machine. He also showed it at the Great Exhibition. Hussey was contemptuous of Bell's efforts. Bell's machine, which had in fact been demonstrated in England before Hussey received his American patent in 1833, required too much tinkering and repairing to be a practical implement. Its cutter with one half of the shears fixed and the other vibratory, turning on the iron bolt that confined them to the iron bar across the front of the frame, was, in his opinion, a bad principle and never likely to succeed.[20]

Though there were other reaping machines shown at the Exhibition the two Americans carried the palm for practicality. Their machines were tried at several places during the harvest. At Tiptree Hall, where Alderman Mechi was then lavishly spending on spectacular farming the money he had acquired by the sales of his patent razor, McCormick's machine did well, but Hussey's would not work. At a further trial to determine whether the Society should award medals to both inventors, Hussey's machine failed to qualify because it sometimes clogged. The machine was being managed by Dray and Co., Hussey's English agents, a firm who intended to manufacture under licence. Hussey thought it well to come over himself, and in a field belonging to Mr. Crosskill (?), Grovehill Lane, Beverley, the machine did quite well, as it also did in private trials at Blenheim in September 1851. Meanwhile McCormick's had added to his laurels at the Royal Agricultural College at Cirencester.

The controversy rose to great heights, and as both machines had secured distinctions, McCormick issued a challenge to all other makers of reapers to compete in a trial at Marton, Middlesbrough,[21] under the auspices of the Cleveland Agricultural Society. H. S. Thompson says that this trial was at Guisborough.[22] It was a trial by jury. Twelve practical farmers judged the performance of the machines in the field visually, and came down in favour of Hussey's by a majority of eleven to one. Honours were now even. Both machines had a cachet, and everybody was at liberty to make his own choice between them.

The cutting apparatus on Hussey's machine was a series of knives like arrowheads. They moved between projecting bosses of the same shape which acted as sheaths to the knives when at rest and stays to the corn when in work. This action was like that of a chaff cutter in which a sharp knife passes close to a metal plate, the knife being so arranged as to have a drawing cut. The metal plate gave the requisite stiffness to the straw or other material operated upon.

Several English implement makers took up the Hussey machine in preference to McCormick's, amongst them Garrett's. No fewer than one thousand five hundred were said to have been distributed over England within a couple of years of the Exhibition. This was too easy. "The old Scotch reaper [Bell's] like a giant refreshed by a long sleep, came suddenly forth at the beginning of harvest and threw down the gauntlet and challenged its younger American imitators to a trial of skill!" Bell's reaper completely defeated the Hussey–Crosskill at the Highland Society's show at Perth, and afterwards on Keillor Farm, belonging to Mr. Hugh Watson. Bell is said to have wished to exhibit his machine at the Great Exhibition but was dissuaded. If he had done so, he might have been vindicated before. Apparently his machine proved better than a Hussey-type designed by a Northern Irishman named Robinson against which it was pitted at trials in Belfast before the British Association.

It is not surprising that the shears type of cutter had been adopted by the Americans, who apparently copied it from those machines of Bell's which found their way to America. An anonymous writer on the subject was quite uncertain whether such machines, if perfected, could be of any general use; on the whole he thought not. They were only likely to be used, he said, on large farms, and could never cut laid crops. This was an unfortunate prophecy. Still, it was a desirable machine to save labour, and make the harvest short and merry rather than long and dreary as it so often was. He was convinced that the making of bands and the binding of sheaves were not likely to be effected by machinery. He was wrong. In less than twenty-five years this was accomplished. But he was right in prophesying that stooking must always be done by hand. He thought that perhaps an exchange of parts between Bell's and McCormick's machines might result in a perfect reaper.[23]

What combination of parts this writer had in mind he did not disclose; but one combination was tried by Lord Kinnaird of Rossie Priory, Inchture, who worked with George Bell, the brother of Patrick. After a good many failures Lord Kinnaird bought two McCormick reapers and McCormick visited him. He applied the McCormick driving gear and cutter to Bell's side delivery, and established a small factory for the making of this hybrid product, but did not continue it after the death of the engineer. This machine won the Highland Society's prize for the best reaper in 1858.[24]

No time was lost by British makers after the American machines shown in 1851 had aroused so much interest, and in the next year at the Royal Agricultural Society's Show at Lewes, reaping machines were exhibited by Thompson, Woods, Holmes, Ransome, Mason, Burgess and Co., Crosskill, Samuelson, Garrett and Howard. One of the machines, made by Samuelson, was on McCormick's principles, and the others on Hussey's. Ransome, whose machine was practically identical with Garrett's, arranged with that firm not to enter the trials.

When ripe rye was cut at these trials, Garrett's machine proved the best and Crosskill's next best. But the judges felt that reapers must be stronger and less complicated before they could be generally useful. A footnote was added by A. Hammond to the effect that the reaper could never be an implement on which the farmer solely relied to cut his corn, but it might become a useful addition to the scythe. This opinion was confuted by William Fisher Hobbs in a note immediately following which stated that the principle that corn could be cut by machinery had been established, and makers would soon overcome the manufacturing difficulties.[25]

Patents, of course, continued to be taken out, though it would be tedious to try to catalogue them all. One machine designed in 1852 may be mentioned. It was Ridley's Patent Cutting and Reaping Machine. The cutting apparatus on this machine was two sets of blades, one stationary and one movable, which acted precisely like scissors, the movable blades being worked by springs on an oscillating bar. The claim was made that the cut corn was laid in a continuous line, or in bundles within the framework of the machine. It was like Pliny's machine and said to require a tropical climate.[26]

Trials were annual events for the next few years and then were made only at intervals by the great agricultural societies until the coming of the self-binder in 1876, when they were renewed until that machine had become established as an essential in the farming equipment of the nation.

The years 1853 and 1854 each saw at least two major trials, but they were not definitive because, as in the later trials, manufacturers were constantly introducing improvements that made for better working in the design of the machines, so the prizewinner in any one year was liable to be defeated in the following year, until almost all firms could claim to have been prize winners at some time or other.

The "Royal" tried five machines selected from those exhibited at Gloucester in 1853; Hussey's own improved; Dray and Co's. Hussey; Samuelson's original McCormick; Burgess and Key's improved McCormick, and Crosskill's Bell, the last firm having apparently abandoned the Hussey type. The two American machines were arranged for manual sheaf making by hand raking. This was considered an advantage over Bell's, which laid the cut corn in swathe. Both Ransome's and Garrett's machines had an elementary sheaf gatherer that did not tie, but neither competed at Philip Pusey's farm in Berkshire. The prize of £20 was given to Crosskill's Bell, which had an improved cutting apparatus.[27] Trials between the Bell, Hussey and McCormick machines at King's Park, Stirling, under the auspices of the General Agricultural Association of the county in the same year were indeterminate. By then Hussey had laid aside his clipping shears and adopted McCormick's serrated saw-edge cutter. Crosskill was driving the fans (sails or reel) of the Bell by a belt instead of a chain. The premium went to Bell though his machine was deemed not yet perfect. The Hussey was condemned out of hand as no use in Scotland. The McCormick was considered good but in need of modification for that country. Next year, two Bell's, two McCormick and one Hussey were tried again in Scotland. Hussey's machine won the prize by virtue of its low selling price. For some reason the Crosskill–Bell with its new cutter bar failed to work here this year. The McCormicks did good work. None of the machines shown was deemed suitable for small farmers; a small and cheap reaping machine was still a desideratum. A manual delivery machine invented by Mr. Simpson of Westmains carried two men who tied the cut corn into sheafs and tossed them off for stooking. Its form of shears was not considered desirable.[28]

The failure of the Crosskill–Bell machine at this trial is incomprehensible, because such a machine had been used very successfully by James W. Hunter of Thurston during the 1853 harvest in spite of occasional breakdowns. He cut one hundred and thirty acres in one hundred and forty-eight working hours. The crop consisted of thirty-nine acres oats, twenty-four acres wheat, and sixty-seven acres barley. Besides the advantage of doing the work so speedily, less grain was wasted than by hand cutting.[29]

An oddity was patented by Joseph Burch, of Crag Hall, Maccles-field, in December 1852. Its cutter was two horizontal discs revolving contrariwise. To each perimeter were fixed knives or sickles which crossed each other in motion. It was dragged by a long rope over the corn.

Joseph Whitworth of Manchester patented a reaper like Matthew Gilson's. William Exall of Reading patented another with its cutters on an endless band or chain revolving round two rollers. In spite of all this, the competition was among the Bell, Hussey and McCormick types.

The McCormick was improved in 1854 by Burgess and Key who added side delivery of the cut corn by means of an Archimedean screw. In 1857 they included a conical screw divider, and in 1859 a spring hinge. At the 1855 "Royal" trial at Carlisle, the Archimedean plat-form with side delivery was thought a decided improvement, and though not perfect was expected to be made so. The Burgess-Key–McCormick won the prize that year, though in the previous year at Lincoln the side delivery of the Bell exhibited by Crosskill had been greatly praised. The draught of the Bell was too heavy, and the judges thought its cut should be narrower. In competition with it at Lincoln, Ransome entered a machine, the Automaton, fitted with a gathering arm for side delivery in bundles, but it did not tie them up. Lord Kinnaird's machine did not put up a good show at Carlisle. An Ameri-can machine made by Forbush and Co. was exhibited by John Palmer of Bury. It was very similar to Dray's Hussey that was also on show there and at Chelmsford in the following year. But it was not tried at either place. Only three machines were, in fact, tried at Chelms-ford, Crosskill's Bell; Dray's Hussey; Burgess and Key's McCormick, and all of the makers received prizes. Crosskill's delivery web made of three gutta-percha bands was lighter and reduced the draught. It went some way towards satisfying the judge's wishes and received the highest award. Two farmers reported their experience with Dray's improved Hussey, and Burgess and Key's McCormick in that year. At Salisbury the following year, Dray showed a Forbush machine as well as a Hussey, but the judges gave the prizes to Burgess and Key, Crosskill and Kinnaird in that order. All of these machines had side delivery.[30]

No more "Royal" trials were made till 1860, but in the interval, A. B. Bamlett, then employed on his father's thousand-acre farm, had visited the Yorkshire Agricultural Society's show at Thirsk in 1858, and seen there a trial of reapers. He thought most of them unsatisfactory and, like Bell, made in his barn a swathe delivery reaper. He showed it at the "Royal" show in 1859. He used some of Hussey's ideas in an improved model that won a silver medal at the "Royal" show in 1860. At first, Bamlett's machines were made by Picksley, Sims and Co. of Leigh, Lancs, and by Kearsley of Ripon, Yorks, but the supply from these sources was unequal to the demand, so he established a factory at Thirsk, at a date which is a little uncertain. A few years later Bamlett's reaper won very high praise from the Yorkshire Agricultural Society. The firm of Bamlett has continued to flourish with this and other products till the present day.[31]

In 1860 and 1861 the "Royal" again held trials of reaping machines at Canterbury and Leeds. Only three machines were selected for trial at Canterbury. They were made by Burgess and Key, Robert Cuthbert and Co. and by W. Dray and Co. An award of £10 was made to Cuthbert and Co. for the light draught, compactness, simplicity, strength and durability of the working parts of their machine. The Burgess Key was highly commended, but the Dray retired because it tore off some heads of grain.

A much more elaborate set of trials was made at Leeds of grass mowers, corn reapers, haymaking machines and horse hay rakes. The reapers were divided into three classes: with side delivery; without side delivery and combined reapers and grass mowers. No prize was awarded to the third class as the combination was not considered effective. The entries in the other two classes were fairly numerous. The Burgess and Key and Crosskill machines were the best in the first class, and were tried with a dynamometer, an award of £14 being made to Crosskill and £6 to Burgess and Key. In the second class, Picksley, Sims and Co. received £6 and Cuthbert and Co. £4, the

draught of the latter's machine being thought too heavy for the horses
to haul it all day. The judges felt that mechanical invention as applied
to agriculture had attained no greater triumph than in the production
of the reaper, and that great progress had undoubtedly been made
towards perfecting it.[32]

This progress was summed up by Jacob Wilson. The various
machines differed mainly in respect of the cutting apparatus, then
limited to two kinds, the obtuse angled cutter and the acute angle;
in the mode of delivery, which was by hand to the back or side of the
machine, or by mechanical or self delivery in swathe or sheaf; and in
the draught which was still a choice between the square hauled or
pushed. He also classified the machines and their derivation, demonstrating how greatly the British manufacturers were in debt to the
Americans. Crosskill's machine was Bell's much improved. Burgess
and Key's was McCormick's fitted with Archimedean screw delivery.
Lord Kinnaird's was a combination of McCormick's and Bell's. Kemp,
Murray and Nicholson's was an improved Hussey. Picksley and Sims'
was a patent of Bamlett's machine, and considered likely to holds its
own in Scotland against Scottish makers. Gardener and Lindsey had
produced an improved Hussey, and six thousand one hundred and
fifty-one acres were cut by one hundred and nineteen of these machines
in East Lothian during the harvest of 1860. It was made by Brown
and Young of Stirling. Cuthbert of Bedale, Yorkshire, and Jack and
Sons of Maybole, Scotland, both made improved Husseys. Buchan
and Bickerton were yet another firm to adopt this type, selling sixteen
machines in 1860, sixty-nine in 1861 and one hundred and ninety-four
in 1862. Wood's machine, an American importation, was not popular.
Samuelson's patent Eclipse was cheap.

Wilson rejoiced that "the farmer was thus no longer subjected to
the supercilious and intolerant behaviour of bands of unscrupulous
reapers, but was able to use a machine as an addition to his ordinary
staff at harvest time."[33]

McCormick added, in 1862, the rake arm which raked the cut
grain off the platform of his machine, and won the first prize at the
London exposition,[34] though the Dorsey type of self-raker which
remained the standard type for at least thirty years, was also shown by
Samuelson and Co. of Banbury.[35] No less than forty-five reaping and
mowing machines were exhibited at the "Royal" show at Worcester

in 1863. Though by this time some doubts of the efficacy of the system of giving prizes was beginning to be felt,[36] trials of all kinds of machines continued to be held, and those of reapers were renewed in 1865 at Plymouth, and 1869 at Manchester.

At Plymouth the inferiority of manual to mechanical side delivery was very apparent. Manual delivery involved severe and incessant labour on the part of the attendant. Hornsby's swathe delivery won £25 and Samuelson's self-raking reaper £15. Amongst the other reapers shown, the Beverley Iron Works' machine was very like Crosskill's Leeds prize reaper; Burgess and Key's reaper fitted with McCormick Automaton was erratic in delivery, and Walter A. Wood's did not work satisfactorily. Of the large entry of one-horse reapers, several were much too large and heavy for one horse, a conclusion that was confirmed at Manchester in 1869. Here the judges selected from the stands no less than eighty-four reaping machines for trial, and felt that as the flail had of late disappeared from the barns of this country and been replaced by machinery, so after this successful exhibition will the scythe and the sickle gradually cease to be used in our fields. Bamlett showed twenty-two machines, Hornsby seventeen, Picksley twelve, and Howard a large American collection. There was a variety of new manufacturers, including J. and F. Young of Ayr with their manual delivery machine. William Foster and Sons, Witham, Essex, with their "Star" which had a special cam drive like that used by Bell in 1830; and Brenton of Polbath, Cornwall, showed a machine fitted with a roller plate for sheaf gathering which was released by a foot spring.[37]

The disliked Walter A. Wood self-delivery reaper did exceedingly well when tried at the Glasgow show of the Highland and Agricultural Society in 1875. The advantages were that the delivery rakes were below the driver and therefore in his control, large or small sheaves could be made, and there was an improvement in the knife. The only other machine tried here, that of William Anson Wood, broke down after a few minutes.[38] Next year at the "Royal" show at Birmingham, Walter A. Wood exhibited a sheaf binder which was not attached to a reaping machine; it could only be demonstrated on the stand. This was epochal and the final stage in the evolution of the self-binder.

At the same show the future was prefigured in the mechanically hauled reaper made by Crosskill and hauled by an Aveling and Porter 8 h.p. steam engine. The engine makers were a well-known firm, who, by the agency of steam, could do all sorts of things formerly considered impracticable. This "magnified swather" was tried at Leamington, and pushed its way about the field in what was thought a most extraordinary manner, cutting a width of twelve feet and delivering a swathe so perfect as to surprise most of the spectators and delight all. It received a gold medal. In that year, Hornsby's won twelve of the fifteen prizes for horse-drawn reapers.[39]

The massive steam-hauled machine did not come to anything, but the sheaf binder shown by Walter A. Wood presaged the completion of the reaper binder. Trials were held by the "Royal" at Aigburth of several of these machines exhibited at Liverpool. They were mainly wire tying binders and had been recently shown at Philadelphia. Eight were entered, five were shown, but only three tried. These were all American and none was perfect for English conditions. Some of the machines were new inventions and could only be used experimentally in that harvest. Even at that date two of these experimental machines tied string, but they did not succeed in getting tried. They were made by M. T. Neale and H. J. H. King. The judges were satisfied that the "mere operation of sheafing and tying, unconnected with the question of gathering and delivery" was shown to be an accomplished fact, but the gold medal was not awarded, though the judges were pleased that it was to be kept on offer.[40]

Despite the coming of the binder, John Gregory of South Shields produced, in 1879, another manual and self-back delivery reaper, that was said to have worked remarkably well in trial. But this was not a line of development which could be profitably followed. Self-binders were seen in most gratifying array at Smithfield in 1880, including "Wood's" string tier. The Johnston Harvester Co., an American firm, put out a separate string binding and tying machine which bound with "a regular overhand knot, then considered unique.[41] Samuelson showed another new machine at Smithfield in 1881 having no canvas elevators or belts, but which cut and bound on the same platform. Bamlett, Kearsley (who showed the Johnston), and Harrison McGregor were also represented in that show.[42]

An exhibit that must have aroused general interest at the "Royal" show in Kilburn in 1879, was one of ancient and modern implements.

Bell's original reaper that had been demonstrated at Glasgow in 1829, was included, and in the notice about it in the catalogue, it was stated that a number of these machines had been sent to America in 1834. The exhibit also included a Smith rotary cutting machine, invented in 1834, and still used in 1879 by Mr. McQueen on a farm near Stirling. Sir P. Miles of Leigh Court, Bristol, showed a Burgess and Key swathe delivery reaper made in 1844. Hornsby's and Wood's original mowers, and Bamlett's machines completed the tally of this collection.[43]

In 1879, too, McCormick secured the "Royal" gold medal in trials at Derby for a string-tying binder; Samuelson and Co. and the Johnston Harvester Co. were awarded silver medals; and H. J. H. King of Newmarket was commended. Neither King's nor Bamlett's, however, was yet considered sufficiently developed, the American machines still being in advance. The report contains extensive details of the different kinds of knotters used, but they are too elaborate for insertion here. The machines were very similar to one another. The McCormick, the Johnston and the Samuelson were identical, and Bamlett, Hetherington and King worked from the same patents. Wood was still regarded as unique, and there were some four or more other makers. Separate gleaners and binders were also shown.[44]

When Howard's, Wood's and Hornsby's machines, all string tiers, were tried at Glasgow in 1883, it was found that all of them cut close, clean and even, and they tied perfectly secure and with the same tightness throughout. Howard's and Wood's machines made small sheaves, but Hornsby's won on this point. Howard's and Hornsby's delivered gently, Wood's with considerable velocity. Prizes of £100 were awarded to Hornsby, £50 to Wood, and £25 to J. and F. Howard. The judges, who were experienced Scottish farmers, thought the sheafing and binding superior to hand labour, but the price of the machines, £60, a disadvantage, and the damp climate and greasy undergrowth of Scotland liable to cause many breakages.[45] Again, at similar trials in 1886, Hornsby and Wood won the first and second prizes, though all the machines entered did good work and there were no breakdowns.[46] Nevertheless, T. S. Bissett and Son of Blairgowrie thought sufficiently well of the machine to produce one in 1890 with a chain conveyor and no canvas, rather like a hay and straw elevator. This was a development of their previous activities. They had been in the business since 1862 and had, amongst other things, produced, in 1880, the first machine with enclosed gearing made in this country.[47]

Another American novelty was exhibited at the "Royal" show at Doncaster in 1891. It was the Adriane Harvester and Rear Discharge Binder and it was awarded a silver medal because its construction gave it great advantage in simplicity and lightness of draught. It had but one canvas apron, the usual two vertical and cutter canvases being replaced by revolving sprockets to gather the grain with a revolving disc to shape the butt of the sheaf. Delivery was by a discharge foot which carried the sheaf to the back of the machine and deposited it on its butt out of the track of the horses. It did not figure in the trials the Society held two years later at Chester, which were held to demonstrate "the various improvements tending to greater perfection of work" effected since the previous trials nine years before.

Originally twenty-three machines were entered by nine firms, but fourteen were withdrawn between the show and the trials, leaving only nine made by five firms to be tested, i.e. Samuelson two; Kearsley two; J. and H. Keyworth and Co. one; Massey Harris two; Hornsby two. All these were intended to work with two horses and one man, and all used Manila twine. They were tried in oats, barley and wheat, and dynamometer readings were taken. Hornsby won the first prize of £50 and divided the second and third prizes of £30 and £20 equally with Massey Harris.[48]

Further detailed improvements were steadily made by the different manufacturers, but by the 1890s the reaper binder was stabilized in its general principles. The main improvements had been the substitution of string tying for wire, the reduction of weight, the reduction of draught, some makers using ball and roller bearings for this purpose, and the reduction of the price. Cutting, elevating and sheafing and binding had been greatly improved. By 1890 the best models had good controls by levers in the reach of the driver who could set the reel up or down, backward or forward and could alter the tilt of the cutting platform and finger bar, and the position of the band on the sheaf. But there were no costings to guide the prospective purchaser, and every farmer was obliged to estimate for himself the probable economy effected by the use of the machine.[49]

It was clear that self-binders had come to stay. As James Edwards remarked, they had "been before the public for upwards of a quarter of a century and this ought to be a sufficient period of probation to satisfy the most cautious." This statement indicated that so late as 1900 there were still "cautious" men who had not yet adopted the machine, but reaper-binders were certainly in general use before the outbreak of World War I.

It is difficult, as will be appreciated, to allot credit for the invention. There was certainly a good deal of exchange of ideas across the Atlantic and it is quite clear that after 1851 British manufacturers largely depended, at any rate initially, upon American ideas and patents to enable them to produce and improve their machines, particularly in respect of the binder. That British manufacturers added improvements and materially assisted in the evolution of the modern machine, is no less certain, and many of the firms have achieved world-wide fame.

Many share the credit of creating this boon to the farmer. As one farmer wrote no longer ago than 1922: "Fourteen hands mowing is a pretty sight. But think of the cost! . . . Then consider the time harvest took if the weather was bad. And mowing is hard work and no mistake, if kept at any length of time. (I've done some, so I know.) Then with wheat and oats there was the stooping in tying up, and the bands to make. The thistles (they ought to be absent of course) would prick one's arms to a greater extent than was pleasant."[50]

Even stooking is becoming unnecessary as the combine harvester spreads over the land.

(b) Haymaking Machinery

First cut your grass, scatter it about, gather it in windrows, cock it overnight, scatter it about, windrow it, cock it, and so on to the stack and stack it—such were the old-time instructions for hay-making.

Before the coming of the machine it needed nearly as many men to make hay as the blades of grass they gathered; or so the picturesque sight of an army of haymakers must have appeared to the farmer who had to pay the bill. Women who followed the waggoner to the stack collected every stalk that dropped by the way.

Though a grass mower was, as I have said, invented early in the nineteenth century, it was not till after the coming of the reaper that the grass mower came into use. Meanwhile other operations in hay-making had been provided with mechanical aids.

Middlesex, where so much hay was grown for the London market, was reputed the model district of England and of the world for hay-making a century and a half ago. The methods of that county were advocated by writers from then to 1850,[1] and repeated in 1888.[2]

The process was simple though prolonged, and demanded a great deal of hard work in the heat of summer. A contemporary description runs "Natural meadow and pasture grass, being mowed in its proper season, should be spread in the morning, and before the evening raked into small rows, and those rows made into small cocks; they cannot be made too small, provided they are put together in a round snug manner; on the morrow the cocks should be throwed and spread in rows, and turned and raked together as may seem necessary, and in the evening made into larger cocks, than those the preceding day; thus the process should be continued till the hay becomes fit to carry together, which may be known by its handling light; and on twisting a small wisp as hard as you can with both hands, observe that no moisture appears, or the hay is not sufficiently dry to put together in a rick."[3] For this job all hands were called together, even the children, who probably enjoyed it greatly, and, of course, there was a certain amount of junketing.[4]

It is surprising that in the eighteenth century, with all the enthu-siasm for the seed-drill and threshing machine, two quite complex devices, nothing was invented to simplify the labour of haymaking. Horse rakes there may have been. In 1807 Mr. Ketcher of Burnham, Essex, had one; it was first seen there by Arthur Young, whose men-tion of it is fair proof that it was something of a novelty, though it may have been known before this date. It was used for bean stubble, but obviously could quite easily be employed for other purposes. It was simply a set of curved iron teeth fixed in a beam carried on a framework with two wheels, and provided with handles by which it could be guided and lifted out of work as required.[5] This is not unlike Weir's improved hay and corn rake, described by Loudon, except that Weir's rake was fitted with a lever arrangement for putting in and out of work.

There was also the common or Norfolk horse rake used for barley and oat crops as well as for hay. It was a simpler version with a few straight teeth placed vertically in a beam carried on two wheels, and was said to be capable of windrowing twenty or thirty acres a day, "by simply lifting up the tool and dropping it from the teeth, without the horse being stopped." The horse stubble rake was a heavier and stronger pattern, but how long these had been in existence by 1831 it is difficult to estimate. Although of great service in haymaking as well as in gathering crops that were mown, the saving of manual labour being very large, Loudon does not think it was then in very general use.[6] It is odd that the simple transition from hand raking to horse raking did not take place at an earlier date.

For spreading the hay for drying, the hay fork was used manually right down to the late nineteenth century, though the haymaking machine, or tedder, was designed by Robert Salmon of Woburn in the early years of the century. There is a certain discrepancy in the evidence about the date of its production. Loudon says it was invented about 1800, Ransome that it was patented in 1816, and Cashmore and Newman that it was "invented about 1814."[6a] It was quickly brought into use by the hay farmers of Middlesex, because it was of great advantage in making meadow or natural hay which required much more frequent turning, and needed to be more thinly spread out than "seeds hay." Salmon's machine was quite simple and forms the basis on which all subsequent haymaking machines were constructed. It was an axle on a pair of wheels. The axle shaft carried two smaller wheels, the rims of which were joined at regular intervals by horizontal bars, making a hollow cylinder. The horizontal bars carried curved iron teeth, pointing outwards about six inches long. This arrangement revolved as the machine was drawn along and the series of forks scattered the hay in all directions, and over the driver and the horse as well, if care was not taken to drive to leeward. A crank enabled the raking cylinder to be lifted out of work for travelling. Loudon was not very enthusiastic about it, only remarking that "on the whole it answered perfectly." It was coming into general use near London in 1831, and was improved by Wedlake of Hornchurch, Essex, sometime before 1843. Wedlake's machine had the cylinder in two parts, each working independently. The tine teeth were placed upon a bar, supported by a spring that would give if it met an obstruction, and spring back into position.[7]

Another machine that seems to have been a tedder is said by a contemporary to have been invented in Yorkshire some years before 1834, but I have been unable to find any other reference to it—though it had "since with some improvements been pretty generally adopted." When the horse trotted gently, it did the work much more effectively than could be done manually, though it was necessary to avoid short turns, and in high winds the hay had to be spread on the leeward side, otherwise horse, machine and man got smothered in hay. It was only faintly praised because it did not occasion that saving of labour that had been hoped, "for it does not rake the grass into rows, nor cock it; and when the grass begins to get dry, the violence of its operation is apt to shake out the seed." In Yorkshire its original cost was £4, but in London it was sold at £18. This is all very circumstantial, and if this writer was not confusing the machine he had in mind with Salmon's, it must have been very much like it.[8]

The same writer suggested that a hay rake of a simple construction was still very much wanted and if made like a horse stubble rake would save time and labour. The Americans had then lately exported such a rake, and it was successfully employed in Scotland, where wooden hay sweeps, or swoops, not unlike the modern implement, were in use. The firm founded by John Bright in 1740 and later taken over by William Garner to become Garner and Sons of Melton Mowbray, seems to have made hay-sweeps since 1800. Garner and Sons afterwards absorbed the firm of Thomas Holyoak and Son of Narborough, Leicester, who made the same kind of implements.[9]

The American rake and the stubble rake with curved iron teeth, an implement much approved in East Lothian and Berwickshire, were shown at Drummond's Museum in 1839.[10] They gained some approbation from the Rev. M. Wilson ten years later. He contrasted them with the still prevalent hand tools. "The tedding machine does its work in the morning; the crop tossed and scattered by it lies fully exposed to the sun and the wind throughout the forenoon; and the horse rake gathers the scattered crop into windrows in the afternoon." Unfortunately the rest of the work must be done by hand, cocking and whatever else may have been necessary to protect the hay from the rain.[11] The Scotch horse rake and Wedlake's improvement on Salmon's were again illustrated by J. C. Morton in his *Cyclopaedia*, 1856, together with Ransome's Swath horse rake. This new machine of Ransome's had a series of three sets of teeth working on an axle above the centres of the ground wheels and presenting three several rows which successively came into operation as rakes. Morton thought it very ingenious. Ten years later Copland said that the haymaker was newly invented, an odd statement for such a well-informed writer. He admitted there were several makes, but all were much alike. Smith and Ashby's of Stamford was probably the best type. It was, like Wedlake's, constructed with the rakes in two parts "so that if an obstruction presents itself only one half of the length of the rake is affected by it." The whole rake was thrown out of gear if the machine was backed or turned. This was an opinion that was shared by Donaldson, who estimated that it did as much work as twelve or fifteen haymakers.[12] Copland thought correctly that the horse rake had been in use in one form or another for many years and that it was simple and effective and not likely to be improved upon.

This was twenty years after the Royal Agricultural Society had held its first trial of haymaking machines in 1846. The Society organized other trials in 1857, 1861, 1865, 1869, 1875, and 1895. Already in 1842 the Society had given a prize of £10 to James Lovell of Glastonbury for his invention, a silver medal to Wedlake in 1843 for the best of the four haymaking machines shown in that year, and £3 to the same firm in 1845.[13] Lovell's machine came in for a good deal of praise in 1842. The judges did not like the machines in general use—there could not have been many—because they took the grass or hay round on the rakes and threw it over in the air, whereas Lovell's simply turned and spread it. The teeth were straight and unlikely to become clogged, four rows being fixed on a shaft that revolved immediately over the main axle of the carriage from which it received its motion. The rakes adapted themselves to inequalities in the ground by ascending and descending on the carriage wheels. They revolved in the same direction as the carriage wheels and left the grass spread behind them. They could be readily engaged or disengaged by the driver who rode on the machine. The rake was estimated to do five acres an hour.[14] It is odd that little was heard of this machine thereafter.

It was in 1846 that H. Smith and Co. of Stamford first distinguished themselves with their double-acting haymaking machine. It was awarded £5 after full trial on a crop of good grass. The judges, both

K

at this trial and in 1847, praised its device for raising or lowering it to the ground as the crop required. In 1846 Joseph Cook Grant won £3 for his horse rake invented and manufactured by himself.

When C. W. Tindall wrote in 1895 his report on haymaking machines, he selected the five years from 1857, in which trials of this kind of implement were held,[15] but he omitted to mention that trials were held for several years in succession after 1846. In 1848 Grant of Stamford, and Barrett, Exall and Co. of Reading were runners-up for the medal awarded to Smith and Son of Stamford (Smith and Ashby?), but their machines were not quite so simple in construction. In the following year there was practically no competition, Smith's being regarded superior to all others in all its parts "and perfection of work." It was judged so near perfection that "no one need fear to buy it." The same opinion was strongly held by the Bath and West of England Society who awarded it more than one prize.[15a]

Hensman of Woburn got a medal for a horse rake in 1848, but many others, almost as good, were tried, including Howard's, Busby's, and Grant's. The prize was won in 1849 by Mr. Williams, whose rake did its work "in that way which has so long been desired, the peculiar curve of the teeth causing the hay . . . to rise round their face until its own weight caused it to fall over so that the whole is rolled into a piece like a lady's muff, or the roll of wool from a carding machine, giving the air and wind free circulation through the mass." This also allowed stones and lumps of earth to fall between the teeth. The lever adjustment too was easier than the others.

Progress in construction of haymaking machines was very great in the decade 1840 to 1850; this can be attributed to the efforts of the Royal Agricultural Society, who were perhaps aroused by the fact that no such implement was exhibited at their first show in 1839. Trials went on and medals and money prizes continued to be awarded. Philip Pusey was disturbed to find that though the horse rake would do the work of ten or fifteen women, and was common in many counties, it was unknown in others, and when made known was not adopted. The work of the haymaker, too, was far better done.[16] Practically every implement maker was then making these devices.[17] Nevertheless at the end of the nineteenth century haymaking was still a manual task in some counties and the women of the farms helped.

The forks of a rake made by Thomas Smith of Bradfield, Suffolk, were weighted to counterbalance them. This arrangement tended to keep them from the land and prevented them from sinking in and damaging the ground, and, of course, made the lever for lifting them easier to operate. (Several Smiths seem to have been making implements at this time.)[18] Pusey had already noticed the arrangement whereby the haymaking machine could toss the hay high above itself, or when in reverse, just stir the hay gently and loosen it on the ground.[19] The tines were mounted on springs and one of the praiseworthy parts of the Smith and Ashby machine was that it was on double springs.

The enthusiasm for the reaper was bound to react on the task of cutting grass for hay, and though it had to meet rather different demands, the mower was the same kind of machine. By 1857 the Royal Agricultural Society was able to include mowers in its trials, though cutting with the scythe lasted at least half a century longer.

In 1857 haymaking machines by Nicholson, Barrett Exall and Andrews, Smith and Ashby, H. A. Thompson, Ransome (the same as Nicholson), Wyatt, Samuelson, and Lane were tried, and thirteen competitors entered horse rakes. Of these Nicholson's horse rake scattered the crop easily, the teeth were well shaped and it cleared either backwards or forwards readily without clogging. Mechanically it was simple. The firm of Barrett, Exall and Andrews ran it close. Among the horse rakes Rowsell's windrowing rake got a silver medal, Samuelson's self-relieving rake could be operated by a string, Fisher's had beams of tubular iron, and spring teeth curving forward, and the whole class was considered a credit to the makers and a boon to the farming public. But the chief interest was the mowing machine, these other things having been familiar at shows for ten years or more.

The mowing machines were tried in a small meadow of coarse, rank herbage near Salisbury intersected by open drains "and ill adapted for anything but a severe trial of the tempers of the exhibitors." Clayton and Shuttleworth won a prize of £15 and Drays £5. Lord Kinnaird's machine did not cut close enough to the ground, Mazier's had great difficulty, but Clayton's American Eagle worked very satisfactorily. The knives on this machine were worked by cam from the ground wheel. There were two sets of teeth, the upper moving and the lower fixed. Both these features were acknowledged to be new. Doubtless interest in the machine was stimulated because it was worked by "two cheerful Yankees." The cutters were easily replaced and less liable to clog or choke than the old cutters and guards.

Three years later the judges believed that mowers would soon be all that was desirable. Bamlett's machine, for example, then laid its swathe in a very perfect manner and was considered so important for artificial grasses that it was hoped it would be improved and reconstructed in other respects. This was done and the firm of A. C. Bamlett, Ltd., founded in 1857, has today a very wide reputation for mowers and other machines. The Yorkshire Agricultural Society in 1866 reported that Bamlett's machine was of wood and iron, strong and quick in action and remarkably steady. Its steadiness was due in great measure to the presence of a third wheel projecting in front of the machine and under the pole. It was notable for its steady motion and the absence of friction. It worked well across ridge and furrow.

Some good mowers were tried at Plymouth. Bamlett's was a strong, useful mower, very even, but clogged occasionally. The Burgess and Key was of good compact design. The judges were "much pleased" with the Kearsley which was a strong, well-made machine, cutting evenly and tolerably low. This was a north country firm founded in the late 1820s as iron founders and merchants at the British Iron and Implement Works, Ripon. They started making mowers and reapers about 1857.[20] The mower was wood-framed and the firm, like most others in the business, also produced a combined reaper and mower. The latter, again like most of the others, made good work, but did not cut the grass as closely as it might. The other firms whose mowers were tried this year were Samuelson, Barber, J. and W. Dicker, Child's American Clipper, Picksley and Sims, Wood, and Hornsby. No less than sixteen haymaking machines and eighteen horse rakes were tried at the same time, but neither kind of machine showed any marked change. The judges did not approve of a seat for the driver because the draught was sensibly increased and from this position he could not empty a heavy crop so easily.[21]

Twenty-one mowers and combined mowers and reapers were tried in 1865. This number rose to fifty-two in 1869; in addition, ten haymakers and twenty horse rakes were exhibited. The hay harvest was well on the way to being supplied with adequate labour-saving devices. Five hay collectors made by three firms were exhibited, but I am not quite clear what these were; they were "on the principle of the

American turn-over horse rake" and were not thought well of by the judges.[22]

It was a time of development. New firms were being founded for the purpose of making haymaking machinery and already existing firms were taking up the manufacture of these machines. Harrison, McGregor and Co., Ltd., of the Albion Ironworks, Leeds, began making mowers in 1873, and later made reapers and binders as well as feed preparing machines.[23] Bamford's too, founded by Henry Bamford, of Yoxall, Staffordshire, who went to Uttoxeter in 1839, and invented a new iron water tap at the age of nineteen, added the manufacture of haymaking machinery and other agricultural implements to his original enterprise of making hot air stoves and water barrels.[24]

The judges rather reluctantly admitted that the farmer's interest in mowers was not great in 1869. They thought the show of 1875 "exhibited the performance of the machines in a high degree." Three years later John Algernon Clarke stated categorically that "mowing machines now cut the major portion of the clover and meadow hay on all but the area under small occupations."[25]

These machines had not greatly changed since their first introduction. "The same scissors-like motion and the same principle of conveying power from the bite of the travelling wheel on the ground have been maintained since the first introduction of mowing machines. These two important elements, power and speed, have always seemed to be wedded on very fair terms in these machines; but we may well suppose," said the judges proudly, "that the simplifying and arranging of all their parts, according to their present mechanical construction, must have required many thousands of experiments, especially when we consider what work is performed by them. The knife runs at a very rapid speed, close to an uneven surface, consequently coming into contact with stones, sticks—not unfree from pieces of iron brought in manure—mole and anthills, often of a consistency like glue; at other times driving through an uneven surface as hard as a road, or running full speed into deep uneven furrows." These machines were therefore very different from barn machinery or even reapers, superior material and construction being of the utmost importance. Their development had shown a clear appreciation of these necessities. Strength was then obtained without unnecessary weight, improved wearing parts had been designed, and the machines tried at Taunton in 1875 were far better adapted for heavy and difficult cutting than anything that had previously been seen. Hornsby distinguished themselves in these trials by taking the first prize for one-horse mowers, the other entries being disqualified on account of too heavy draught, and by taking all three prizes in the two-horse class against severe competition, thirty-two machines being entered.[26] By this date, or even ten years before, the machine had developed its modern form. "The cutter bar had been given freedom of vertical movement, so that it could follow the ground closely and adapt itself to ridge and furrow. It could also be raised and lowered and in one make of machine the angle of the knife could be altered."[27] Since 1875, there have been improvements in detail, such as the use of roller bearings and better lubricating systems, but nothing more.

One of the great disadvantages of the haymaking machine was that if care was not taken to watch the direction in a wind, the hay was scattered all over the driver, horse and machine. One of the greatest novelties shown at Taunton in 1875 was a machine fitted with a hood "completely covering the front action of the forks." This was made by Ashley, Jeffery and Luke. The judges, like good and cautious farmers, were not prepossessed by its appearance, but on trial they found it was the only machine that did not clog. The hood was made of a light framework of wood, covered with canvas, a none too durable construction. A current of air was created under it when the machine was working and helped the forks to rid themselves of the hay. It also kept it closer so that it was handled more gently and there was less liability to shed out the grass seeds. Other manufacturers, too, had been concerned about the disposition of their machines but on the whole there was little change since the previous trials.

Seven self-acting horse rakes and nineteen non-self-acting were tried in this year, and Messrs. Nicholson carried off the first prize for self-acting, and the first and second prizes for the other type.

There is little more to relate about haymaking machinery, though so-called new types of these machines continued to appear. Stacking was greatly facilitated by the hay and sheaf elevators that were being introduced.[28]

Another American mower, the Eureka, which was really a new version of one previously shown, was exhibited by Everett, Adams and

Co., Ryburgh, Norfolk, in 1880. It was tried and cut a crop of clover and bents. Since the cutter was set in front of, and between the wheels, the cut grass fell inwards and stood almost upright, looking as if it had not been cut at all. This was considered to "quicken the drying." At this time, too, Ransome's showed a new self-acting horse rake, controlled by a foot lever, and an improved haymaker fitted with alternate straight and curved tines that scattered the hay well and turned the swathe satisfactorily.[29]

Five years later T. H. Ramsden exhibited a combined horse rake and haymaker that was described as a crude attempt to carry out a novel idea. Ramsden had tried to remedy several defects of the existing machines, e.g. the ordinary horse rake stopped lifting when halted to empty, so the hay was dropped on uncleared ground; and the revolving fingers of ordinary hay-rakes could not be set so close to the ground as to prevent their missing and hiding sunken places of wet hay. His machine had a lift like a hay elevator with apron teeth like reaper fingers, pivoted and set in an endless chain. These carried the hay upwards and when it reached the top and the fingers began to descend, the hay was forced on to a projection that delivered it to a revolving drum with projecting edges that acted as a spread. When used as a rake, the drum was removed and a container filled in the same way was fitted. This was not unlike some modern machinery, having something of the same principles as the Wilder Cutclift.

At the same meeting Bamford's showed a Progress Haymaker with the screen (or hood) made of corrugated instead of the usual solid iron, a substitution that probably made for lightness.[30]

John V. Gibbons, of Haseley Ironworks, Tetsworth, Oxfordshire, showed the Haseley Hay Tedder in 1889. His design was another attempt to smooth the rough action of the ordinary haymaker that Ramsden had tried to overcome. The Haseley was fitted with a series of spring forks working with a very similar action to the Darby Digger. Motion was given to three throw crankshafts by annular geared wheels on the travelling wheels. On each crank were fitted four tined forks, made of $\frac{1}{4}$ in. spiral spring steel, mounted on a shaft slung about the middle of the crank which was connected by two flat iron bars to a pivot on the fore part of the framing. The inventor called it a Hay Kicker.[31] This was a type of machine that gained some popularity in the 'nineties and was made by a good many firms. Five firms exhibited examples at Warwick in 1892: Ogle and Sons, of Ripley, Derby; J. V. Gibbons; Barford and Perkins; Ransome; W. N. Nicholson and Son, Ltd. It was then remarked that these machines had been introduced from America nearly thirty years before and were first shown at the Bristol meeting of the Bath and West Society in 1864.[32]

Nicholson's had been awarded a silver medal at Plymouth in 1890 for their Snapdragon horse rake. At this show Davey Sleep exhibited a combined charlock cleaner and horse rake; Lankester and Co. showed a hay-loader for attachment behind a wagon that pitched up the hay from the windrow, and Blackstone and Co., of Stamford, presented their Rutland Mower.[33] This was not, of course, Blackstone's first entry. As long ago as 1846 they had exhibited a haymaker, and when they opened their new works in 1877 they had already a reputation for their machines. By 1892 they were making a wide range of implements besides haymaking machinery, but their latest production was a new one-horse swathe turner.[34]

In spite of Blackstone's swathe turner, the judges were disappointed at the machines entered for the trials of hay- and clover-making machines at Darlington in 1895. They did not find that engineering science had much advanced the design of such machines in the twenty years since either the 1875 trial or even that of 1869. Eleven haymaking machines were tried and nine clover-making machines, but the first prize machine in the first class (Nicholson's) was much the same in principle as that which won so long before. They were most disappointing when worked on uneven ground, self-adjusting forks which they lacked being essential. The shakers always will work better than the tedders. There was much room for improvement for the difficulties were not insuperable. "There was a great want of a machine for putting out of swathe into windrow, say eight rows into one."[35]

The hay-kicker was improved upon by the swathe turner, and it is curious to find no notice of Blackstone's machine, so-called, in the *Journal of the Royal Agricultural Society*. In 1896 Jarmain's swathe turner, the Haseley, was tried. It was then recognized as a novelty. Instead of rake teeth or kickers, it turned the swathes by means of two rotating winged cones at the rear of a light frame which was carried on two wheels. At the back of the frame was a shaft with three pinions driven by an endless chain. It worked on two six-winged cones carried on short arms, which rotated at right angles to the direction of draught.

65. Fair Haymakers. From S. Baring Gould, *Book of the West,
Devon.* 1899.

66. Mowing with the Scythe. From L. C. Seguin, *Rural England*, 1885.

67. Bamlett's Two Horse Mower. From an old catalogue lent by the firm.

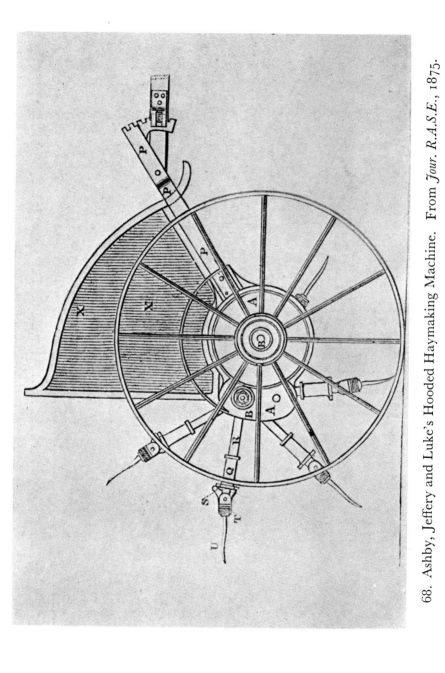

68. Ashby, Jeffery and Luke's Hooded Haymaking Machine. From *Jour. R.A.S.E.*, 1875.

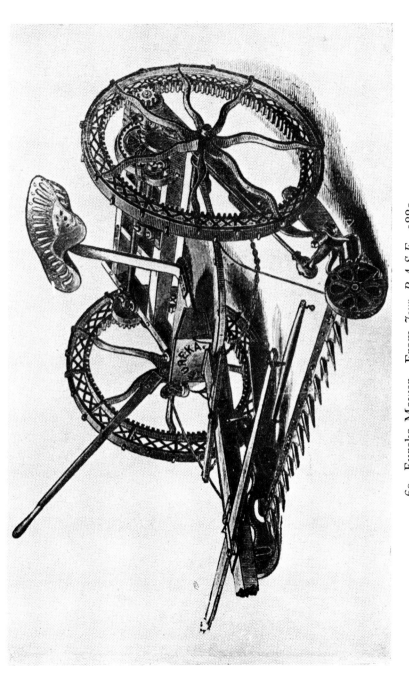

69. Eureka Mower. From *Jour. R.A.S.E.*, 1880.

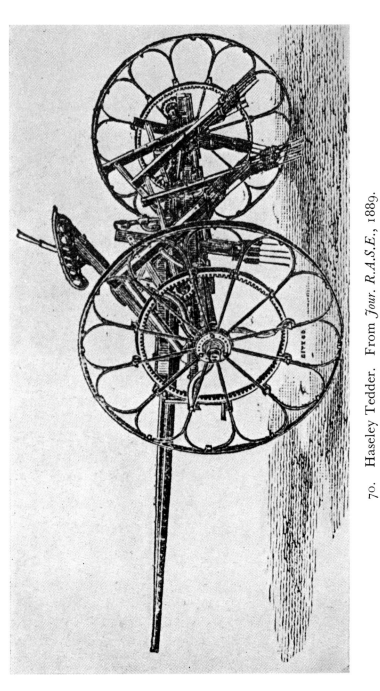

70. Haseley Tedder. From *Jour. R.A.S.E.*, 1889.

71. Nicholson's Hay Tedder. From *Jour. R.A.S.E.*, 1895.

72. Barford and Perkin's Tedder. From *Jour. R.A.S.E.*, 1895.

73. Jarmain's Swath Turner, the Haseley.   From *Jour. R.A.S.E.*, 1896.

74. Blackstone's Swath Turner. From *Jour. R.A.S.E.*, 1907.

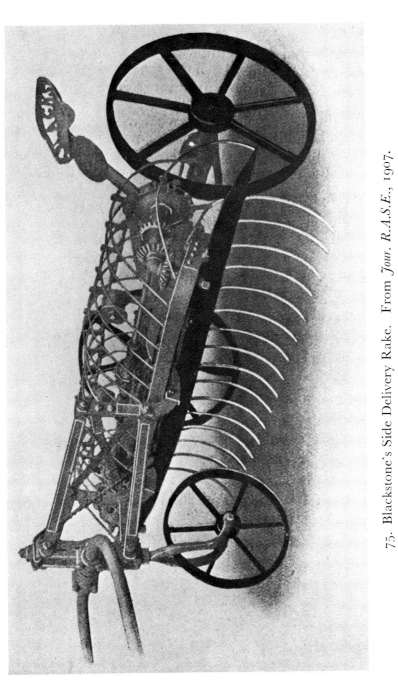

75. Blackstone's Side Delivery Rake. From *Jour. R.A.S.E.*, 1907.

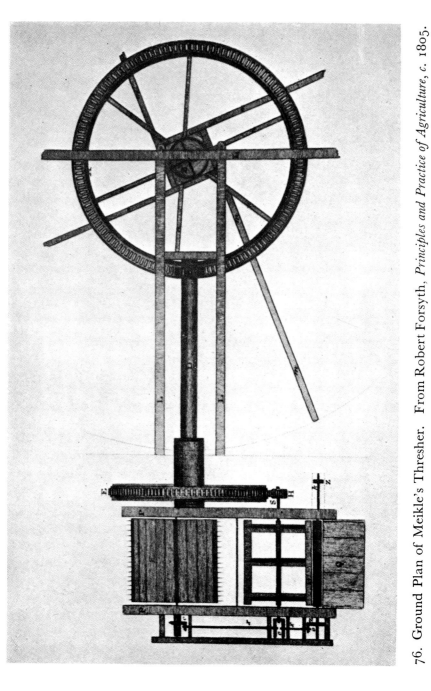

76. Ground Plan of Meikle's Thresher. From Robert Forsyth, *Principles and Practice of Agriculture, c.* 1805.

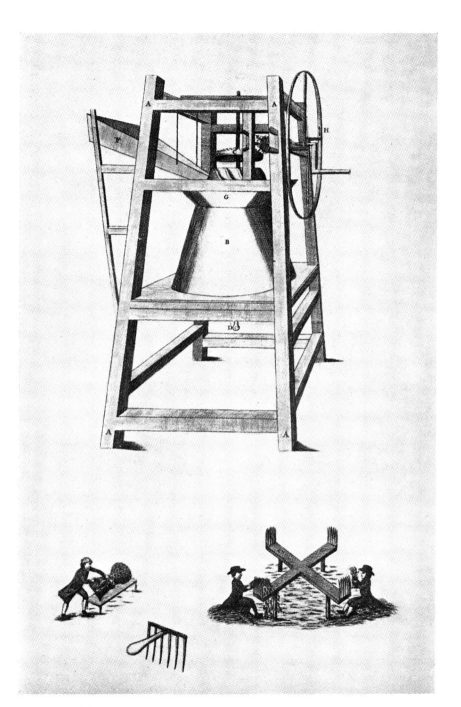

77. Winlaw's patent Mill. From *Annals of Agriculture*, Vol. VI.

78. William Spencer Dix's Thresher. From his *Remarks on the Utility* . . . , 1797.

79. James Sharp's Winnowing Machine.   From Agricola Sylvan, *Farmer's Magazine*, 1772, Vol. II.

80. Threshing Machines from the *London Encyclopaedia*, *c.* 1810.

These wings were placed diagonally to the spindle so that, when revolving, each wing struck the sward a few inches in advance of its predecessor, and continuing its revolution lifted or shoved the grass over it. Springs gave to the inequalities of the ground. This machine made excellent work when tried. It was much improved by 1903.[36]

Blackstone's swathe turner came into its own at Lincoln in 1907 when it won the first prize in competition with the machine of Martin Cultivator Co. Jackson and Son withdrew their machine early in the trial. Blackstone's also won the.prize for a side delivery rake. It had the advantage of being able to deliver the crop to either side, though the draught was undoubtedly heavier than that of its competitors.[37]

With, the coming of these machines, practically all the necessities of mechanical haymaking by horse traction, were met, and little further development could take place. The farmer could now be supplied with a machine which could do the job. It had taken nearly a century to make the full transition from manual haymaking to the use of machinery. Only half that period had been required to develop the mowing machine, and indeed much less if John Algernon Clarke's statement in 1878 can be accepted at its full value—which of course it can not.

A word must be added about hay collectors and loaders which did not, for technical reasons, come into general use till after the first World War.[38] A collector for use with horses was, however, illustrated in Loudon, but it was probably only an idea. The conception may have been of earlier date than Loudon, but the design is not so very different from the modern hay sweep. A type of this implement was seen in use in Scotland in the 1880s by Primrose McConnell. The Scottish implement used by John Speir of Newton Farm, Glasgow, was an adaptation of an American machine. McConnell bought it and developed it, and Cottis of Epping made some hundreds for customers mainly in the South of England. Finally Speir had one made to pass through narrow gates, and found it satisfactory in Scotland. But neither this implement nor the loader, which had been developed on the same lines as the hay and straw elevator, came into general use till after 1918.[39]

CHAPTER FIVE

THRESHING THE GRAIN

FOR COUNTLESS CENTURIES the grain won by arduous manual labour was trodden out by cattle, rubbed out by a wooden framework dragged over the threshing floor by animals, or knocked out by the flail. The ancient Israelites were conjured by their prophets "not to muzzle the ox that treadeth out the corn,"[1] and it has been suggested that when Gideon threshed barley by the winepress in secret against the Midianites,[2] he did so with a primitive flail.[3] In general it was with the flail that the grain was threshed right up to the beginning of Queen Victoria's reign,[4] though a threshing machine had been invented nearly a century before and was being used by advanced farmers in England and many more in Scotland.

Like so many other agricultural machines, the origin of this one is not very easy to determine. It was held by Michael Menzies' contemporaries, or near contemporaries, that he was the first man to attempt to prevent the losses in threshing by the flail, by making a machine to do the work. He is described quite categorically in different accounts as the brother of the Sheriff Depute of East Lothian, as living in Edinburgh, and as a native of Culterallers in the upper part of Clydesdale. There is little doubt that a machine was, in fact, made by a man named Michael Menzies, wherever he lived. It was an arrangement of flails fixed in a beam and worked by a water-wheel. Trials made with it were so satisfactory that a great deal of work was done in a given time, but, owing to the velocity of moving the flails, they soon broke, and the invention fell into disgrace.[5] Apparently three of these machines were erected in East Lothian.[5a] One at Roseburn near Edinburgh was inspected by a delegation of the Honourable the Society of Improvers in the Knowledge of Agriculture in Scotland. The delegation consisted of two advocates, Alexander Boswell and Charles Maitland. The apparatus was turned by a great water-wheel, and straw already threshed by hand was put through to show what it would do. Twelve bolls were threshed and a quarter of a peck of good grain recovered, demonstrating that the machine threshed more perfectly than was possible by hand flailing. The delegation also saw a smaller machine with a wheel of only three feet diameter, "moved by a small quantity of water." They reported that the machine, which is stated to have been patented, would be of great use to farmers in threshing and saving labour as "with it one man could do the work that normally demanded the efforts of six."[5b]

A more explicit description is given by Martin Doyle who quotes it from an unstated source. "It consisted of a number of instruments fixed in a moveable beam and inclined to it at an angle of ten degrees. On each side of the beam on which the flails were fixed, floors or benches were placed for spreading the sheaves on. The flails were moved backwards or forwards upon the benches by means of a crank fixed on the end of an axle, which made about thirty evolutions in a minute." I think this means that the sheaves were placed on either side of the beam carrying the flails, and that the beam made a half turn which caused the flails to strike the floor on one side of it and then to be carried backwards in a half-circle above the beam to strike the floor on the other side. If that is so, it is no wonder that the flails wore out quickly or were broken by the force of the blows.

Perhaps this was the machine invented at Dalkeith, said to have been written about by George Thomson in 1735,[6] but beyond a bibliographical reference to his pamphlet, I can discover nothing about it.

A machine working on the flail principle, apparently rather like Menzies', was invented soon after by a Mr. Craw of Netherbyres in Berwick. He is described as a very ingenious and learned gentleman in both mechanics and mathematics and was regularly consulted "on all difficult matters." He succeeded in making a thresher in which "the effect was produced by impulse, a stroke in imitation of the flail; ten or more in succession, with incredible force gave their blows upon the sheaves, which beat out the grain most completely; but from the number of people to attend the operation, as also the crude state of the first discovery, the threshing sticks and their then misconstructed tackling went often amiss." The machine was abandoned till further improvements could be made, but Craw did not succeed in making them and the road was left open for others who worked on different principles. [6a]

The next recorded attempt was made in 1758 by a Mr. Stirling, a farmer in the parish of Dunblane, Perthshire. One writer, however, mentions that Mr. Moir, of Leckie in Stirling, invented at an earlier date a machine on the principle of the horizontal flax mill, to the scutchers of which the corn was presented by hand. It headed everything but oats. [6b] Stirling's machine was also on the principle of the flax mill. It had an upright shaft carrying four arms enclosed in a cylinder three and a half feet high by eight feet diameter within which the shaft and arms were turned rapidly by a water-wheel. The corn was put in by hand at the top of the cylinder and the arms beat out the grain. Both the straw and the grain fell out on the floor where they were separated by riddles and fanners which were also driven by the water-wheel. [7]

This was ingenious and probably rather effective. It is said to have been carried into Northumberland by a Mr. Edward Gregson about 1774. With it a man could thresh eighteen bushels of wheat in a day, and this may have meant by manual operation because the work was so hard that it was dropped after the death of Gregson. His brother told John Bailey and George Culley that it was probably the same machine as that described by David Meldrum in a letter to William Charge of Cleasby, Yorkshire. This machine, said Meldrum, was the same as the flax mill, capable of threshing one hundred and fifty bushels of oats a day. The oats dropped through a screen into a winnowing machine that dressed them. Such machines were becoming general in Northumberland by 1794. [8]

At the same time as Gregson brought Stirling's idea from Perthshire to Northumberland (if he really did so), two other men were working on the idea in Northumberland, and perhaps a third, but of the last only his name, Smart of Wark, remains. The first two were Mr. Ilderton or Elderton of Alnwick, and Mr. Oseley, or Oxley, of Flodden.

Ilderton's machine threshed by rubbing instead of beating out the grain, as Smart's is said to have done. The sheaves were carried between an indented drum about six feet in diameter and a number of rollers of the same description ranged round the drum. They were pressed towards the drum by springs so as to rub out the grain when the drum was turned round. Upon trial this machine did not prove very satisfactory because it worked slowly and bruised the grain.[9]

Apparently Oxley's machine was erected for Sir John Delavel, Bart., but was never made public. Robert Brown stated that he obtained the following details from the mechanic who helped to dismantle it after it had been tried and proved more expensive than threshing by flail. It had two fluted rollers, and, in place of a drum, had a double set of arms connected at the ends by crossbars. "The scutchers were framed of two pieces of wood about three inches broad, one and a half inch thick at one end, and three quarters of an inch at the other. They were connected with the cross bars by leather straps. A circular breast was fixed beneath the centre, about three inches from the scutchers, so as to allow the corn to pass between them; and the unthreshed corn was laid upon a board at the level of the centre of the scutchers and drawn in by two fluted rollers."[10]

Various stories are told about Sir Francis Kinlock, Bart., of Gilmerton in Scotland, who saw Ilderton's machine and undertook to improve upon it. One relates that while doing so, "he saw a flax mill, made for poor families, worked by a man. It struck him that it would thresh corn, and he got one made with the addition of two smooth rollers, for taking in the corn; the work being too hard for a man, he sent it to Mr. Meikle's mill to have it tried by water."[11] Robert Somerville said that after seeing Ilderton's machine it occurred to Sir Francis to enclose the drum in a fluted cover, and to fix on the outside four fluted pieces of wood capable of being raised a little from the circumference by springs so as to press against the fluted cover. This arrangement rubbed out the grain as the sheaves passed, but it still bruised the grain too much.[12]

Both Forsyth and Robert Brown stated that Kinlock had a model of Ilderton's machine made, possibly by the then late Mr. Rastrick of Morpeth. Sir Francis tried several improvements and had other models made. One of them was at one time kept in the warehouse of the Board of Agriculture in London. It is quite clear that either a large model or a full-size machine of this kind was sent by Sir Francis to Andrew Meikle, who was either a civil engineer of Houston Mill, near Haddington, or a millwright of Know Hill. He was to try it, driven by the water-wheel of his barley mill. The speed at which it was driven smashed it, as it did a larger model tried in the same way.

Everyone was interested in the subject, and Arthur Young thought that it was extremely desirable that a machine for threshing corn should be designed as a substitute for the clumsy method of hand flails, but his idea of the direction of design was erroneous. Inventors should proceed along the lines of a range of flails fixed on one side of the threshing floor, worked by machinery from behind, and kept in motion by a a horse in the same way as in a mill, with space enough in front for men to move about and lay the corn under the flails with forks.[13] He could not then have been aware of Menzies' failure along these lines, or he would hardly have made this proposal.

Despite Robert Brown's defence of his compatriot, there is little doubt that Andrew Meikle owed the basis of his idea for a threshing mill to Sir Francis Kinlock's version of Ilderton's threshing machine. Martin Doyle stated that Meikle spent a good deal of unsuccessful labour on the flail principle before he hit upon the true plan of two revolving rollers between which the sheaves passed,[14] but this, in fact, could not have been Meikle's own idea. He adopted the principle of scutchers "acting on the sheaves by their velocity and beating out the grain in place of pressing or rubbing it out." He made a model in which the grain was beaten out by the drum, to which it was presented through two plain feeding rollers, afterwards altered to fluted ones. The first machine on this principle was made by Meikle's son for Mr. Stein of Kilbogie in 1786. It worked satisfactorily,[15] he received several orders, and erected ten or twelve machines in this neighbourhood. When this had been done "he applied to Kinlock to take out a patent," but was told that Kinlock did not look upon it as an original invention and that a patent would be useless. Some time later (in 1788) Meikle took out a patent in his own name for England only "for the making of a machine, whose leading principle had been applied to the same purpose, at least two years before."[16] This patent, however, did not become effective because Meikle failed to enforce it for some years and then it became impossible to do so, the infringements were so numerous.

Most of the threshing machines erected towards the end of the eighteenth century were designed on Meikle's principle, and therefore a good part of the merit belongs to him. Slight and Burn wrote in 1858[17] "he is entitled to this as having produced the first really effective machine there can be no question, but there can be as little that those who pioneered the way and brought the machine so near this mark deserve their share of the merit. The previous machines appear to have contained the essential parts of the threshing apparatus, the feeding rollers and the beater or scutcher; and though it is usually alleged that Meikle gained the palm by having devised the drum with its beaters" yet the closed cylinder was not essential, and in these authors' opinion it was possible that a beater upon open arms might be better.

None of these accounts mentions either Winlaw's rubbing mill, or William Spencer Dix's machine, both of which were eighteenth-century inventions. It is doubtful whether more than units of them were ever produced. Winlaw's was the earlier. The inventor, William Winlaw, had a considerable "manufactory" in Margaret St., Cavendish Sq., where he made agricultural implements. In advertising these Winlaw tells the story of the development of his rubbing mill.[18] The premiums offered by the Society for the Encouragement of Arts and other societies in Europe not having produced any tangible result, Winlaw was approached by "several noblemen and gentlemen his employers" to construct a model threshing machine. He says that the model "when tried, had not the desired effect; the plan of which was stampers or levers, raised by a cylindric shaft, planted or set with studs or lifters in a spiral form, from the one end to the other, which lifted the stampers in a regular succession; being disappointed in my expectations, my next attempt was a larger one, on a different plan, with flails at a great expense; which method, at first, I thought could not fail of success, but when tried it was also found incomplete." He had, however, been told of one of this kind that did work, probably Menzies'. His own experiments convinced him that a machine with stampers or flails simply could not be made to answer. His own success was in making one "on the following plan, of a conical, spiral rubbing mill, for separating the grain of wheat or other corn from the heads without threshing." He thought it could be used for cleaning clover seed, rape seed or canary seed or for husking rice. The ears of corn had first to be stripped from the straw by using a comb like a rippling comb for flax, and the ears were then fed into the machine. It came in for some praise in the next number of the *Annals*, both as saving time and cost in this arduous operation.[19]

Dix's machine was another rubbing mill. It was intended to be worked manually, and the corn was rubbed out of the ear by a flat circular slab that was rotated in a tub rather like a grinding mill. It consisted of a hopper to which the corn was passed by two ribbed rollers. Dix himself said that the flail was by then (1797) scarcely used in Scotland, and was much out of use in many parts of England, but this must not be taken literally. By far the greater part of threshing was done by the flail until well into the nineteenth century. "Threshing and winnowing machines," wrote Dix, "are getting daily more into use," but the process was slow enough.

The winnowing machine in a primitive form had been brought into effective use before the threshing machine. It was introduced to Scotland by James Meikle, the father of Andrew Meikle, the threshing machine inventor. James Meikle went to Holland under the patronage of Andrew Fletcher of Saltoun, who had lived in Holland and had seen the barley mill used there. On his return he sent Meikle, who was a millwright in his neighbourhood, to Holland, to bring back details of the mill for making pot barley. Meikle did this and constructed fanners for creating an artificial wind to winnow grain. These were sails fitted to four or more radial arms which revolved manually by a wheel gear so as to create a draught. Formerly farmers had been dependent on the wind blowing across the barn through two open doors. Meikle is said to have had a strong, though uncultivated, genius for mechanics and it was inherited by his son.

By 1794 these fanners were said to be used by every husbandman, and to be made by almost every country carpenter. They had certainly travelled a long way if they were really brought to Holland from China.[20] By about 1770 this simple apparatus had been elaborated, and one made by James Sharp from a pattern supplied by Mr. Duckett, cleaned and sorted the grain and waste. The wheat and chaff were thrown into the hopper and the chaff and dust blown out at the end. The ears of corn, sticks and stones, etc., were separated into different drawers, the clean wheat coming out of a screen in front. I am not quite certain what this description means and the drawing is not much help, but the machine was evidently quite effective, though how many were then actually in use it is difficult to decide.[21] Marshall estimated that it was well known "as a curiosity" but only established in common practice in the single county of Yorkshire in 1796, having been introduced into the Vale of Pickering about 1760. Originally it had been made by Sharp. Winlaw was still making it in the 1790s. Marshall thought that the original failed to take in Yorkshire because "the gentlemen neglected to oversee its use." Luckily Marshall's father saw one used by "a sensible, substantial yeoman." He copied it with some improvements of his own. Since then it had been generally adopted in Yorkshire, and scarcely any of the larger farmers were without a "Machine Fan," some of the smaller farmers joining forces to buy one. By the end of the century the sails were made of sheet iron instead of boards.[22]

At first the apparatus was a simple fan turned by hand that directed a blast of air across the stream of mixed grain and chaff as it fell downwards from the hopper. The blast of air blew the lighter chaff out of the machine, but the heavier grain fell and was discharged at the side. The same arrangement was used in the later machine, but the grain and chaff put into the hopper fell on to a pair of shakers that allowed the grain to pass but held everything larger. The blast upwards through these shaking screens blew out the chaff, but the waste held by the shakers was carried forward by them and discharged by a chute to the side of the machine. The falling grain dropped on to a sloping screen, small enough to retain it as it passed downwards along to a point of discharge, but permitted small weed seeds to drop through.[22a]

Bailey and Culley reported that it was "in universal use" in Northumberland at this time, and was first invented by "a farmer of a mechanical genius called *Rogers*, who lived at Cavers, near Hawick and whose grandson, a carpenter there, still makes them." Old Rogers saw an old machine cast aside in a granary at Leith in 1733, undoubtedly one of Meikle's. When he got home he made one and sold it to Mr. John Gregson of Wark. Other farmers in the county soon followed his example.[23] By this time many threshing machines had a "winnower" under them, the corn and straw being thrown together on a screen through which the grain dropped into the winnower, the straw being raked off by hand, until Bailey invented (or so he claimed)

L

the "circular rake." Bailey fitted this device to his machine at Chillingham about 1790. It was rapidly adopted and was added to all the threshing machines lately erected in the county.[24]

There was no very complete information available to the reporters of the day about the degree to which the threshing machine and winnower had been adopted. Its use must have been very sporadic even in Scotland where it originated. George Patterson, of Castle Huntley introduced it to the Carse of Gowrie in 1787, and only seven years later some sixty-one machines, either worked by water or horse-power, had been erected there.[25] George Meikle put up one at Kilbogie, Clackmannan, in 1787. This was driven by water, and four others of this type were to be found there in 1795. Many, worked by horses, the larger by four, the smaller by two, had also been built. Fanners had long been used in the county.[26] The Reverend Mackay of Reay sent the Board a model of a threshing machine of his invention, and another was promised by Mr. Mann of Delny, but nothing more was heard of these inventions.[27]

In Ayrshire the threshing machine had been found of superior utility, and was usually worked with two horses. It was introduced into Midlothian soon after its invention and became "very general." It was frequently used "by those who possessed large farms" in West Lothian. There were a good many in Clydesdale, but in Galloway the first and only person to erect a threshing mill was Mr. William Ross of Stranraer. They were expected soon to come into general use in Banff, and had made great progress in Berwick where there were about fourteen. None was used in Dumbarton and there were only a few in Dumfries, mostly horse-driven. There were eight in Elgin, an unspecified number in Fife, and were being ordered at the rate of six or eight in six months from John Nicoll, millwright, in Stonehaven, Kincardine. The machine had appeared in Kinross and it was coming fast into use in Perthshire and had already found its way into Roxburgh. There were "only a few" in Selkirk, but "several" in Stirling.[28]

This information is quite incomplete, the most that can be said is that in the advanced districts of Scotland the threshing machine was being adopted by a great many farmers at the end of the eighteenth century and that the "fanners," as the winnowing machine was called, was probably more widely used still.

England had been slower. The threshing machine was used on some of the farms in Northumberland where there were very large areas of grain. William Marshall reported that Yorkshire was favourably inclined, though Isaac Leatham knew of only one threshing machine in the East Riding in 1794, there being some doubt in the minds of the farmers about the cleanness of its work. The neighbouring county of Lancaster, though "not a corn county," had several, one of which worked by water power. It belonged to Colonel Mordaunt of Hallsall.

It threshed and winnowed, and ground or crushed corn for provender at the same time, a process that is no more clearly described. The Rev. Croxton Johnson had a similar machine, the description of which indicates that both the threshing and grinding were done by friction or rubbing. Mr. Harper had a large beater type thresher, which he himself had designed. It is reported not to have damaged the straw, which was a serious defect of this type.

Hand threshers had also been introduced into Lancashire. They required two men to turn, a boy or girl to feed and another to take away the straw. Mr. Jones of Arnold, and Mr. Wright of Runby in Nottingham, had these machines. Threshers are not mentioned in Stafford, but Mr. Joseph Cornforth, of Bushbury near Wolverhampton, a manufacturer of drills, etc., made a winnower or dressing machine of "the very best construction."[29] It is doubtful if any threshers were yet in use in Wales, though one Cardiganshire landlord was expecting to set one up in 1800. He remarked then that there was one good model of a winnower at Vaillalt, and another at Mr. Jacob Jones's at Aberystwyth.[30]

So far the threshing machines erected had been permanent installations. The next step was to make them portable. Already at the turn of the century Thomas Wigful of Lynn Regis, Norfolk, was experimenting along this line. In June 1803, he was able to show a machine at the Woburn Agricultural Meeting that could be moved on its own low wheels.[31] The progress made in the design of threshers in the eighteenth century formed a firm foundation upon which the nineteenth could build. An effective threshing machine had been designed, and to it had been added the revolving rake and shakers and the dressing fan. It could be driven by horse, wind or water power, and could be erected by local labour. The winnowing machine, too, had been made efficient and was widely used, perhaps more widely than the thresher. All this was largely due to the work of Andrew

Meikle, though many others had played their part and it was unfortunate for him that he did not reap any adequate financial reward for his ingenuity and industry. He lived to an advanced age, being eighty-six in 1805.[32]

Twenty-five years later the threshing machine was in use all over the country, and the fears of the labourers, and indeed of some farmers and others that they would lose their winter work if the machine was employed, were justified. Whether this fear was correct or not, they were sufficiently convinced of it to rise in rebellion and to destroy the machines. The revolt began in Kent in August, 1830. It went on to September and spread through Sussex, Hampshire, Devon, Wiltshire, Oxford and Dorset. There were also disturbances in Norfolk, Suffolk, Essex and Northampton, and they spread as far as Hereford, Yorkshire and Lincoln.[33]

The thresher worked by horse gear exerted an uneven strain upon the horses, and I have heard or read somewhere, that horses occasionally suffered from giddiness as well as from the uneven draught of the machine. The giddiness was unavoidable because horse gear demanded a round walk. Walter Samuel of Niddry invented a gadget before 1839 to equalize the draught, but what exactly it was, and whether it was ever generally used, is not known.[34]

A hand-power machine had long been in use on the smaller farms. It was probably of the type of which a specimen came into the possession of Mr. E. Rhodes, of High Harrogate, about twenty years ago. This is now in the Science Museum. It apparently rubbed and scutched the grain out of the ear between two rollers fitted with projecting spikes. Both grain and chaff fell together through a shute with a plate below, to be winnowed at a convenient season later. The machine was improved upon by Barrett, Exall and Andrews, of Reading, in 1843, and three years later many hundreds were said to have been sold. In it the concave or breasting was made to expand or contract so as to maintain a uniform space between it and the drum, thus adapting it to all kinds of grain or seed. The adjusting screw was fitted with a pointer showing on an index how to adjust it for any particular grain. The firm made a portable thresher on the same principle, fitted with a winnower. The horse gear was simple and when mounted on wheels formed a compact carriage for the machine that was within the capacity of one horse.[35]

Barrett's hand thresher was believed to have the greatest merit for originality at this time. Several others were thought to have been copied from it. Two had been shown at the Royal Show at Liverpool in 1842. They were Ransome's and the Earl of Ducie's. In the second of these, the corn went round the drum and was scutched off by the revolving action of eight narrow blades. Some separation was effected but it was by no means complete. Ransome's machine shook out the grain by hard blows of the beaters, and was worked, rather like one of the contemporary manual fire engines, by pushing and pulling bars on either side, the reciprocating action being transformed into rotary motion by connecting rods. The work was very equal in both machines. At this show, too, Ransome's exhibited a steam disc engine for driving a threshing machine.[35a]

The number of threshing machines exhibited at the Royal Agricultural Society's other shows now began to increase with some rapidity. Only two of the eight machines tested completed the trials of the "Royal" Society at Cambridge in 1841; they were those made by Ransome and May of Ipswich, and Garrett and Sons, of Leiston. In 1846 Earl Ducie won a £10 prize at Shrewsbury for his fixed combined threshing and dressing machine.[35b] Richard Garrett and Sons secured a prize of £25 for their bolting threshing machine, and Richard Hornsby was awarded £3 for a winnower. The next year Garrett's were again awarded £20 for the best threshing machine, and Cooch and Son won a prize for their seed dresser and winnower.

Eight threshing machines were submitted by Crosskill, Knight of Northampton, Grasby, Garrett, Ferrabee and Langdale. Garrett's and Hornsby's were both considered good, but Garrett's had a parallel movement in the concave, described as "a great improvement." It was fitted with a patent cylindrical wire drum. Ferrabee's machine was portable, being mounted on wheels and provided with a lifting jack. It had an iron frame drum and concave. The trial on which the judges formed their verdict only lasted a few minutes with each machine and was therefore open to some criticism.[36]

Cooch's seed dresser had been improved since the 1845 show by enclosed blast and slide control of the air to the fanners, amongst other details. The firm of Cooch and Sons was founded in 1800 by John Cooch of Harlestone, Northamptonshire, who farmed five hundred acres. He made ploughs and repaired farm implements for some time before he invented and patented his corn and seed dressing and winnowing machine. Both businesses were carried on by the son and grandson until 1880, when Henry Cooch gave up farming except for fifty acres of land. In 1891 Henry Cooch purchased premises at Commercial Street, Northampton, while retaining his Harlestone works and home. The business, of which the mainstay during the whole of the nineteenth century was the corn and seed dressing machine, is still carried on by Mr. J. F. Cooch and his two sons as a private limited company. The demand for dressing machines fell off as threshing machines came into general use, but a good trade continued to be done with corn and seed merchants whose grain required better dressing than the farmers' crops. Besides the prize in 1847, the firm was awarded the first prize in 1841 and again won it in 1872.[37]

In addition to the firms who exhibited at "Royal" shows, Wedlake's of Fairhyte Ironworks, Hornchurch, Essex, were then making threshers for two, four, or eight horses.[38] In the following year that famous firm now known as Marshall, Sons and Co., Ltd., was founded by William Marshall, engineer and millwright. He entered upon the manufacture of portable engines about two years later and had produced some one hundred and seventy-nine thousand engines, boilers and threshers by 1921.[39]

It was natural that steam power should be applied to threshing at about this time, and in 1848 the machines were first tried by horse-power and then, if the makers wished, by steam power. Cambridge complained of the judges' decision in this year. Trials of both threshers and corn dressers continued almost regularly as an annual event, the number of competing firms varying slightly from year to year. Threshers were exhibited by Dean, Crosskill, Hensman, Abbey, Barrett and Ashton, Holderness and Gilson, Rawlings; corn dressers by Hornsby, Holmes, Garrett, Kilby, Williams and Taylor, Cooch, and Nicholson. The favour of the judges passed from one make to another, not without stated reasons of course, but though they considered the threshers shown much improved by 1850 "in lightness and draught," they thought that it was disgraceful that they were not yet as perfect as cotton mills. They then preferred the fixed machine with dressing apparatus included.[40]

A model of a portable horse-driven machine of this date used to be on view in the Science Museum. It was originally shown at the Great

Exhibition of 1851, and was compact in appearance. It included patents of the previous decade and was described in Spencer and Passmore's *Handbook* as follows: "The drum has five straight iron blades as beaters and the concave is of ribbed iron plates separated by spaces covered with wire screens. The corn is threshed out of the straw by the rapidly revolving beaters, which knock out the grain as the straw is being carried round in the small space between the drum and the concave, the empty straw finally being ejected at the lower end of the drum. Here the straw passes over a wooden grid which recovers any short ears that may have been carried round unthreshed. The grain threshed out drops into the space at the bottom of the machine and is removed at intervals through the side doors provided. The concave is hinged and the clearance is readily adjustable by screws." A two horse-power machine and one of six horse-power of the same kind, won a prize in 1852.[41]

The corn from these machines was afterwards finished in a corn dresser, but eventually, as Mr. Cooch's letter quoted above shows, the thresher was fitted with a dresser that obviated the necessity for this separate process, except when preparing the grain for seed. Some of these machines were fitted with self-acting straw shakers that removed any grain remaining in the straw.

The first combined threshing and dressing machine was produced by Charles Burrell and Sons, Ltd., of Thetford, Norfolk, in 1848, and was awarded a prize medal at the "Royal" show at York in that year. This firm was then long established, having been set up by Joseph, James and William Burrell in 1770 as a small foundry and smithy making ploughs. It was awarded a silver cup at Coke's Holkham sheep-shearing festival in 1803 for an improved drill for sowing crushed oil-cake manure with wheat, turnips and other crops. In 1847 they began to manufacture portable steam engines, and in 1853 traction engines. For half a century or more their threshing sets were well known. In 1920 the firm was absorbed in that of Richard Garrett and Sons, Ltd., of Leiston.[41a]

The beater drum was opposed to the peg drum type, both of which became standard as the century advanced, the former being sometimes known as the common Scotch threshing machine. Some experiments for the purpose of comparing the work of the two types were made by William Watson, millwright, of Errol, Perthshire, in the 1840s.

The beater drum cylinder was four feet long, twenty-six and a half inches by twenty-eight and a half inches diameter and it had four to six beaters longitudinally on the cylinder, bolted to arms. The beaters were made narrow so as to lessen air resistance and not to break up the straw so much. Its rate was three thousand five hundred feet a minute. There were two opinions about it, as there are about most things. Its great fault was in the placement of the drum in relation to the shakers, which frequently caused the drum to take the straw round with it, though it could be adjusted. The light corn and unthreshed "heads" were carried "down back" away from the floor where the marketable grain fell.

The peg drum machine differed from the beater in the construction of the cylinder. The corn passed between two rollers, which retarded its progress until the grain was separated by the blows of the pegs attached to a revolving cylinder four and a half feet long by twenty-five feet diameter. It revolved at four thousand feet a minute. This machine had not been generally adopted because, William thought, it worked too fast to ensure complete separation of the corn from the straw. Another objection was that the men were exposed to the dust, and this made them careless. But many owners and users thought the peg beater preferable, because less attention was required in feeding.[42]

One of the disadvantages of the beater type was that it was inclined to bruise the grain. Tizard attempted to overcome this difficulty by fitting a conical drum which was said to give the beaters a whipping action and thus prevented the grain from being injured.[43] It seems that the injury was more likely to be caused by the speed of working and consequent violence of the impact rather than in any other way.

A modification of the beater bar was patented by Mr. J. Goucher in 1848 to overcome this difficulty. Diagonal channels were cut in the face of the bars providing clearing spaces for the straw and grain and ensuring that the straw was carried round. This is largely the modern form of beater bar and secured the desired effect.[43a]

By this time the threshing machines produced by two or three of the leading makers were recognized as good sterling implements that might safely be purchased. One firm, not identified, sold fifty-six machines in 1849 and 1850, and one hundred and ninety-two machines in 1851 and the first nine months of 1852. Another firm sold as many in 1852 as in the previous three years—not a very precise statement. A third firm turned out five a week and stated that the customers preferred a machine that dressed as well as threshed. Clayton and Shuttleworth won the Royal Society's gold medal that year with a machine that was "a decided advance," worked well and saved an important amount of labour. This machine was fitted with a shaker and riddle and won the prize in competition with eight other "formidable competitors."[44] The firm had been founded ten years before and set up by two brothers at Stamp End, Lincoln, for making portable engines. At about this time Tuxford's of Boston produced a combined engine and threshing machine of which nineteen were made. Clayton and Shuttleworth produced a portable steam engine with the first single horizontal cylinder in 1848, and by 1851 their output had reached two hundred and fifty-seven. Threshing machines were looked upon as a separate department, but apparently about one thousand per annum were being turned out by this firm in 1891.[45]

Several firms entered corn dressing machines in 1852. Hornsby's won the prize and secured high commendation for the unrivalled capability in chaffing of their machine and its excellence as a finishing machine.[46]

In 1853 Ransome and Sims won the prizes for the two-horse and six-horse gear-driven machines, though Barrett and Exall ran them close. The great fault of the latter was the confined space under the threshing part and the consequent difficulty of getting at the threshed corn. Ransome's six horse-power was esteemed of better workmanship. Barrett's close drum casing, being only one inch from the concave, was unsuitable for strong districts. The other machines entered were indifferent, though Hart's dressing apparatus was efficient, giving perfect separation and delivery in different directions of straw, cavings, chaff and corn, the last being carried by a short elevator to a mouth feeding into sacks. Unfortunately this spout was beneath the machine and had to be continuously watched to ensure the rapid changing of sacks when one was full, but this necessity is equally present in a modern machine. The machine had a close drum but beaters projecting one sixteenth of an inch above the casings. Henry Brinsmead, of St. Giles, near Torrington, Devon, won a silver medal that year for an improved and simple method of shaking straw, which was considered likely to supersede the then present shaker, but it is not described.[47]

The improvements made in threshing machines had fast out-stripped the expectation of the most sanguine in the opinion of the judges of the following year, having attained a high degree of perfection in the short space of three years. Not long before the farmer had been content to thresh an increased quantity of corn by the application of steam power to the old threshing box. Soon he found he must have his corn partially dressed, but by 1854 he must have it finished, sacked and weighed for market, and for those last improvements was much indebted to Clayton and Shuttleworth. Humphries' machine was also commended as arranged for simple draught, light, and doing perfectly good work with damaged barley. Since the introduction of these combined threshers into nearly general use, screening, blowing and finishing had become the most important operations in a dressing machine, of which nineteen were tried.[48]

It was premature to say, as the judges did in 1855, that the threshing machine had by then "entirely superseded the flail," but the remark that it was as important as the plough was not far wrong. Corn dressing machines were a necessary adjunct to the threshing machine and were in an advanced state of development, though further improvement could still be hoped for. An example of this was Ransome's six horse-power steam driven machine with Brinsmead's shaker and Worby's separators attached. The judges were agreeably surprised at the great general improvement in these machines, but felt that their weight (two and a half to three tons) was getting too heavy for easy transport. Clayton and Shuttleworth were complimented on their machine, and for the adoption of the revolving screen patented by J. H. Nalder and Knapp. The screen won a prize though the whole machine was disqualified because it required too much power to drive it.

J. H. Nalder was the son of a yeoman of Oxfordshire who farmed at Alverscot. He had a taste for engineering and became an apprentice to Clayton and Shuttleworth. On completion of his apprenticeship, he set up the Challow Works, Berks, in 1858. The rotary screen, which was apparently a joint invention, was universally accepted in threshing machines for separating the head and tail corn, and the firm of Nalder and Nalder not only turned out one thousand seven hundred threshers but also more than eight thousand grain separators by 1891. They had won in 1879 and 1882 "Royal" medals.[49]

Knapp was a member of a firm that had already over a hundred years of life, having been founded in 1745 as wheelwrights and smiths. Besides their corn drills they made steam threshers and helped in the invention of the rotary screen. At a later date they gave up this branch of business and concentrated more on the lighter implements, making various improvements in the "Suffolk" drill.[50]

The machines entered by both Tuxford and Humphries in the 1882 trial were commended, but this trial, compared with that in 1858, was insignificant. No less than eighty-nine machines of various power were entered for the trials of that year. The mere bulk of entries made the dismayed judges remark that it was "unquestionably the most important trial of this kind of machinery ever undertaken." Engineers examined the machines for simplicity of construction and workmanship, and the judges awarded points on the quality of work. The whole were divided into six classes and in the result Clayton and Shuttleworth won four prizes and Garrett and Hornsby one each.

This trial was too overwhelming in numbers, and the Society restricted the 1860 trial at Canterbury to non-finishing machines. In 1863 only finishing machines were examined. The trend of the times was indicated by the entry of only three horse-driven machines, those of Wallis and Haslam, Tasker and Sons, and Hansman and Son, the judges remarking that little attention had been paid to this type since the introduction of steam power. The judges at Bury St. Edmunds in 1867 proposed that no more horse gear machines should be tried because they considered that where such machines were still used they were a sign of backward agriculture, and it was a positive mistake to encourage by prizes, machines that ought to be bygones in English Agriculture. There was a dispute in 1860 between the Society and some of the firms, leading to the non-attendance of several. Nineteen machines limited to eight horse-power were entered, of which four broke down, nine required more than eight horse-power to work them and the remaining six were tried. They were made by Gibbons, Humphries, Savory, Forster, Gilbert and Turner.[51]

By 1862 it was felt that no one machine was the best. What ought to be done was to combine the best features of each into one perfect machine. The finishing machine with double and treble blast had such numerous bearings and driving straps that the cost of repair of the bearings was enormous, and Henry Evershed doubted whether they were economical. They needed simplification. Garrett's, for example obtained a blast of air by a fan fixed to the drum spindle. Willsher had lately adopted an arrangement for driving the shakers and cavings screen, either with or without a riddle box and corn screen, from one crank spindle and with one strap. Clayton and Shuttleworth's new elevator consisted of spades or scoops fixed on the same spindle as the blower. By revolving rapidly the elevator threw the corn up into the second dresser. Evershed added that it "awns the barley or chobs the wheat" so as to dispense with the straps of the former elevator and barley awner. Ransome's rotary screen, though ingenious, could not be included among the novelties tending to simplify the machine. Evershed's opinion was that the single blast machine would last ten years, the double only eight.[52]

The method of working the double blast machine made by Wallis, Haslem and Steevens was for an attendant to stand in the closed recess, or "dickey," in front of the hopper, or "mouth," and to throw the corn into the bottom of the hopper, the sheaves having previously been opened and placed on the platform. The corn was caught by the ribbed beaters of the drum which made about one thousand revolutions per minute. It was carried round through the space between the beaters and the concave which delayed its passing so that the grain was knocked out of the ears of corn and dropped through a grid in the concave, the long straw being delivered at the opposite edge. The grain, chaff and short straw dropped through the bars of the concave, slipped down an inclined board to the higher end of a sloping sieve, or caving riddle, the larger pieces of straw passing along to the end of the riddle, where they fell on to the caving board for removal. The corn fell to a lower vibrating frame carrying a board on which it travelled until it dropped over the edge to a finer screen. Through the meshes of this screen or chaff riddle, a revolving fan drove a continuous blast of air, so that chaff and other light particles were blown away, heavier grain falling through the riddle. Thence it was carried to the side of the machine where it was raised by a cup elevator to the top. It was then allowed to fall in front of the blast from another fan so that any remaining light particles were removed and the grain separated by a dividing board into two grades which dropped into separate sacks attached to external hooks.

The long straw thrown out by the drum fell upon three inclined grids or shakers, reciprocated by a three-throw crankshaft, so arranged that the shakers, while they tossed the straw and so released any entangled grain, slowly worked it to the end of the machine, where it fell upon the straw board, ready to be carried away and stacked. Any grain that passed through the shakers was received on a vibrating inclined board, down which it slid to the other grain coming from the concave.[53]

In Shearer's thresher of about the same date, a fixed barn machine, the bars of the beaters on the drum were fitted with short, sturdy spikes. The concave was closed by a sheet of iron so that the grain and chaff, as well as the straw, were carried round and thrown upon shakers of normal modern pattern. The grain, chaff and short lengths of straw fell out of the shakers straight on to the caving riddle. Here the straw was stopped and grain and chaff fell through to be caught by the lower shoe. The cavings riddle and lower shoe were both rocked backwards and forwards, throwing the cavings forward and dropping the grain and chaff into the first dressing shoe. There the chaff was blown clear and a single sieve separated the large weed seeds and allowed the mixture of grain, broken and shrivelled grains and small weed seeds to fall into the elevator trough. This mixture was then carried up at the side of the machine and fell into the second shoe where the process of the first dressing was repeated. Larger weed seeds were separated and thrown clear and the grain and small weed seeds passed out at the side of the machine. A separate seed cleaner was necessary to clean the grain of small weed seeds and small and broken grain.

Ransome's portable was fitted with shafts to enable it to be moved by horses. This machine threshed, cleared the grain from the straw and from weed seeds and chaff, but did not clean the sample by removing the broken or shrunken grains. The sheaves were fed at the top and rubbed between the eight plain beaters on the rotating drum and the bars of the concave, which was adjusted at the top, at the bottom and at the join of its two halves. Precise adjustment was necessary to prevent loss by incomplete threshing or by grain being discharged through the ribs of the concave with the chaff and broken straw to the cavings riddle. The straw was thrown into the shakers, which were fifteen spiked rollers, triangular in cross section, and set parallel to one another across the machine. Grain held by the straw was shaken clear and fell between these rollers, the straw being carried along to fall clear of the machine. The cavings riddle was jogged from side to side and was designed to separate broken short lengths of straw, while grain and chaff passed through it and were guided by the lower shoe into the dressing shoe. This dressing shoe was also jogged and was equipped with two sieves and a fan. It was really a winnower. The fan blew the chaff clear of the grain; the upper sieve stopped large weed seeds and passed the grain; the lower sieve stopped the grain and passed the small weed seeds. Arrangements were provided to discharge weed seed and grain at different spouts, those for the grain having hooks for sacks to receive it.

Among the recognized, if not the essential, adjuncts of the threshing machine, whether portable or fixed, was the straw elevator, of which several new and cheaper forms had been shown at Battersea. The judges at the Worcester show in 1863, held the opinion that those first in use, which were in the form of a tall frame mounted on a separate four-wheel carriage, were not easy of transport or stowage and were too costly, the price being £50 or £60. Wright of Boston's Stalking Machine, of which no drawing is provided, was self-contained and packed very compactly, and when modified, according to Ransome's patent, was "but an appendage of the threshing machine when travelling. A long net, strained and raised by shears composed either of telescopic iron tubes, or wooden poles, which slide out to a length of thirty feet, supersedes the cumbersome wooden frame which is so commonly seen standing exposed to the summer sun." Campaign's elevator, exhibited by Clayton and Shuttleworth, was considered better if the straw had to be delivered to a considerable distance and height, but no description or picture of it is added. [54]

At this show, too, a novel corn elevator for use inside the threshing machine that had been invented by J. W. Bruckshaw was exhibited by J. S. Underhill. It was an ordinary fan spindle with blades upon it driven at speed. The corn from the riddles fell into the cave containing these fan blades which, like a series of cricket bats, struck the grain so as to raise it to the required height, but there must have been some danger of damaging the corn. The blows were also supposed to separate the chaff from the grain. Four years later this was still the only machine fitted with the appliance. [55]

Daniel Crowe of King's Lynn showed a portable threshing machine, with engine attached, at Bury St. Edmunds in 1867. The engine both drove the thresher and propelled it when travelling, which it did "with perfect ease," although the whole affair weighed seven tons one hundredweight. Having the fore wheels placed under the carriage it was able to turn in its own area. It had been brought all the way from Towcester using only sixteen pounds of coal per mile. The driving arrangements were good and the engine was so carefully enclosed as to ensure that there was no danger of fire. The drum could be adjusted to suit the varieties of corn and all the straps were under cover. The machine was considered capable of some improvements in detail but likely to be of great use for letting out.[56] I do not think, however, that it ever developed into anything important.

A grand review of progress was made by the large trials of 1872 when prizes were offered for the best steam portable combined threshing and dressing machine, the best with no corn screen, the best straw elevator worked by steam and by horse gear, and for the best corn dressing machines and screens. Rather detailed specifications of the competing machines are supplied, but the main features have already been given, and it would occupy too much space to repeat them here. One tiny thing was noticeable. Though the trial of each individual machine only lasted twenty minutes or so, a good many bearings ran hot. Pusey's remark at the 1851 trial that the thresher was the most complicated agricultural machine in general use, was obviously as true in 1872 as when it was made. Indeed the machine had become more rather than less complicated. In 1858 only four of fifty-five trials of steam threshing machines showed perfectly clean work; other faults were general. In 1867 the judges were not satisfied with the work of the finishing machines, but the 1872 trials demonstrated a great improvement. In the previous three or four years, some of the largest manufacturers stated that they sold fifty multiple blast machines to every one single blast machine. The judges thought it probable that in seven years' time the single blast machine would be as antiquated as the horse-gear drive was in 1867.

Most threshing was by then done "by hired machines," or by agricultural contractors, and it was necessary for those who worked by contract to have machines that suited all customers. This was one reason for the preference for finishing machines. Another was that a somewhat wasteful application of steam power was much cheaper than the most economical manual labour.

This had long been known theoretically, and was daily becoming more recognized in practice. These expensive and complicated machines had by their economy superseded the sixpenny flail, remarked the judges. In spite of the enormous increase in power required, steam threshing cost less than half as much as flail work. No figures were given in support of these contentions, but their validity must have been apparent or they would not have been so obviously accepted. Part of the power was wasted on the straw which was often much broken. It was asked whether a modification could be made to prevent this, and so get threshing done with the expenditure of less power.

It had already been recognized that the feeding mouth of the thresher was dangerous. The self-feed invented by Mr. Wilders, a tenant farmer of Croxton Kynil, Grantham, solved this problem, though it was never generally adopted, and serious accidents continue to happen even today. Other contrivances for lessening or preventing this risk, impeded the proper feeding of the machine. Wilder's invention was fitted to Clayton and Shuttleworth's double blast machine. This feed consisted of a series of shakers with wooden ratchet teeth which conveyed the untied sheaves to the drum, loosening them well in the process. It had an adjustable rake at the mouth to regulate the feed, and could be instantly stopped by throwing the belt off the fast pulley by a lever at either side. It seems simple and effective, and was one of the first of many attempts to render this machine less dangerous. A hood covered the mouth and prevented waste of grain while the cost, £15, was trifling compared to its worth. It could be fitted to any machine.

Nine steam power elevators and ten horse gear were tried. The judges commented that it was only a short time since stacking by horse-power was tried by those who could afford to make experiments in agriculture for the public good. In 1872 elevators had been long enough in use to justify their purchase by many who adopted the sound advice:

Be not the first by whom the new is tried
Nor yet the last to lay the old aside.

The steam-driven elevators were shown by Wallis and Stevens; Tasker; Nalder; Albert Waston; Marshall, Russ Morris and Co.; Stephen Lewin; and Clayton and Shuttleworth. Three of the ten horse-driven machines were "pitchforks" rather like a modern grab; all the rest were much like the modern elevator. Eleven were tried the following year, it then being assumed that clear delivery of twenty-five feet high would meet the requirements of most farms. In this trial the prize went to Tasker.

Some thirty-two corn dressing machines were entered in 1872, and twenty-two were tried. Very few presented any novelty in construction, only differing in minor details. The very general adoption of finishing machines had reduced the necessity for each farmer to keep a hand-worked dresser, though one was often useful. Dressing had, in fact, begun to get outside farming scope, being really the job of the maltster and the miller.[57]

After seeing Wilder's self-feed, the Society decided to offer a gold medal for a guard, and in 1874 there were fifteen entered of which eleven were presented for trial. They were various types of self-feed, some of which could not act as guards, and some greatly impeded the feeding. The following year J. P. Fison was awarded £20 for his drum guard, and Tasker received £10.

Fison's guard was a revolving cylinder, having a wooden frame cased with sheet iron. It was driven by a two-inch belt from the shaker spindle at one hundred revolutions per minute and covered the full width of the mouth of the machine. It was supported at either end by two balanced levers connected with a swinging feed board hung on pivots. Eight wooden bevelled projections were screwed into the circumference of the cylinder at equal distances apart. The spindle of the cylinder rested in movable dies in slotted iron brackets, allowing an extreme play of three and a half inches up and down. When compressed down, either by a person slipping on the guard or an extreme weight of corn upon it, the belt was slacked off, and the cylinder stopped revolving. Tasker's was much simpler, being only a hood. The other entries were considered only partial guards.[58]

Robey and Co., of Lincoln, received a gold medal from the Highland and Agricultural Society at this time for a new design said to embody many improvements. It had the lower part of the framework left open so that the working could be observed. It was supplied with a self-feeder that could be quickly stopped, and it threshed six quarters of grain per hour. The new feeding apparatus came in for high praise. This Society also gave a gold medal to George W. Murray and Co., of Banff, in 1876. The only information supplied about the machine was that it did its work in a satisfactory manner.[59]

M

By then harvest work was greatly facilitated by stacking machines and hay and sheaf elevators. Nalder and Nalder won a silver medal for their straw elevator as attached to a threshing machine, i.e. working in conjunction with it. It had been shown at Kilburn in the previous year, but there had been no opportunity of trying it there.[60]

Another essential was presented to the public in 1881. This was Dederick's Hay Press, called the Perpetual Press. It was put on the English market by J. H. Ladd and Co. In 1882, it was demonstrated baling straw. The hay or straw was fed into a hopper by hand. At regular intervals the traverser was withdrawn, and a fork, or board, descended and forced the hay into a chamber below the hopper. Here it was subjected to the compressing action of a reciprocating traverser moving backwards and forwards underneath the hopper. The downwards and sideways action folded the hay, which was held in its position by steel springs when the traverser receded. The bale was tied with wire and the machine was worked by two men. It was awarded a silver medal. The following year at York the Society offered a prize for a straw trusser, and a silver medal was given for Howard's machine. This was not a compressor, but the straw fell direct from the thresher between two revolving aprons and was carried forwards and downwards much as the cut corn was carried up to the binding table of an American self-binder. There it collected against weighted levers, balanced to move at a given weight of straw when the binding mechanism was started. This was like an Appleby binder knotter, and used twine.[61]

Seven years later when they again offered prizes for these machines the Society was astonished at the extent of the entry. Of the four classes those driven by steam were the most important, the horse-driven and manual presses and old hand hay presses being already in the background if not actually superseded. There were four steam-driven machines. One by Samuelson, designed by Pilcer, an American, and the others by Howard, Ladd and Foster. The judges were not satisfied that any of them was both efficient and economical. The trials were specially interesting because all four machines were entirely different in their mode of working, which led the judges to believe that the steam power hay and straw press of the future was still to be designed. All except Howard's absorbed a great deal of power in proportion to the work done, while the cost per ton was generally greater than the best hand presses. When Ladd and Pilcer had stopped their open leakages of power, and Howard had substituted machinery for men (six were required to operate his machine) some future trials might, they thought, introduce farmers to an economical as well as efficient press of this kind. The efficiency was to hand, but the economy might be greatly improved, a hope that has been completely fulfilled. Four horse-driven, nine manual and nine old hand-power hay presses were also tried.[62]

Minor improvements continued to be made in the mechanism of the thresher. Foden produced a novelty in 1883. It was so arranged that the exhaust fan did the work usually done by the first and second winnowers, and also acted as a chaff lifter and chaff cleaner. This saved power, both blast fans as well as their shafts, pulleys and straps being dispensed with. Two years later Ruston Proctor produced a machine without cranks in which one plain straight shaft was used to drive the shakers and the winnowing shoes by external eccentrics on each side. The eccentrics were connected by two crossbars passing through the machine from side to side and giving motion to the shakers. Two pairs of rods from the eccentrics drove the shoe and the caving riddle. While this was helpful the judges recalled that other makers before them had reduced the number of wearing parts. Nalder and Nalder were the first; they were awarded a medal at Reading in 1882 while Foden won one for his use of the exhaust fan in 1883. Gibbons and Robinson's machine, exhibited at Shrewsbury, dispensed with eighteen bearings and joints requiring oil. Moreover, in Humphries' new improved machine the shoes were connected with the shakers rather like Nalder's arrangement. Clayton and Shuttleworth adopted Foden's exhaust fan.

Ransome produced in 1866 another guard to make threshing machines safe. This was a self-acting feeder with a cylinder in the mouth. Above the revolving cylinder was a fixed shaft carrying three curved tines which moved backwards and forwards and were driven by a connecting rod and crank from the cylinder spindle. The cylinder and tines were enclosed in a wood casing and fixed above the drum mouth, forming a complete protection for the operator. The sheaves with the bands cut were placed on an inclined board and fell on to the cylinder which carried them forward to the drum, whilst the looped and curved tines assisted in so separating the straw that an equal and continuous stream, directed by an internal and swinging plate, was carried to the drum.[63]

The last of the major trials of these machines held during the nineteenth century was at Cardiff in 1891, and only one class was open to competition, the "Combined Portable Threshing and Finishing Machine" for which three prizes of £100, £50 and £25 were offered. In place of the thirty competitors in the two classes of 1872 only nine exhibitors entered. From these two circumstances it can be deduced that only one type of machine was in demand at the end of the nineteenth century, and that the severe competition for the business had eliminated some of the early makers. But, of course, the nine original entries may not have included all the firms who were making threshers; and, indeed, four entrants eventually withdrew, leaving only five machines. These were made by James Coultas, E. Foden Sons and Co., W. Foster and Co., Gibbons and Robinson, and W. Tasker and Sons.

Though James Coultas' machine had won a £10 prize in a competition arranged by Lord Yarborough—the firm's Perseverance Ironworks was at Grantham—it did not do too well at these trials. This is the more surprising because the firm was old-established, having been founded by its owner, who is believed to have come from Yorkshire in or before 1853. They had been highly commended for their dressing machines so long before as 1859, and between that time and 1891 the Coultas drills had taken many prizes. The Coultas folding elevator proved very rapid in work in 1873.

Foster's machine had faults, breaking too much of the best wheat, and though it made a clean sample of barley it did not separate the seconds from the best corn as well as it might have done. Gibbons and Robinson's machine did good clean work, but poor feeding handicapped its performance. In this respect the Foden operatives excelled, causing their machines to do a great deal of work in the given time. Tasker's machine, too, did pretty well. In the result the judges placed Foden first and Gibbons and Robinson and Tasker jointly in second place.[64]

Finality in any machine is rarely achieved, but it may be no exaggeration to say that the harvest had become mechanized by 1891. The corn was reaped and bound by the binder, and it was often ricked by means of elevators. At the appropriate time it was threshed and dressed and sacked for market by the combined threshing machine or stacked by the help of the elevator. This was of immense advantage to the farmer, but was still looked upon somewhat askance by the labourer.[65]

It would be wrong to terminate this chapter without a passing glance at the early attempts at crop drying, in particular the apparatus patented by W. A. Gibbs, of Gilwell Park, in 1866, and modified in 1874, 1876 and in 1880.[66] The idea was simple. Hay and cut crops were wholly or partly dried by a current of air drawn by a fan from the smoke-box of a portable engine in conjunction with waste steam or— as the Royal Agricultural Society's Report of 1869 has it—"The products of combustion are driven through a chamber containing the corn or are brought directly in contact with damp hay which is being constantly moved." It raised quite a furore in agricultural circles. Gibbs received a medal from the Royal Society of Arts for the principles upon which the machine was founded. The drying chamber was in two compartments, the flow of drying air being controlled by a valve which let it into each compartment alternately, so that while one was being used for drying the other could be emptied and refilled. A four blade induction fan was used.

Such an idea was bound to be imitated, and at the same show at Manchester, Daniel Adamson and Co., of Hyde, near Manchester, demonstrated their plan for driving a current of air through sheaves of corn stacked round a wire frame. Davy Paxman and Co. dried threshed grain by a system of steam-heated cylinders through which the corn was propelled, being heated from steam in the jacket of the cylinder and a blast of dry hot air from a furnace.[67]

In 1878 the "Royal" society offered a prize for an efficient method of doing this job, but no inventor was confident enough to submit his apparatus for trial. They were more successful in 1882 when seven contrivances were shown. Gibbs's apparatus was in a class by itself, using the method of hot air drying. Six exhaust fans for drying in the stack were shown, and some system of ventilation assisted by hot air through the stack. One of the exhaust fans was produced by Gibbs the others by the Agricultural and Horticultural Association, Ltd., by A. C. Bamlett, James Coultas, R. A. Lister and Co., Ltd., and by Charles D. Phillips, whose ventilation system was by C. Kite and Co. Very complex trials in drying hay and barley stacks were carried out, but the results were not sufficiently satisfactory for the judges to award the prize, a decision which greatly annoyed Gibbs.[68] After two decades crop drying was forgotten and has only been revived in recent years.

CHAPTER
SIX

BARN AND MISCELLANEOUS MACHINERY

THERE IS NO mention of barn machinery in an encyclopaedic work issued in 1756 as *A Compleat Body of Husbandry*; so whatever feed may have been prepared for the livestock was prepared by hand. Of course the new forage crops and roots were then only slowly coming into production, and apart from kibbling beans and peas, or chopping up a few roots with a knife or chopper, or cutting whatever hay may have been to hand in the same way, there was little feed preparing done. The beasts had to survive as best they could.

Less than ten years later a primitive chaff cutting machine, called a "cutting box," was invented. This was to be used for cutting horse meat. Thomas Comber, Jun., of East Newton, Yorks, thought that the advantage of this machine was that the better and the worse forage was mixed so that the animals could not pick and choose. The action of the knife against the end of the box caused a scissors-like cut. A Kentish farmer was much taken with the idea and could not sufficiently commend its use, though he thought the ploughmen would oppose it, because the cutting of the horse meat was pretty tough work "and they do not, in general, love to do more than they can help." Comber believed the machine would be improved if the knife handle was lengthened and three parallel knives were fixed in a frame to work in notches in the sides of the box, so as to give a chopping action and make three cuts at the same time.[1]

Early in the 1760s the Society for the Encouragement of Arts offered a premium of £20 for a machine to slice turnips. Some people may have thought this an odd subject for the Society, but turnips must be cut for cattle and the Society had learned that in Carinthia where very great quantities of turnips were fed they were always sliced by a rude machine. In England at that date they were always sliced by hand. If an easy method of slicing turnips could be discovered, the risk of the animals choking from attempting to swallow whole roots would be avoided. The work of cutting straw and hay was more difficult, Agricola adds, yet there was a cutting box for this purpose, and he was confident that some such machine as that for cutting up sausage meat could be adapted for slicing turnips.[2]

An improved chaff cutter, made by James Edgill, of Frome, Somerset, had a single spiral knife. It was illustrated, if not widely used, early in the 1770s. It was probably found only in Somerset, a famous grazing and dairy district. James Sharp included in his catalogue a hand mill for splitting beans, and grinding malt, barley and oats. The closeness of grinding in this machine was controlled by a notched bar and roller.[3]

Multiplication of types of chaff cutters was rapid. One was fitted with a roller or bar arranged with a foot lever below the machine. The operator depressed this lever to draw the roller or bar down upon the hay or straw as it was pushed forward for cutting. It was thus held firmly in position while the knife operated. At the turn of the century a great variety of chaff cutters was on the market, but scarcely one was cheap enough for general use, so the common cutting box was still employed on most farms.

Winlaw's successors and other manufacturers had produced a type in which the straw was regularly brought forward by "an iron cylinder contrived for the purpose, as the implement is turned round, and cut by means of three knives fixed on the whole." One of these was McDougall's; others were Cook's (or Cooke's) and Nailor's.[4] McDougall used a weight at the cutting end to hold the straw in position, but this system had been patented by James Cook in 1794. Cook also introduced "fixed and rotating blades," the latter being attached to the spokes of a wheel. The fixed blade was attached to the end of the box and the rotating blades were so arranged that the cutting action was similar to that of a pair of scissors. Both the weight and the scissors mechanism are found in the modern chaff cutter, so that the general principles of the modern machine were set out in 1794.[5] It would be impossible now to find material to catalogue all the chaff cutters made during the next few decades, and it is not necessary to do so. That illustrated by J. C. Loudon in his *Encyclopaedia of Agriculture*, 1831, and made by Weir, shows little change.[6]

The early shows of the R.A.S.E. saw a plethora of these machines. They were numerous, of superior construction and highly finished workmanship in 1841; excellent chaff cutters of all sizes, fashions and capabilities abounded in 1842 and were said to be universally used both in that year and 1843, while there was an immense number and variety of this indispensable implement in 1844, and the number was beyond all precedent in 1845. One type, the Earl of Ducie's, was driven by Dean's travelling (= portable) steam engine in 1843.[7]

In spite of all this, Samuel Copland, writing twenty years later, said that the design of the improved chaff cutter was so recent that almost every farmer was using the old type, the box about three feet long by six inches wide "open except at the cutting end, where a square piece of board is placed, connected by a string with a treadle below." The operator forced the straw along the box under the loose plank with a fork fastened to the frame, and pressed the treadle with his foot to squeeze the hay. At the same moment he cut off the end of the hay close to the end of the machine with the knife which was hung loosely to the side by a lifting joint—the very same machine depicted and described in *Museum Rusticum* a century before. Working this gadget required, as Copland rightly remarked, considerable dexterity and practice.

The then modern implement had mostly two knives, some cutting with a convex and some with a concave edge. The knives were fixed by screw and nut to the arms of the flywheel and presented a bevel edge to the end of the machine. The frame, legs and trough were of cast iron and the hay or straw, on being put into the trough, was caught and pressed forward between rollers. The rollers were driven by a flywheel set in motion by a winch. Those made by Richmond and Chandler, fitted with toothed rollers for pushing forward the hay, had met with general approval.[8] There were many others; Ransome, for example,

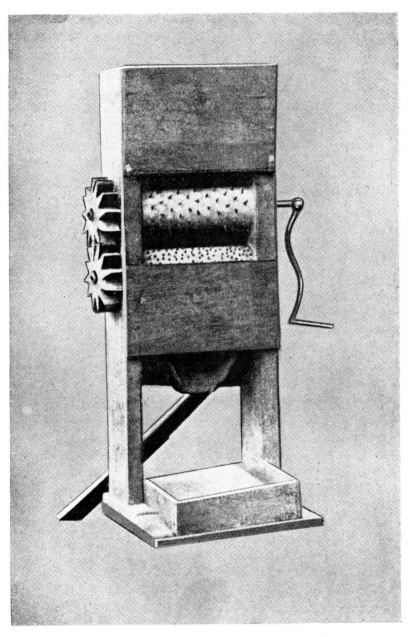

81. A Hand Threshing Mill. *Harrogate Herald*, 1930.

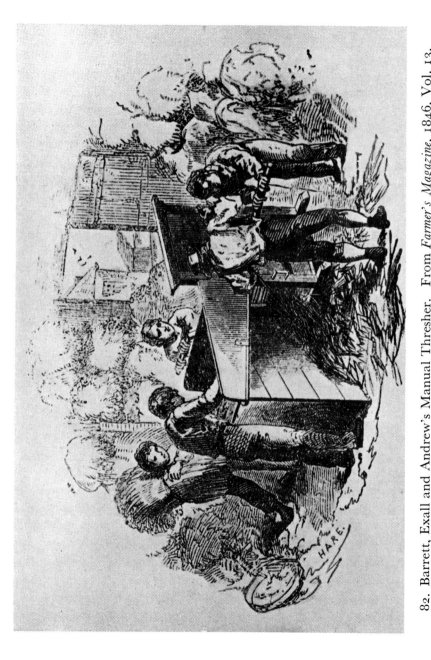

82. Barrett, Exall and Andrew's Manual Thresher. From *Farmer's Magazine*, 1846, Vol. 13.

83. Barrett, Exall, and Andrew's Horse Gear Thresher. From *Farmer's Magazine*, 1846, Vol. 13.

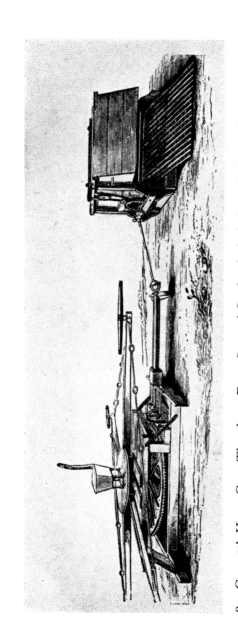

84. Garrett's Horse Gear Thresher. From Samuel Copland, *Agriculture, Ancient and Modern*, 1866.

85. Wilder's Self Feeding Thresher. From *Jour. R.A.S.E.*, 1872.

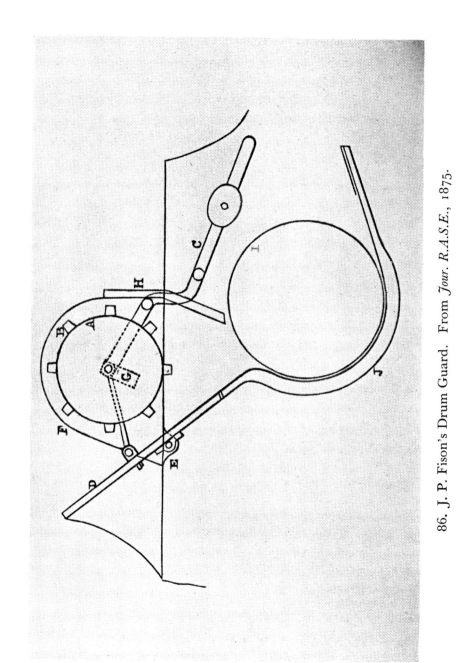

86. J. P. Fison's Drum Guard.   From *Jour. R.A.S.E.*, 1875.

87. Perpetual Baling Press.   From *Jour. R.A.S.E.*, 1881.

88. Ransome, Sims and Jefferies' Self Feeder. From *Jour. R.A.S.E.*, 1886.

89. Cutting box. From *Museum Rusticum*, 1764, Vol. I.

90. Sharp's Chaffcutter. From *Farmer's Magazine*, 1776.

91. Sharp's Grinding Mill. From *Farmer's Magazine*, 1776.

92. Macdougall's Patent Chaff Cutter. From R. W. Dickson.
Practical Agriculture, 1805.

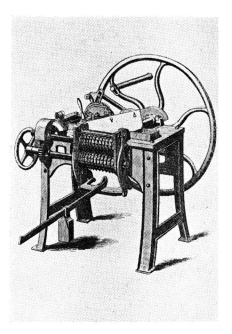

93. Walker's Chaff Cutter. From
John Donaldson. *British Agriculture*,
1866.

94. Ransome and Uley Chaff Cutter. From John M. Wilson, *Rural Cyclopaedia*, 1849.

95. Root Cutter, etc. From *New Royal Encyclopaedia, c.* 1820.

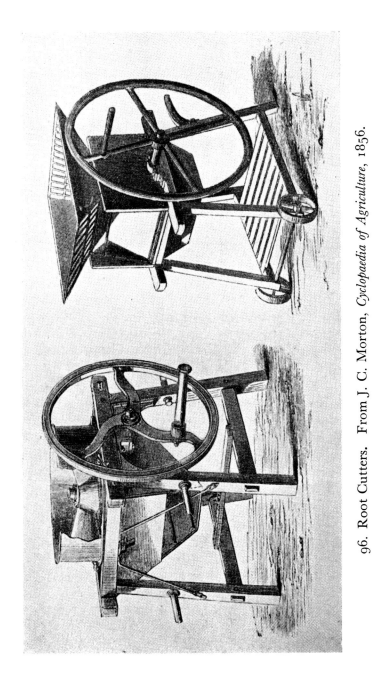

96. Root Cutters. From J. C. Morton, *Cyclopaedia of Agriculture*, 1856.

had offered various types made of wood and iron since 1844.[9] Walker's chaff cutter of about the same date as Richmond and Chandler's seems to have been much along the same lines.[10]

Apart from the large chaff cutter which is fed automatically from the threshing machine, and gadgets for regulating the speed of the feed in relation to that of the knives which governed the length of chaff cut, and the introduction of the modern clutch in the mechanically driven machine,[11] "these changes were in principle final." Nevertheless, the leading agricultural societies continued to hold comparative trials at intervals during the latter part of the nineteenth century. For example, the Highland and Agricultural Society held one at Glasgow in 1889.[12]

The root slicer or cutter was developed at the same time though perhaps not so rapidly. A newly invented machine for slicing was illustrated in the *New Royal Encyclopaedia* of about 1820, and described as being adjustable to cut pieces of any size. The mechanism was probably a series of circular knives on an axle turned so that the edges revolved above the level of the floor of the hopper and thus cut into the roots placed there. By 1831 Loudon could report that the turnip slicer was of different forms, the older type being similar to a straw cutter of the original construction. A better model consisted of a hopper and knives fixed upon a flywheel. In this the turnips pressed upon the knives "by their own weight," and "a man turning a wheel cut a bushel in a minute." Gardener's turnip slicer, which was the premier machine for at least two decades, was an improved form of that machine. There was also a cutter fixed to a handle and used by striking into the root as it lay upon the ground. This, too, continued to be used until at least the middle years of the nineteenth century.[13]

A more ingenious device intended to cut the turnips and spread the pieces over the pasture for the grazing stock to eat, was designed by G. Townsend, of Sapcote, Hinckley, Leicestershire. The apparatus was a cutting disc fixed horizontally underneath the hind part of a cart driven by a toothed wheel clamped to the spokes of the cart wheel. The turnips were apparently intended to be cut as they fell against the blade, but the description is not very clear, and it is doubtful whether the device ever went into production. Something not unlike this was shown, much later, by Kemp and Nicholson, of Stirling, in 1910.[14]

A great variety of turnip cutters was shown in 1842 and the judges reluctantly gave a premium to Sanders and Williams, of Bedford. They thought the machine so important that a premium ought to be awarded only after an extensive trial in the field during the winter. By this date feeding of roots was so general that the machine had become almost indispensable. At this show H. and T. Proctor, of Bristol, were awarded £3 for a combined turnip and chaff cutter. It produced at a single operation a mixture of the two kinds of foods, or it could cut the two feeds separately. Gardener's implement was still universally esteemed in 1844 and many thousands were in use, in spite of the competition it had to face. It was considered the most simple, durable and effective, but in the following year this Banbury firm met with formidable rivals in C. Phillips and Co., of Bristol, who were then awarded £5 over its head.[15]

Pusey had strongly recommended the use of the turnip cutter in his paper in the first volume of the *Journal* of the R.A.S.E. He had deplored the slow rate at which the farmers were then adopting it, but by the mid-1850s its use had been greatly extended.

The simplest form of cutter, other than the hand chopper, acted by direct pressure somewhat like a nutcracker, the one cheek being an open "harp" of cup-shaped edges, and the other a block fitting those edges. The pressure was manually exerted by bearing down on the handle. The roots placed one at a time in the block were cut into slices which then fell beneath the gadget. The finger-shaped piece was preferable for feeding to the slice, and most machines were designed to cut fingers. A cutter fitted with a series of parallel oscillating knives, shaped like a segment of a circle with the curve running over the level of the bottom of a hopper, was then much used in Scotland. Another form had straight, vertical oscillating knives, and others had disc cutters working in an enclosed box below the hopper. Gardener's (nobody is very decided how this name is spelt) was still thought the best. It had a cutting cylinder so designed that it produced the approved finger-shaped pieces, which pieces fell into a basket or box below. If the cylinder was reversed it cut slices. By 1856 Gardeners, of Banbury, had been taken over by Samuelson "who makes enormous numbers of these machines." Wedlake's cutter was a pair of interlocking conical shaped cylinders fitted with cutting teeth designed to allow the roots to feed themselves from the hopper by gravitation.[16] Nevertheless Burgess and Key won the prize at the Great Exhibition in 1851.[17]

Besides the machine that cut the roots into slices there were also root pulpers which cut or rasped the roots into very small shreds. One of these was produced by a firm called Bush and Barter and another by Bentall, of Malden, Essex. It consisted of a cylinder to which were fixed twelve rows of hooked teeth, eight in each row. An Archimedean screw was fixed close underneath this cylinder, so that the teeth in the cylinder might correspond with the threads and pass through them in revolving. "By this united action" the roots were completely pulped.[17a] Obviously, root preparing machines had advanced to efficiency by the late 1860s and were well adapted for driving by steam, or horse gear if steam was not installed.

The use of grinding mills for crushing or bruising oats for horse feed and beans and peas is probably fairly ancient. There is, unfortunately, little information to be gleaned about their develop-ment. A smoothed roller was used for cracking oats to make them more digestible, and some two centuries ago Isaac Wilkinson, of Lancaster, patented a machine, fitted with cast-iron rollers, for "crushing, flattening, and bruising or grinding of malt, oats and beans." James Sharp was selling a hand mill for the same purpose twenty years after this patent was granted in 1753.[18]

The use of fragments of the cake residue from oil manufacture, rape seed and so on, as manure, was introduced at the beginning of the eighteenth century, if not earlier. A machine for breaking up the cakes became more necessary than ever when these residues began to be used as concentrates. It was not until 1845 that a prize was offered for a linseed cake crusher. It was won by Dean of Birmingham, a firm that had large experience in the manufacture of mills for crushing bones for bone manure. Earl Ducie's oat and bean mill was still pre-eminent at that time, but not equal to Dean's for linseed. Ducie's machine, invented by Richard Clyburn, had won a silver medal in 1843. It carried two rollers of different diameter with vertical V-shaped grooves which worked into each other. The different velocity of the rollers gave a bruising action, the fineness of the crushing being regu-lated by adjusting the rollers. At this show James Spencer, of Hopton, near Wirkworth, was awarded £5 for his mill on the fluted roller principle, but these were only two of the very numerous designs sub-mitted. Hornsby won £5 for a cake crusher, the crushing detail carrying conical pointed case-hardened teeth. This machine again won a premium in the following year when £30, a large award for those days, was given to Messrs. Ransome for their horse gear and barn machinery. This included a corn and seed crusher which was judged the best implement of the kind yet brought before the public. Dean's bone mill was the only mill for fine grinding in that year, though Stratton, of Bristol, showed Robert Fry's simple and cheap hand mill.

And so it went on. The Ducie cake crusher won a prize again in 1846 when some machines by Ransome, Nicholson, Garrett, Stratton, Sharman and Ferrabee were tried. Wedlake and Thompson also won a prize and Nicholson was commended for a very strong cake crusher.[19]

By 1860 the trials of barn machinery were very extensive. They included chaff cutters, oilcake breakers, root pulpers, turnip and root cutters and slicers, grinding mills with steel and stone grinders, linseed and corn crushers, bone and bone dust mills, etc. The number of firms engaged in making these machines was very large. A few of them were Ransome, Garrett, Hornsby, Blackstone, Bentall, Richmond and Chandler, Ashby and Co., Hunt and Pickering, Turner of Ipswich, Picksley and Co., Crosskill, Cornes and Son, Tasker, Woods and Son. The equipment of the barn on a large farm was now very elaborate; it remained so to the end of the century. A large variety of power-driven barn machinery was tried at the Royal Show at Bury St. Edmunds in 1867 and 1870.[20]

The business of making these machines became rather specialized, and Ransome passed over their production to Messrs. Hunt and Tawell, of Earls Colne, Essex, in 1872.[21]

Thirty years later the Highland and Agricultural Society conducted trials of grist mills at Dundee. The machines tried were made by Blackstone and Co., Nicholson and Sons, Woodroffe and Co., William Balfour of Pittenweem, Barford and Perkins, and R. G. Morton of Errol.[22] This was a year after the Royal Society had carried out similar trials at Plymouth.[23]

The cultivation of the potato as a staple was one of the developments of the nineteenth century, though in some parts of the country fairly extensive acreages of the crop had long been grown. It is a crop that needs a vast deal of labour in planting, raising and sorting, especially when all these jobs must be done manually. The demand for seasonal labour is still large, but by the middle of the nineteenth century active minds were already busy in devising machines to alleviate the drudgery of this work.

Possibly the earliest attempt was a digger of the elevator type patented in 1852. J. Hanson patented a device for digging potatoes by means of rotating forks similar in principle to the modern rotary spinner as long ago as 1855.[24] In 1858 three more patents were taken out, two were of the spinner type and one of the plough with skeleton mouldboard of prongs which sifted the dirt from the potatoes.[25] From then till 1876 some thirty-five other patents for potato diggers were granted. But it was not till twenty years after the first invention that the Highland and Agricultural Society held the first trial of these machines on a farm near Perth. There were six firms: J. Bisset and Sons of Blairgowrie; William Dewar of Killis, Dundee; Low, Duncan and Co.; James Mollison, Ruthven; James Robertson of Coupar-Angus; and R. Stewart, Buttergask, Coupar-Angus. All these diggers did their work extremely well, the machines being easily hauled by two horses, and every exhibitor was awarded a silver medal.[26] J. and R. Wallace's potato digger was shown at Glasgow in 1875, but further trials at Aberdeen demonstrated that all the machines removed the potato from the soil too rapidly, and thus injured the skins so that they could not be advantageously stored in pits. Accordingly, no award was made.[27]

Although Aspinall's patent, which had been placed second at Aberdeen, won no award, it was given a silver medal at the Royal show at Birmingham in 1877. It was a machine with a revolving extractor or separator driven by spur gear from the travelling wheels. It had a pair of wheels with a main frame between them, having a central draught pole and a seat for the driver, after the fashion of a grass mower. Potato and soil were together lifted by the share and broken and separated by being passed through a cylindrical cage travelling backwards and having an indented or waved circumference. This was in two parts, an outer and an inner cage, and did two lots of riddling to clear the earth. The haulm was cleared by a gadget like the roller of a turnip drill.

Ten years later the Society offered prizes for different types of digger; the first was won by Powell and Whitaker who had shown Lewis's patent in 1884; the second went to John Gregory Destoe, of South Shields. Powell's machine was a spinner, running loose, the weight causing it to turn, the soil falling through and the tubers being gently laid aside. There were two classes at these trials, one for machines that sold for less than £5 and the other for those that sold at a higher price. Machines were entered by J. D. Allen and Sons; William Elder; Alexander Jack and Sons; Robert Kyd; Penney and Co.; Powell and Whitaker; and Moorhouse A. Thompson, of Berwick. Implements costing more than £5 were demonstrated by John Cooke and Son, William Elder and John Gregory. An American machine by Lankester and Co., was also shown. The second class was confined to ploughs with some arrangement of skeleton fingers in place of the mouldboard, while the cheaper machines were all spinners.[28]

Diggers with tail shakers behind a ploughshare continued to be made. John Perkins and Son, of Lichfield, showed one in 1893. James Holt, of Altrincham, exhibited a machine equipped with three sets of spinners, and Ransome submitted their machine with a hemp net to prevent damage by too violent working. In the following year John Wallace and Sons, of Glasgow, showed a machine with the diggers arranged to revolve horizontally. Ransome had a novel arrangement of the forks, provided with eight arms and working in a kind of slow motion so that the potatoes were not delivered with great force into the hempen net receiver. By 1910, though the spinner type was more usual, the elevator type was still being made.[29] By this time the spinners, which were at first set in a vertical plane that occasionally missed some of the plants, had been redesigned so that the ends of the tines followed "a path which was an ellipse, the major axis of which was horizontal." Though mechanically rather complex, these machines were successful; they have been superseded since.[30]

Planting potatoes, too, was a tedious and arduous job if done manually, as it had to be until after the middle of the nineteenth century. A patent for a planter was granted to J. Baird in 1857. The specification was "A suitable frame carries one or more shares in front to open up furrows into which potatoes are dropped at regular intervals by a rotary distributor, divided into compartments with doors or valves operated as required. A rotary feeding device with cups takes the potatoes singly from a receptacle and delivers them into the compartments of the distributor. Shares are mounted at the rear of the implement for covering the potatoes."[31] About twenty more patents, aside from dibbers and ploughs, were taken out in the next eighteen years, but the general principle had been laid down by Baird and most later machines were on those lines.

Six planters, said to be much improved since some earlier trials, were exhibited at Glasgow in 1875. They were the products of William Dewar, Kellas, Dundee; Alexander Guthrie, Craigs, Montrose; Charles Hay, Merchiston, Edinburgh; G. W. Murray and Co., Banff (Ferguson's patent); and J. W. Robinson and Co., of Liverpool (Aspinall's patent). One of the two machines put up by the last firm was only designed to sow on the flat and so was not tried. The other was tried, with Guthrie's and Murray's. Though the machines were not perfect, the improvement in design was very noticeable. After some indecision the judges awarded £10 to Guthrie for his double-row planter, and £10 to Robinson, a decision against which Murray entered a demurrer noting that the judges had missed the finer points of his machine. They very reasonably replied that his representative should have described them at the trial.[32]

Wright's patent made by Coultas had received a silver medal from the "Royal" Society two years before. It was very similar to a turnip drill with the seed box very much enlarged. It had a sort of cup feed on revolving chains, working like a dredger, which rose through the box filled with seed potatoes. Each cup took one potato and was inverted as it entered the top metal tube that was the feed. The potato fell on to the cup back below. This was slightly cup-shaped. The potato dropped into the furrow opened by a double mouldboard plough fitted to the lower part of the frame. An award of £15 was made to this firm in the following year, 1874, when a prize was offered for a patent potato drill and these drills were tried along with all kinds of seed drills. As the judges remarked, "The want of some implement to facilitate the operation of potato planting has been much felt of late years by large growers of potatoes." There was a growing shortage of labour and the planters already on the market were inclined to sow two or three instead of the one seed ensured by hand planting.

Another silver medal was awarded in 1880 to G. W. Murray and Co. for a two-row planter. The potatoes were carried in a container, and, as in Wright's patent, a series of cups, arranged like the scoops of a dredger, formed each a link in an endless chain, though only hooked into each other. On the end of each cup was a tail, which, as the chain turned over the supporting wheels, rose up through the bottom of the succeeding cup, ensuring that the seed left the cup at the right moment, and cleaned it of dirt. This was considered an important improvement. The machine could be arranged to plant at three different spacings. A prize was again offered seven years later, but no award was made because there was no noticeable improvement and extreme irregularity of planting was a fault in most of the machines.

An ingenious arrangement was brought out by Arters, of Canterbury, in 1891, taken up by Ransome in 1892 and awarded a silver medal in 1893. In this machine the potatoes in the hopper were spiked one by one, and dropped into a cone-shaped feeding tube which discharged them into a furrow made by a plough body on the frame. The spikes were replaced by a finger and thumb arrangement in 1898.[33]

Another troublesome job was sorting the chats from the ware potatoes. Maunder exhibited a Potato Separator in 1863. It was a riddle on an inclined plane. It had two compartments floored with wooden laths resting on rollers, which were placed at smaller intervals in the upper compartment than the lower. The smallest potatoes and the dirt fell through the first set of laths, and the dirt again dropped through a screen bottom in the lower chamber. The seed potatoes fell through the wider spaced laths in the lower chamber and the large ones were carried along to the end. Motion was given by a crank to the rollers which caused the laths to vibrate sufficiently to keep the potatoes moving. The wooden floor was to prevent bruising. Here again, the obvious principle of shaking and differently spaced riddles, is still in use.

Nineteen years later the East Yorks Waggon Co. produced a sorter with the modern type of riddle, and in the following year Lightfoot, of Stockton-on-Tees, produced a machine with flat screens which had the advantage that diseased potatoes could be hand picked, an impossibility in a machine with tubular screens like the East Yorks Waggon Co's.[34] Henry Cooch, the great grandson of the founder of the firm of Cooch and Son, designed a sorter in 1885 that became widely known and was awarded a silver medal by the R.A.S.E. in 1911.[35]

No attempt has been made to give all the names of all makers of potato sowing, harvesting, sorting and cleaning machines. Such a list would not only be difficult to compile but would be inordinately long. Nor is it possible to make any estimate of the rate at which the growers adopted the machines. They were probably just as cautious in taking up these things as they had been in accepting others, though they probably became quite enthusiastic when they were convinced of their usefulness.

Many other devices were being invented as the later years of the nineteenth century progressed. Mechanical sheep shearing clippers were introduced from Australia in the last decade, and the "Royal" Society staged a trial of them in 1893, but it is pretty doubtful whether these machines were used very generally before World War I. No statistics of the production of agricultural machinery were collected then.

Amongst other gadgets was a thatch-making machine; this, like the mechanical hedge cutter, has quite recently been revived, but perhaps the most important development of this time was the introduction of the cream separator and the milking machine.

Though the cream separator had been known for some time in Germany, Denmark and Sweden, it was not till 1879 that the de Laval was shown at the Royal Show at Kilburn, where it was awarded a silver medal, being the most novel exhibit to be seen there. There was some doubt of its practical value for the farmer though its merits in producing perfectly fresh cream, in dispensing with ice and in saving space and apparatus were recognized as of great use in a factory. This machine, once again in its early form, contained practically all the principles of the modern machine. The milk was put into a metal bowl that was caused to revolve at from 3,500 to 4,000 r.p.m. This caused the heavier portion, the skim milk, to fly to the sides whence it was forced upwards and discharged through an appropriately placed pipe. The cream remained and was discharged as seen in the diagram. Three machines were shown in 1881, a German like the Laval, made by Lefeldt, but very cumbrous; the Laval, and the Neilson Peterson, a Danish product. A competition was held in 1882 and two gold medals offered, but although ten machines were entered, owing to an impending action for infringement of patent, only two firms showed four machines on two distinct principles. A gold medal was given to the Laval exhibited by Hald and Co. Its competitor was the Hamburg or Peterson, a rather more complicated apparatus.

These two makes continued to compete alone for the next few years, the British Dairy Farmer's Association adding their gold medal to the Laval award in 1884. This machine was shown in a slightly

N

improved form in 1887 and encountered some new competition in 1888 when the Victoria separator made by Watson, Laidlow and Co., of Glasgow, was exhibited by Freeth and Pocock. This was a self-skimming machine that emptied itself completely and was easily cleaned. It was also shown at the Bath and West Society's Show in the same year. The Laval A.I. encountered still more competition in 1889 when Lister's showed a power-driven machine, the Alexandra; and at the Bath and West Show there were five power-driven machines— the Laval A.I.; Turbine Cream Separator; Victoria in two sizes; Lister's Alexandra. Manual machines were by then being produced by Laval; the Dairy Supply Co. (Laval type); Burmeister and Wain; the Aylesbury Dairy Co. (Star); Freeth and Pocock (Victoria); and Lister (Alexandra).

The Victoria manual machine was used in the working dairy that had become a feature of "Royal" shows by 1889. It had a finish about the design that was pleasing and was very effective in action, but in that year the Bath and West Society thought there was little to choose between the Laval machine and that of Koeford and Hanberg exhibited by Lister. The latter was, in fact, the best designed machine, well proportioned, compact, well shielded, the gravity kept low and a smaller spindle used, making for safety. It was lifted easily for cleaning and was secured by three long bolts, another safety precaution. Lister's Alexandra was placed best by this Society and Laval good. The Victoria was noticed for several novelties but was criticized on account of the difficulty of cleaning it.

Next year the Dairy Supply Co. produced an elaborate "Instantaneous" butter-maker by placing a refrigerator between the separator and churn, Hall's Refrigerating Plant having been shown for the first time in 1889. In the Lister "Alexandra" of 1890 the milk was heated to 80° before it entered the separator by means of a jacketed steam chamber which formed the bottom. For three or four inches above this a loose diaphragm rested on a small ledge in the side of the tub. This checked the heated milk in rising so that the bulk of the upper milk remained comparatively cool. On leaving the separator the skim milk was passed through a jacketed vertical cylinder and boiled, after which it was cooled over a refrigerator and canned for sale. The milk was prevented from scumming or sticking to the sides of the boiler by an ingenious stirrer revolving inside it.

With all this development the "Royal" judges were justified in claiming that the trials held at Doncaster in 1891 were the most important that had so far been held in the United Kingdom. Earlier trials by this society and by other societies had been limited to one firm, or at most two, and the trials were quite superficial. The exhibitors of both power and manual machines were the same five as mentioned before, but the Laval machine was supplied with a novel fitting. This was an arrangement of thin steel discs fitted into the drum (bowl?) placed one above the other, loosely arranged about the spindle and kept apart from each other by projections on them. The first prize was awarded to the Dairy Supply Co. for their Alpha-Windsor machine.

One Waldren, of Chilcombe Farm, near Bridport, became an enthusiast for the separator. He kept a dairy of sixty Devon cows whose average yield was four hundred and twenty-eight gallons in 1887. He induced some of his neighbours—the district was much occupied in and famous for dairy farming—to lend him their skim milk, made in the ordinary way of placing the whole milk in shallow trays and skimming off the cream by hand after it had been allowed to set for a period of time. He put the skim milk through his separator. He found that he could get a quart of cream from five gallons of this milk and by an elaborate set of costings proved that this meant a profit of £16 13s. 4d. per lactation of ten cows in favour of the separator, the capital expenditure being £50 for a two horse-power engine and £40 for a separator, which would clearly be recovered in the first year in a dairy of his size, provided that his calculations could be relied upon.

The next R.A.S.E. trials of cream separators were not held till 1899 but the Laval, the Humming Bird that worked like a humming top with a string, and Freeth and Pocock's Express were shown in 1894, while Lister's put on an elaborate "Farmer's Cream Separating Plant" in 1895. A new machine, a Butter Accumulator, made by Wahlin, of New York, which separated and made butter in one continuous operation was shown in 1896. The Dairy Supply Co. produced a sterilizing and bottling plant, and a large-scale Swedish system was also shown. The Melotte Cream Separator appeared in 1898, and was tried with three other power machines in 1899. They were made by Watson, Laidlow and Co., Glasgow; "Fram" Dairy Machinery Co., of Holborn Circus; the Farmer's Surprise, of the Dairy Supply Co. All these produced manual machines as well. So did Pond and Son, of Blandford, Dorset, who showed the Swedish Crown, and Vipan and Headly, of Leicester, who showed two machines. All these machines proved capable of separating the quantity of milk claimed for them. There were various shaped discs in the bowls of the Melotte, the Farmer's Surprise, Watson and Laidlow's machine and the "Fram." Finality had not yet been reached, but the judges were convinced that the day of the empty bowl had passed because the various discs and plates enormously increased their capacity. Several machines were again shown in 1904, in 1908 and in 1910. In the last year the Dairy Supply Co., the Titanic Co., of Euston Road, R. J. Fullwood and Bland, Watson, Laidlow and Co., and R. A. Lister and Co. were the exhibitors.[36]

The milking machine, which was a later development in this country than the cream separator, has been claimed as an "entirely Scottish invention,"[37] but this would, I think, be difficult to establish. Attempts had been made to produce a milking machine as early as 1862, and suction machines of the modern type were tried in America in 1878.

The American milking machine of 1862 was exhibited in the United States Section of the International Exhibition of that year. The *Illustrated London News* thought its advent meant that the poetry of rustic life was being lost.[37a] "The mower," it went on, "is no longer required at the scythe, nor the reaper at the sickle; that bent figure at the barn door swinging to the music of the flail is gone; the whistle of the ploughboy is gradually dying in the distance; and now we are called upon to dismiss the ruddy milkmaid. A machine has been invented for milking cows. . . . The teats of the cow just drop into four elastic tubes placed under them, in communication with an exhaust apparatus and a reservoir. The quick movement of two handles creates a vacuum, and the udder is instantaneously emptied of its contents in four continuous streams. While the operation is distressingly practical [sic], it is very cleanly and we believe agreeable to the cow [a more than doubtful proposition]. The milk is withdrawn at the rate of a gallon a minute. The patent of the 'cow milker' has been sold to Watkins and Keene, of Birmingham, for £5,000 and a royalty to the original inventors; it is stated that the two firms have already received orders sufficient to cover the expenses of the patent, and that the machine is rapidly being adopted by the great dairymen throughout the country." A prize medal was awarded to this machine but the buyers of the patent were over-optimistic and little more seems to be heard of it. The R.A.S.E., encouraged by the numerous machines brought forward in America, Germany, Denmark and Sweden since about 1840, offered a prize in 1879, but no entry was made.[38]

The Scottish machine invented by Mr. Stewart Nicholson, of Bombie, Kirkcudbright, assisted by John Gray, was shown at the "Royal" show at Doncaster in 1891, where it was awarded a silver medal. Cow's horns with indiarubber cushions were fixed on the teats of the cow. Flexible pipes from these passed to another pipe connected with an airtight milking pail. An air pump, driven by hand or power, created a vacuum, and the milk was thus drawn from the cow into the bucket, the passage of the milk being seen through a narrow window. When the milk was all drawn from the udder, the horns fell off and then the operator passed one tube from teat to teat to strip the cow. This was a continuous suction apparatus. Although the report of the R.A.S.E. declared that it had overcome the difficulty of earlier machines which had drawn the blood down into the teat so that it was left in a congested state, showing that an unnatural pressure had been applied, the inventors soon found on their own farms that this difficulty persisted.[39] Perhaps this was why John M'Cullock said that machine milking had been found defective and entirely given up by 1875.[40]

Mr. Steward Nicholson was considering the possibility of designing a milking machine in 1888, but he was not the first in the field, a machine being patented in 1889 by William Murchland, of Kilmarnock, a sanitary engineer or plumber. This was a continuous suction machine, the vacuum being created by water and worked by gravitation. Richard Henderson, reporting on it in 1890, said that the principle was even then no new one, and that numerous milking machines on the same lines as Mr. Murchland's had been designed, but with no useful practical result. They were either too complicated or too cumbersome to be easily manipulated.

Murchland's apparatus was first erected on David Shaw's farm at Haining Mains and, like most other farming inventions, suffered from the antagonism of the workers, in this case, girl milkers.[41] There was a lack of competent hand milkers in this, the premier dairy district of Scotland, and possibly this encouraged the farmers to take up the milking machine. John Speir, of Newton Farm, Newton, Glasgow, who used one of Murchland's from March 1892, thought that it did not milk sufficiently clean, but he found no other disadvantage. He felt that mechanical milking could be tried without any anxiety.[42]

In that year W. N. Nicholson and Sons, of Newark-on-Trent, showed a Danish machine, Jens Neilsen's patent, a very crude affair, suspended from a cradle fitted across the back of the cow. The milking was done by an apparatus consisting of "two pairs of cushions, covered with india-rubber, having an approaching, rocking and receding movement, produced by eccentrics working on either side driven with a chain and crank handle. The upper edges close first on the upper part of the teat and as they open the lower edges close in a similar manner. . . . " Suction was obtained by this pressure, not unlike hand milking, but the machine was difficult to fit, and was found to strip the front and not the back teats when it was tried at Heathcote Dairy Farm, belonging to Lord Warwick. The cows did not object to it, but the one in the picture certainly looks a trifle astonished. The labour of working the crank handle was at least equal to hand milking, so there was little or no saving.

It was not until the pulsator principle was adopted that the milking machine became a really practical machine. This was patented by Dr. Alexander Shields, of Glasgow, who showed the Thistle Mechanical Milking Machine at the Royal Show in 1895. This machine produced intermittent suction similar to that of a calf sucking and the cows stood quite quietly while it was working. The suction was not always successful and the machine failed to work with some cows. It had several disadvantages from the practical point of view. "All the moving parts were driven directly by mechanical power and the pulsator had to be placed quite near the power source and connected to the power source by a long range of tubing, entailing great waste of power." In other words the vacuum make and break operated at the pump itself and through the whole overhead pipe system. This required a large air pump and was very noisy. I have been told that it could be heard as far as two miles away when working soon after dawn at the morning milking. It was described in the R.A.S.E. *Journal* as like "the Laidley worm in the gruesome Northumbrian legend, taking ten cows' milk to breakfast." It was found impossible to keep the milk tubing reasonably clean. Large volumes of air had to be passed through the tubes to release suction and give pulsation, causing contamination of the milk and adding greatly to the cost of maintaining the vacuum. The cost of the machine was also very high. Nevertheless a great many were erected both in this country and abroad.[43]

The Highland and Agricultural Society in 1898 carried out trials of milking machines in what was rather an original way. They set up a committee of experts who visited farms where milking machines had been installed and judged the machines on efficiency and cleanness in milking, effect on teats and udders of the cows, quality of milk, facilities for cleaning the parts of the machine and power required. Only two types were available for examination, the Murchland and the Thistle. As a result an award of £50 was made to the Murchland that fulfilled the conditions laid down and was a practical success.[44]

Two years later the R.A.S.E. held a trial. Again only two machines were entered, the Murchland and the Lawrence and Kennedy. The latter was an adaptation of the Thistle, that company having become defunct. One of the directors, Mr. Kennedy, aided by Mr. Lawrence, a Glasgow engineer, made and submitted the Kennedy and Lawrence Universal Cow Milker. This machine applied the new principle of producing the pulsation near to the cows themselves by a small vacuum-driven motor on top of the milk pail. If placed between the two cows it was possible to milk them at the same time. The difficulties previously experienced were at once overcome. It was the first really practical milking machine, though the R.A.S.E. judges thought that neither of the machines efficiently fulfilled the requirements demanded and recommended that a prize should be offered for future competition.

Primrose McConnell, that great enthusiast for mechanized farming, installed about 1903 a milking machine on his farm where he had a dairy of eighty to one hundred cows. It cost him no less than £240, but he found that after he had been using it for some time the yield dropped, though at one time he was so favourably impressed that he would almost have given it a testimonial. His men were keen to make it a success, one being a born mechanic and McConnell himself was in the milking byre at five a.m. to help with the work. Later he borrowed a friend's apparatus by a different maker but still the yield went down. Then he designed and made a set embodying the good points of both. This proved simpler and more efficient. He tried it with fourteen cows, some of which were special pets that would allow him to do anything with them, but still the yield would drop; so he concluded that the milking machine in its three varieties had been no less than a disastrous failure.[45]

This dismal pronouncement did nothing to stop development. J. and R. Wallace, of Castle Douglas, showed their machine in 1905 and were awarded the R.A.S.E. silver medal. There was a shortage of good hand milkers and a really good machine would be a boon. By 1908 this machine had been altered and improved so that it appeared to the judges to have overcome "the difficulties hitherto experienced in being harmful to the cow." It was on the same general principles as the Lawrence–Kennedy machine, but instead of having one small pulsator on each pail for milking two cows, it had a tiny motor fitted to the bottom of each teat cup. Consequently it had more moving parts and was more delicate in construction.[46] In 1910 Vaccar, Ltd., produced a machine for cows milked in the field. A small air pump mounted on top of a hermetically sealed can maintained a vacuum of about thirteen pounds and the teats were pressed by indiarubber tubes that carried the milk to the can. Thus on the eve of World War I the way had been prepared for the modern developments in machine milking.

Before the days of cream separators and milking machines there was little apparatus that could be described as machinery in use in the average farm dairy. There were always cheese presses of one type and another and a wide variety of churns, some of them shaken by an astonishing set of horse gear.[47] By the end of the century there was a sufficient variety of power and other churns for the R.A.S.E. to hold a trial in 1894, but the development of pasturizing, refrigerating and sterilizing plant came rather later.

CHAPTER SEVEN

BRIEF RETROSPECT

WRITERS OF DIDACTIC treatises on farming during the four centuries here reviewed made lists of the articles required to stock a farm. Included was a catalogue of the implements necessary, or considered necessary, at the different dates. These lists indicate the degree of mechanization then possible, if not practical, on every farm. They show the slow progress of invention until the industrial era, when it became possible to make almost any type of machine in large numbers, and, with the development of good roads, canals and railways, to transport the machines to every corner of the land.

The first of these writers was Fitzherbert in 1523. He does not provide a list and the only implements he describes are ploughs and harrows. Thomas Tusser, half a century later, added a roller and supplied, in not unamusing verses, a long list of hand tools, including flails, sickles and scythes. Barnaby Googe in the last years of Elizabeth did the same. Trenching ploughs were added in the late seventeenth century by John Worlidge. The first real advance in mechanization was the production of the seed-drill and the horse hoe in the reign of Queen Anne by Jethro Tull, after nearly a century of theorizing about drilling by his English predecessors.

A little later the winnowing machine was produced in Scotland

and the threshing machine soon afterwards in the same country. During the eighteenth century a large number of types of seed-drill and of cultivating implements were devised, including the spiky roller. Iron ploughs, too, were made, and development took place both in the theory and practice of plough design. It might be said that the advanced farmer of the later years of George III's reign required more than one design of plough, different harrows and cultivators, rollers, seed-drills suited to sowing cereals, roots and manure; and, if he was absolutely up-to-date, a threshing machine worked by hand, wind, water or horse-power, and a winnowing or dressing machine.

During the nineteenth century, and especially in the long reign of Queen Victoria, mechanism advanced apace. The reaping machine was experimented with and became practical by 1851; the grass mower following shortly after. The threshing machine was perfected during the same period, and a dressing apparatus was usually included in it by the end of the century.

Steam engines were applied to driving the miscellaneous barn machinery that was rapidly developing into its modern form. This was followed by the application of steam to ploughing, cultivating and other operations of arable farming. It reached its climacteric just before World War I.

During all this time the ordinary implements were being improved in the factories, where they were now made. Standardization enabled the farmer to obtain spare parts.

The growing acreage of potatoes created a need for special implements and machines for dealing with this crop, and the last two decades of the century saw the introduction of the new dairy machinery.

Such in brief outline is the development that has been described in some detail in the preceding chapters. It was this development that laid the foundation for the very rapid mechanization of farming in Britain during the past few decades.

NOTES

CHAPTER I

¹ *Walter of Henley's Husbandry*, ed. by Cunningham and Lamond, pp. 16 and 17.

² *The Shepherd's Life*, 1910.

³ Jour. Min. Agric., XXXI (Feb. 1925), p.985.

⁴ *Palladius on Hosebondrie* (Early English Text Soc.), p. 150. Sarmint—Latin, Sarmenta, clippings from plants, especially vines.

⁵ *The Boke of Husbandry* in *Certain Ancient Tracts*, 1767, p.72.

⁶ *Surveyinge*, 1523(?), Ch. XXXIV.

⁷ Robert Plot, *Natural History of Staffordshire*, 1686.

⁸ *Five hundred points of good husbandry,*1577, ed. by William Mavor, 1812.

⁹ Janus Dubravius, *A Newe Booke of Good Husbandry*, tr. by George Churchey 1599, p.14. *Maison Rustique*, tr. by Richard Surflet 1600, p. 679. John Norden, *The Surveyor's Dialogue*, 1607, pp. 188, 231. Gervase Markham, *The Inrichment of the Weald of Kent*, 1625, p. 16. Gabriel Reeve, *Directions for the Improvement of Barren and Healthy Land*, 1670, p. 32. John Smith, *England's Improvement Revived*, 1670, p. 37.

¹⁰ *Maison Rustique*, 1600, p.637.

¹¹ *The Surveyor's Dialogue*, 1607, pp. 193, 198.

¹² *Most improved and long experienced water works*, 1610.

¹³ John Aubrey, *Memoirs of naturall remarques in the county of Wiltshire*, ed. by John Britton, 1847, p. 51.

¹⁴ George Boswell, *A Treatise of Watering Meadows*, 1779.

¹⁵ John Worlidge, *Systema Agricultura*, 1675, p. 23. Richard Blome, *The Gentleman's Recreation*, 1686, pt. VI, p. 209. Francis Forbes, *The Improvement of Waste Lands*, 1778, *et al.*

¹⁶ *The English Improver Improved*, 3rd ed. 1653, pp. 10, 36, 67–71 (1st ed. 1649).

¹⁷ Robert Plot, *Natural History of Oxfordshire*, 1677, pp. 249, 356.

¹⁸ Stephen Switzer, *Practical Fruit Gardener*, 1724, pp. 24, 25. Jethro Tull, *New Horse Houghing Husbandry*, 1731, p. 15. A. Hunter, *Georgical Essays*, 1770–2, III, p. 145 ff.

¹⁹ Wm. Ellis, *The Modern Husbandman*, 1750, Vol. I, p. 109.

²⁰ *Modern Land Steward*, 1801, p. 254. John Johnstone, *Account of Elkington's System*, 1801, p. 166. *Third Report of Select Committee*, 1836, p. 7. *Quarterly Journal of Agriculture*, IV, 501 ff. and XI, 68 ff.

²¹ John Evelyn, *Discourse of Earth*, 1676, pp. 86, 87. Tim. Nourse, *Campania Foelix*, 1700, p. 39. Robert Maxwell, *Select Trans. Soc. of Improvers*, 1743, p. 17. Wm. Ellis, *op. cit.* John Lawrence, *New System of Agric.*, 1726, p. 61 ff.

R. Bradley, *Riches of a Hop Garden*, 1729, p. 10, and other works. A. Young, *Farmer's Letters*, 1767, p. 240.

[22] *Six Weeks Tour*, 1768, pp. 55, 61.

[23] *Eastern Tour*, 1771, Vol. I, pp. 66, 80, 190, 230, 248, 391. Vol. II, pp. 200, 227, 481. Vol. III, pp. 29, 141, 357. Vol. IV, p. 80.

[24] Richard Bradley, *Complete Body of Husbandry*, 1727, p. 33 ff. William Ellis, *Chiltern and Vale Farming*, 1733, p. 326. *Reports of House of Commons Select Committee* 1836, III, p. 7.

[25] *The Modern Husbandman*, 1750, I, p. 109.

[26] *The Whole Art of Husbandry*, 4th ed., 1716, I, p. 49.

[27] *English Improver*, 1649, p. 28.

[28] Robert Dossie, *Memoirs of Agriculture*, 1771, Vol. II.

[29] *True Theory and Practice of Husbandry*, 1777.

[30] *By a Society of Gentlemen*, 1766.

[31] *Memoirs of Agriculture*, 1768, I, pp. 12, 79.

[32] *Farmer's Tour through the East of England*, 1771, I, p. 61; II, pp. 237, 483, 518 ff.

[33] *ibid.* IV, p. 473 ff.

[34] *Farmers' Practical Instructor*, 1826, p. 97.

[35] *Museum Rusticum*, II, p. 307.

[36] James Brome, *Travels over England*, 1700, pp. 56 and 100.

[37] John Johnstone, *An account of the mode of draining land . . . system practised by Mr. Joseph Elkington*, 3rd ed., 1808.

[38] Ernle, *English farming, past and present*, 1932, p. 363.

[39] A. Lawson, *Farmer's Practical Instructor*, 1826, p. 535, Fig. VII.

[40] *Quarterly Jour. of Agric.*, N.S. 1847–49, p. 372 and 1849–51, p. 563. *Jour R.A.S.E.*, IV, p. 269 ff.; V, p. 273.

[41] *English Farming Past and Present*, 1932, pp. 363–364.

[42] *Scottish Jour. of Agric.*, VI (1923), p. 82. An early recommendation of the herring-bone pattern of drains is to be found in Gabriel Plattes, *A Discovery of Infinite Treasure*, 1639, p. 51.

[43] G. E. Fussell, *The Dawn of High Farming in England*, Agric. History, April 1948, pp. 83–84. Scott Watson and Mary Elliott Hobbs, *Great Farmers*, 1937, *Farmer's Magazine*, September 1846, p. 191–197.

[44] *Jour. R.A.S.E.*, I (1840), pp. 252–256 (drawing on p. 252).

[45] Josiah Parkes, *Report on drain tiles and drainage*, IV, 1843. Jour. R.A.S.E., pp. 369–379. *Evidence on the antiquity of thorough drain-draining*, collected by Ph. Pusey, *ibid.*, pp. 23–49.

[46] Josiah Parkes, *On the influence of water . . .*, *ibid.* V (1844–45), pp. 119–160. *On the cheapest method of making and burning draining tiles*, *ibid.*, pp. 551–559.

[47] J. Bailey Denton, *On land drainage . . . by loans . . .* Jour. R.A.S.E., 1868, pp. 123–143.

[48] Henry Evershed, *The agric. of Staffordshire*, Jour. R.A.S.E., 1869, p. 307, 308. Lawson, *op. cit.* p. 98 cf. William Lester, *History of British Implements*, 1804, p. 186 ff. Andrew Gray, *Ploughwright's Assistant*, 1808, p. 137 ff.

Reports of H. of C. Select Committee, 1836, ii, 80; iii, 6. *Quarterly Jour. of Agric.*, IX, p. 388 ff. and N.S. 1849–51, p. 562.

⁴⁹ A. Lawson. *Farmer's Practical Instructor*, 1827. p. 98
⁵⁰ *Patent Spec.*, Nos. 2195 and 2373.
⁵¹ *Jour. R.A.S.E.*, 1843, pp. 38 and 40.
⁵² Arthur Young, *General View . . . Agriculture, Essex*, 1807, II, pp. 166–203.
⁵³ Thomas Rudge, *General View . . . Agric., Gloucester*, 1807, pp. 260–263. William Marshall, *Review of the County Reports*, 1818, ii, p. 439.
⁵⁴ *Letters and Papers . . . Bath and West Society*, 1799, ix, p. 110.
⁵⁵ *Annals of Agric.*, 1801, v. 36, p. 399.
⁵⁶ *Jour. R.A.S.E.*, 1851, p. 639.
⁵⁷ *ibid.*, 1850, p. 459.
⁵⁸ *ibid.*, 1854, p. 367.
⁵⁹ *ibid.*, 1859, p. 326.
⁶⁰ J. C. Morton, *Cyclopaedia of Agric.*, 1856, art., Drainage.
⁶¹ Dan Pidgeon, *The evolution of agricultural implements*, Jour. R.A.S.E., 1892, p. 255.
⁶² Dan Pidgeon, *The Development of Agricultural Machinery*, Jour. R.A.S.E., 1890, p. 261.
⁶³ *Jour. R.A.S.E.*, 1881, p. 620.
⁶⁴ Dan Pidgeon, *Jour. R.A.S.E.*, 1892, p. 256.
⁶⁵ R. Scott Burn, *The Practical Directory for the Improvement of Landed Property*, 1881, pp. 186–191 and *Outlines of Modern Farming*, 1888, p. 166 ff.
⁶⁶ pp. 44–45.
⁶⁷ *Land drainage from the field to the sea*, 1919, pp. 154–162.

CHAPTER II (A)

¹ In the book of that title, privately printed by E. Parmalee Prentice, New York, 1947.
² Dan Pidgeon, *The evolution of agricultural implements*, Jour. R.A.S.E., 1892, p. 49–50, cf. J. B. Passmore, *The English Plough*, 1930, Plate II.
³ Vinogradoff, *The Growth of the Manor*, 1905, p. 44 and notes 15 and 16 cf. *The Standard Encyclopaedia of Modern Agriculture*, 1910, p. 250.
⁴ H. G. Richardson, *The Medieval Plough Team*, History, March 1942, pp. 287–296.
⁵ *Walter of Henley's Husbandry*, ed. Lamond, 1890.
⁶ Vinogradoff, *Villeinage in England*, 1892, p. 315 citing Harl, M.S. 1006.
⁷ *Annals of Agriculture*, XXIX (1797), p. 511–520.
⁸ *Facts and Observations relative to sheep, wool, ploughs and oxen*, 3rd ed., 1809, cf. John Worlidge, *Systema Agricultura*, 1675, p. 233. John Lawrence, *A new system of Agric.*, 1726, p. 56. Edward Lisle, *Observations on Husbandry*, 1756, p. 34.
⁹ *Certain ancient tracts . . . reprinted 1767*, Husbandry, pp. 1–2.

[10] *The Epitome of the Art of Husbandry*, 1669.

[11] *Foure bookes of Husbandrie*, 1577.

[12] See Arthur Bryant, *The England of Charles II*.

[13] See Thomas Tusser, *Five Hundred Points of Good Husbandry*, 1573, ed. by Wm. Mavor, 1812.

[14] Ed. of 1568, fol. XI.

[15] Gervase Markham, *The English Husbandman*, 1613, Chap. III and IV.

[16] *ibid.*, *The Whole Art of Husbandry*, 1631, pp. 36 *et. seq.*

[17] Samuel Hartlib, *His Legacie or an enlargement of the Discourse of Husbandry used in Brabant and Flanders*, 1651, pp. 5–7, cf. *ibid. The Compleat Husbandman*, 1659.

[18] *Agricultural Mechanism*, 1810, p. 1.

[19] Ad. Speed, *Adam out of Eden*, 1659, p. 84.

[20] *The English Improver*, 1649.

[21] J. B. Passmore, *The English Plough*, 1930, pp. 6 and 9.

[22] *ibid.*, p.9.

[23] J. W., Gent, *Systema Agriculturae*, 1675, p. 255.

[24] J. Sha, *Certaine plaine and easie Demonstrations of divers easie ways . . . for Improving . . . barren land*, 1657, p. 2, Anon. *An Easie and profitable order in tilling of Ground to improve it and make it fertile* (c. 1657), p. 4.

[25] Robert Plot, *The Natural History of Staffordshire*, 1686, p. 352.

[26] *Observations in Husbandry*, 1757, p. 36.

[27] *op. cit.* pp. 223–226.

[28] *Whole Art of Husbandry*, 1707, pp. 36–44.

[29] *Ichnographia Rustica*, 1718, III, pp. 225–238.

[30] *New System of Agriculture*, 1726, pp. 55–58.

[31] *Chiltern and Vale farming explained*, 1733, pp. 307–326.

[32] *op. cit.*, pp. 39 and 40, cf., Switzer *op. cit.*, p. 225.

[33] John Houghton, *A Collection of Letters for the Improvement of Husbandry and Trade*, 1681–83, ii, pp. 34–36.

[34] J. Allen Ransome, *The Implements of Agriculture*, 1843, p. 13.

[35] *Chiltern and Vale Farming*, p. 161.

[36] *Essays on Agricultural Machines*, 1810, cf. Rev. John M. Wilson, *Rural Encyclopaedia*, 1849, art. Ploughs.

[37] Dan Pidgeon, *op. cit.*, 1892, p. 53.

[38] *Patent Spec.*, No. 518.

[38a] Robert Brown of Markle, *Treatise of Rural Affairs*, 1811, i, p. 232.

[39] Matthew Peters, *Agricultura, or the Good Husbandman*, 1776.

[40] *The Modern Improvements of Agriculture*, 1774, p. 23 *et. seq.*

[41] *Observations on the tillage of the earth and the theory of implements adopted to this end*, 1777.

[42] *A letter on the Construction and Use of the Improved Foot Plough*, 1784.

[43] Matthew Peters, *Agricultura*, 1776, Intro.

[44] *The Rational Farmer*, 1771, p. 99.

[44a] R. W. David Ure, *General View . . . Agric. . . . Kinross*, 1797, p. 26.

[45] T. Sullivan, *Remarks on Ploughing*, Farmer's Magazine, March 1845, p. 198

[46] *Essay on the construction of the Plough*, 1795.

[47] *The Ploughwright's Assistant*, 1808.

[48] *Mathematical Construction of the Plough* in *Essays on Agricultural Mechanics*, 1810.

[49] Capt. Thomas Williamson, *Agricultural Mechanism*, 1810.

[50] Vol. I, p. 409 *et. seq.*

[51] *The Implements of Agriculture*, 1843, p. 25.

[52] Dossie, *op. cit.*, i, p. 12.

[53] *Facts and Observations on Sheep, Wool, Ploughs and Oxen*, 1809, pp. 129–130.

[54] *Annals of Agriculture*, XXIX, p. 514.

[55] p. 113.

[56] *ibid.*, XXIX, p. 118.

[57] Thomas Day, *History of Sandford and Merton*, 1783, iii, pp. 299, 300.

[58] *Annals of Agriculture*, III, 50.

[59] *Annals of Agriculture*, XXIX, 520. Prizes were at this period given on other tests of excellence, as, for example, a prize of "five guineas and a silver cup by the Bath Society in 1784 for ploughing 442 acres of land with a pair of horses without a driver." *ibid.*, III, 50.

[60] *Annals of Agriculture*, XXIX, p. 332.

[61] *Annals of Agriculture*, XIX, p. 332.

[62] *ibid.*, p. 511.

[63] *ibid.*, p. 331.

[64] *Letters and Communications addressed to the Bath Agricultural Society* (Ed. 1788), II, p. 185.

[65] *op. cit.*, p. 141.

[66] *Annals of Agriculture*, XXXII, 154. Journal R.A.S.E., 3rd series, VIII, p. 9.

[67] *Annals of Agriculture*, XXXII, 154.

[68] *Facts and Observations on Sheep, Wool, Ploughs and Oxen*, p. 143.

[69] *For an account of measurements of draught with a dynomometer in 1839*, see Jour. R.A.S.E., I, 140, 219.

[70] e. g. Cardigan, *Annals of Agriculture*, XXIX, 278; Sussex, *ibid.*, p. 587; Manchester, XXXII, 635; Lancaster, *ibid.*, 629.

[71] *R.A.S.E. Journal*, IV, 467.

[72] *ibid.*, 453.

[73] *Journal of Bath and West of England Soc.* (1871), III, p. 197.

[74] Arthur Young, *Eastern Tour*, 1771, ii, p. 212. *ibid.*, *Gen. View . . . Agric . . . Suffolk*, 1794, p. 24. William and Hugh Raynbird, *The Agric . . . of Suffolk*, 1849, pp. 91, 181–182, 195.

[75] Young, *Eastern Tour*, ii, pp. 523–560, *ibid.*, *On the Husbandry of Three Celebrated Farmers*, 1811, pp. 20–21.

[76] *ibid.*, pp. 33–37. Somerville, *op. cit.* pp. 129–132.

[77] J. C. Loudon, *Encyclopaedia of Agriculture*, 1825, Art. Plough. Rev. John M. Wilson, *Rural Encyclopaedia*, 1849, Art. Plough.

[78] *op. cit.*, p. 191.

[79] *Rules, Orders and Premiums of the South Devon Division* (of the Society), 1792, p. 18.

[80] *Annals of Agriculture*, 1799, XXXII, p. 154, cf., Jour. R.A.S.E., 1897, p. 9.

[81] Somerville, *op. cit.*, p. 141 ff.

[82] J. Edward Ransome, *Double Furrow Ploughs. A lecture to Framlingham Farmers' Club*, 1872, lent to me by Messrs. Ransomes, Sons and Jeffries, Ltd. cf. *British Husbandry*, 1837, i, p. 183, ii, p. 15. Loudon, *op. cit.*, 1825.

[83] *Ransome's Royal Records*, 1789–1939, n.d., pp. 39–41. *Patent Specn.*, 1468.

[84] *Rural Economy of Norfolk*, 1787, i, pp. 53, 54.

[85] Robert Brown of Markle, *op. cit.*, i, p. 236. Richard Parkinson, *The English Practice of Agriculture*, 1806, p. 212.

[86] William Pitt, *Gen. View of . . . Leicester*, 1808.

[87] Charles Vancouver, *Gen. View of . . . Hampshire*, 1813, p. 94.

[88] Sir John Sinclair, *Hints on the Netherlands*, 1815, p. 81, f.n.

[89] Somerville, *op. cit.*

[90] In C. W. Johnson and Edward Cressy, *The Cottages of Agricultural Labourers*, 1847.

[91] *Descriptions of some of the utensils in husbandry . . . sold by James Sharp*, n.d., c. 1773.

[92] William Marshall, *Rural Economy of the Midland Counties*, 1796.

[93] *Rural Economy of the Southern Counties*, 1798, i, pp. 59, 60.

[94] *Standard Cyclopaedia of Modern Agriculture*, ed. by Prof. R. Patrick Wright, 1910, p. 250.

[95] Williamson, *op. cit.*, p. 195.

[96] *Rural Economy of the West of England*, 1796, i, pp. 123–125, 294, 310, ii, p. 117.

[97] cf. Henry Hamilton, *The Industrial Revolution in Scotland*, 1932.

[98] *Analysis of the Statistical Account of Scotland*, 1825, p. 232, cf. M. Martin, *A Description of the Western Islands of Scotland*, 1716, p. 53.

[99] See my *The Breast Plough* in Man, XXXII (1933), 116.

[100] John Randall, *Observations on the Structure and use of the spiky roller in Museum Rusticum*, 1766, vi, pp. 371–374, cf. Randall, *The Semi-Virgilian Husbandry*, 1764, App. p. 1.

[101] *New Experiments in Husbandry for the Month of April*, 1736, p. 17.

[102] *Museum Rusticum*, 1766, VI, Editor's note. Thomas Bowden, *The Farmer's Director*, 1776, p. 41.

[103] John Mortimer, *Whole Art of Husbandry*, 1707, p. 43, *et. seq.*

[104] *Rural Economy of Norfolk*, 1787, i, p. 59. *Modern Improvements*, 1774, p. 18. Wm. Amos, *Minutes of Agriculture*, 1804, p. 74.

[105] See his *Treatise on Agricultural Subjects*, 1822, and *British Farmer*, 1825.

[106] I have *The Third Report of Drummond's Agricultural Museum*, 1835.

[107] *Catalogue of the Museum of the Highland and Agricultural Soc.*, 1844.

[108] *A Cyclopaedia of Practical Husbandry*, 1839, Art. Plough.

[109] See also David Low, *Elements of Agriculture*, 1843, and James Hunter, *The Improved Scotch Swing Plough*, 1843.

[110] *The English Plough*, 1930, p. 22.

[111] Philip Pusey, *Present state of the science of agric. in England*, Jour. R.A.S.E., 1840, p. 8.

[112] *op. cit.*, p. 74.

[113] See Rev. John M. Wilson, *Rural Cyclopaedia*, 1849. G. H. Andrews, *Modern Husbandry*, 1853. John C. Morton, *Cyclopaedia of Agric.*, 1856. James Slight and R. Scott Burn, *The Book of Farm Implements and Machines*, 1858. J. Donaldson, *British Agric.*, 1860. Samuel Copland, *Agric. Ancient and Modern*, 1866, etc.

[114] *The Wheelwright's Shop*, 1923, p. 155, cf., *Mark Lane Express*, June 5th, 1922, a letter on *Farming Fifty Years Ago*, by J.M.B.

Chapter II (B)

[1] Much of the material used here is reproduced by permission from an essay on "Steam Cultivation" that appeared in *Engineering*, Aug. and Sept. 1943.

[2] Robert Scott Burn, *Mechanical aids to steam culture*, Jour. of Agric., 1857, p. 545, cf. John Algernon Clarke, *Account of the application of steam power to the cultivation of the land*, Jour. R.A.S.E., XX, 1859.

[3] Ernle, *English farming past and present*, pp. 369–370, 387.

[4] *Chronicles of a Clay Farm*, 1857.

[5] Burn, *op. cit.*, pp. 546–547. Forbes, *The progress and present position of steam as applied to agric.*, Jour. of Agric., 1865–66, p. 493. Samuel Copland *Agric. Ancient and Modern*, 1866, i, p. 593.

[6] pp. 248–251.

[7] p. 240.

[8] Forbes, *op. cit.*, p. 493. Copland, *op. cit.*, pp. 592–605. Slight and Burn, *op. cit.*, pp. 228–234. J. Donaldson, *British Agric.*, 1860, i, 217–221.

[9] *Mechanics Magazine*, Aug. 14, 1852 (lent by Rothamsted).

[10] Much of the information in Clarke's paper is summarized in Baldwin Latham *On the application of steam to the cultivation of the soil*, Trans. Soc. Engineers, 1868.

[11] Burn, *op. cit.*, p. 548.

[12] An old Norfolk Farmer, *Steam Culture*, Jour. of Agric., 1861, pp. 116–133.

[13] Samuel Copland, *op. cit.*, pp. 599–600, provides an estimate.

[14] *ibid.*, p. 603.

o

[15] *The History of the Royal Agricultural Society of England,* 1839–1939, p. 93.

[16] *Mechanics Mag.,* November 24, 1855. *Pat. Spec.* 618 of 1855.

[17] H. S. Thompson, *Agricultural Progress and the Royal Agric. Soc.,* Jour. Roy. Agric. Soc., XXV, 1864, cf. Ernle, *English Farming past and present,* p. 370.

[18] *op. cit.,* p. 500.

[19] *History of the English Landed Interest,* II, (1893), pp. 153–154.

[20] *An economic history of modern Britain, II. Free trade and steel,* 1932, pp. 267–268.

CHAPTER III

[1] There are two authoritative modern studies of the history of the seed-drill and seed drilling to which this chapter necessarily owes a great deal. They are: T. H. Marshall, *Jethro Tull and the "New Husbandry" of the Eighteenth Century,* Economic History Review II (Jan. 1929), pp. 41–60, and Russell H. Anderson, *Grain Drills through thirty-nine centuries,* Agricultural History, 10 (Oct. 1936), pp. 157–205.

[2] *Rural Economy,* 1770, p. 314.

[3] *Who invented the sowing machine?* (trans'd title), Nouva Vita Rurale, VII, Nov. 1935, pp. 264–267.

[4] A. J. des Carrieres, *A dissertation on Virgil's description of the ancient Roman plough,* 1788. Dedication.

[5] W. L. Braley, *Some 4730 years of grain drill history,* Farm Implement News, May 1, 1930.

[6] Ernle, *English farming past and present,* 1912, p. 104.

[7] Sir Hugh Plat, *The newe and admirable Arte of Setting of Corne,* 1601, Chap. I.

[8] *ibid.,* chap. 4.

[9] *ibid.,* chap. 5.

[10] Ed. Maxey, *A New Instruction of Plowing and Setting of Corne,* 1601, D. 3, E, 2 ff.

[11] *Pat. Spec.* No. 115.

[12] Gabriel Plattes, *A Discovery of Infinite Treasure,* 1639, p. 50.

[13] Ernle, *op. cit.,* p. 171.

[13a] Samuel Hartlib, *Legacie,* 1651, pp. 89.

[14] (In two letters addressed to Hartlib), p. 9.

[15] Walter Blith, *The English Improver Improved,* 1652. Address to the Industrious Reader.

[16] *ibid.,* p. 12.

[17] *Systema Agricultura,* 1669, p. 47 ff. *A Complete System of Husbandry and Gardening,* 1716, p. 76 ff.

[18] Ernle, *op. cit.*

[19] *op. cit.,* p. 169.

[20] Phil. Trans., 1670–75 (60), 1035–1065.

²¹ See Anderson, *op. cit.*, p. 165 f.n. Braley, *op. cit.*, and the Italian article quoted above.

²² Anderson, p. 165.

²³ See Marshall, *op. cit.* Anderson, *op. cit.*, cf. my *More old English farming Books; Tull to the Board of Agriculture*, 1950.

²⁴ *op. cit.*, p. 43.

²⁵ *Rural Economy*, 1770, pp. 315, 320–341.

²⁶ Mills repeats all this in his own *New System of Practical Husbandry*, 1767, ii, p. 1, *et. seq.*

²⁷ Anon., *The Farmer's Compleat Guide*, 1760, p. 35.

²⁸ *The Construction and use of a newly invented Seed-Furrow Plough*, 1764.

²⁹ A. Hunter, *Georgical Essays*, 1770–72, iii, Essay 3.

³⁰ *Farmer's Mag.*, 1777, ii, p. 190, *Description of Utensils of Husbandry sold by James Sharp*, 1773.

³¹ *Annals of Agriculture*, 1785, iii, *Reviews of Publications*.

³² David Young, *National Improvements upon Agriculture*, 1785, App. 388–400.

³³ In his book *The Extensive Practice of the New Husbandry*, 1786, p. 1.

³⁴ George Winter, *A New and Compendious System of Husbandry*, 1787, pp. 295–315.

³⁵ *The description and use of the new invented Universal Sowing Machine*, 1786.

³⁶ *Cooke's Improved Patent Drill and Horse Hoe*, 1789.

³⁷ *Phytologia*, 1800. Appendix.

³⁸ William Amos, *The Theory and Practice of Drill Husbandry*, 1794, pp. 123–180.

³⁹ J. Allen Ransome, *Implements of Agric.*, 1843, pp. 101–103. Richard Noverre Bacon, *Agric. of Norfolk*, 1844, p. 335.

⁴⁰ Marshall, *Norfolk*, 1787, i, p. 59.

⁴¹ Anderson, *op. cit.*, p. 175, f.n. 17.

⁴² See *General View* of each of the counties mentioned, 1794 edition.

⁴³ *Gen. View of Agric. of Suffolk*, 1794, pp. 24, 25, 55, *ibid.*, 1804, pp. 69–75, 350–408.

⁴⁴ *East Anglian Daily Times*, July 6th, 1901, cf. J. Allen Ransome, *op. cit.*, p. 104. Richard Noverre Bacon, *Norfolk*, 1844, p. 336.

⁴⁵ Bacon, *op. cit.*, pp. 337, 338. Ransome, *op. cit.*, p. 106–109.

⁴⁶ *Agricultural Magazine*, July 1811, viii, p. 59.

⁴⁷ Ransome, *op. cit.*, pp. 109–112.

⁴⁸ Robert Forsyth, *Principles and Practice of Agriculture*, 1804, ii, pp. 261–268. R. W. Dickson, *Practical Agric.*, 1805, i, Plate viii. Richard Parkinson, *Experienced Farmer*, 1807, i, pp. 325 and 348. Robert Brown, *Treatise on Rural Affairs*, 1811, pp. 289–307.

⁴⁹ J. C. Loudon, *Encyclopaedia of Agric.*, 1831, pp. 387–388, 408–413.

⁵⁰ George Robertson, *Rural Recollections*, 1829, pp. 278–279, 330, 430.

⁵¹ *Quarterly Jour. of Agric.*, 1829–31, ii, p. 247, *et. seq.* Anon., *British Husbandry*, 1837, ii, p. 74. David Low, *Elements of Practical Agric.*, 4th ed., 1843 (1st 1834), p. 176.

[52] Anderson, *op. cit.*, p. 177.

[53] *Mechanic's Magazine*, Jan. 4, 1840. Ransome, *op. cit.*, pp. 113–114. Bacon, *op. cit.*, p. 341.

[54] Philip Pusey, *On the present state . . . of Agriculture . . .* Jour. R.A.S.E., 1840, i, p. 8.

[55] Anderson, *op. cit.*, p. 189, cf., Jour. R.A.S.E. for the years mentioned.

[56] *Catalogue of the Museum*, 1844.

[57] Advertisement already cited. Ransome, *op. cit.*, p. 117.

[58] J. C. Morton, *Cyclopaedia of Agriculture Art. Sowing Machines.*

[59] John W. Wilson, *Rural Cyclopaedia*, 1849, iv, pp. 286–287. James Slight and R. Scott Burn, *The Book of Farm Implements*, 1858, pp. 271–310.

[60] John Donaldson, *British Agriculture*, 1860, i, pp. 205–213. Samuel Copland, *Agriculture, Ancient and Modern*, 1866, i, pp. 619–624.

[61] J.B.M., *Farming Fifty Years Ago*, June 5th, 1922.

[62] A. J. Spencer and J. B. Passmore, *Handbook of the Collections illustrating Agricultural Implements and Machinery*, Science Museum, 1930, p. 19.

CHAPTER IV (A)

[1] *Liber commodorum ruralium*, 13th century; first printed at Augsberg, 1471.

[2] *Whole Art and Trade of Husbandry*, 1614, p. 40.

[3] Adam Dickson, *Husbandry of the Ancients*, 1788, ii, pp. 358 and 364.

[4] Vol. IV, 1787, p. 161.

[5] Arthur Young, *General View of the Agric. of Lincoln*, 1799, p. 70.

[6] Anon., *Patent Report on Reaping Machines and their inventors*, Qtrly. Jour. Agric. N.S., 1853–55, p. 614. A. Lawson, *The Farmer's Practical Instructor*, 1827, p. 134. J. C. Loudon, *Encyclop. of Agric.*, 2nd ed., 1831, p. 422.

[7] *Patent Report as above.* This is largely relied upon for details of patents granted before 1850, supplemented by J. C. Loudon *Encyclo.*, James Slight and Robert Scott Burn, *Book of Farm Implements and Machines*, 1858, p. 343 ff., James Slight, *Report on Reaping Machines*, trans. H. and A. Soc., XIII, 1851–53, pp. 183–195, Jacob Wilson, *ibid.*, XIX, pp. 123–149.

[8] Lawson, *op. cit.*, p. 135. Robert Brown, *Treatise of Rural Affairs*, 1811, i, p. 308.

[9] *Overlooked Pages of Reaper History*, Chicago, 1897.

[10] *Qtrly. Jour. of Agric.*, 1828–29, i, pp. 136–154.

[11] Vol. II, p. 122.

[12] Loudon, *op. cit.*, p. 424.

[13] Rev. P. Bell, *Some Account of Bell's Reaping Machine*, Qtrly. Jour. of Agric., 1853–55, pp. 185–195.

[14] *Implement and Machinery Review*, July 1876, p. 537.

[15] *On the working of Bell's Reaping Machine*, Qtrly. Jour. of Agric., 1832–34, pp. 84–89.

[16] A. Lawson, *op. cit.*, p. 135. Richard Noverre Bacon, *The Agric. of Norfolk*, 1844. William and Hugh Raynbird, *The Agric. of Suffolk* 1849.

[17] *Report on Reaping Machines*, as above.

[18] *Jour. R.A.S.E.*, 1851, pp. 587–648.

[19] See *Roots in Chicago one hundred years deep*, 1847–1947 (published by the International Harvester Co., Inc.).

[20] *Overlooked Pages of Reaper History*, Chicago, 1897, p. 516.

[21] *ibid.*, p. 51.

[22] *Account of a subsequent trial of the American Reapers*, Jour. R.A.S.E., 1851, p. 644.

[23] *Rival Reaping Machines*, Qtrly. Jour. of Agric., 1851–53, pp. 478–491.

[24] *Implement and Machinery Review*, 1876, p. 537.

[25] *Jour. R.A.S.E.*, 1852, p. 316.

[26] *Mechanics Magazine*, Aug. 21, 1852. James Wilson in Trans. H. and A. Soc., 1863–65.

[27] *Jour. R.A.S.E.*, 1853, p. 368 ff.

[28] *Competition of Reaping Machines*, Qtrly Jour. of Agric., 1853–55, pp. 175–178; 541–546.

[29] *Trans. H. and A. Soc.*, 1853–1855, pp. 190–197.

[30] *Reports on the Implements*, Jour. R.A.S.E., 1854, p. 367 ff.; 1855, p. 509 ff.; 1856, p. 577 ff. and pp. 339 and 341; 1857, p. 441 ff.

[31] *Implement and Machinery Review*, Dec. 1879, p. 2620. Bamlett's Catalogue of 1870, and other information supplied by the firm.

[32] *Jour. R.A.S.E.*, 1860, p. 490 ff.; 1861, p. 457 ff.

[33] *Trans. H. and A. Soc.*, 1863–65, pp. 123–149.

[34] *Roots in Chicago*, as above.

[35] Dan Pidgeon, *op. cit.*, Jour. R.A.S.E., 1892.

[36] H. S. Thompson, *Agricl. Progress and the Royal Agric. Soc.*, Jour. R.A.S.E., 1864.

[37] *Jour. R.A.S.E.*, 1865, p. 384 ff.; 1869, p. 530.

[38] *Trans. 4, Ser. Vol. VIII*, 1875, App. A., p. 10.

[39] *Jour. R.A.S.E.*, 1876, p. 596 ff.; 1890, p. 292. *Implement and Machinery Review*, Sept. 1876, p. 634.

[40] *Jour. R.A.S.E.*, 1877, p. 578 ff.; 1878, pp. 103–133.

[41] *Implement and Machinery Review*, Nov. 1879, p. 2555; Jan. 1880, p. 2681.

[42] *ibid.*, Jan. 1881, pp. 3331–3339.

[43] *Jour. R.A.S.E.*, 1879, p. 757 ff.

[44] *Jour. R.A.S.E.*, 1881, p. 601 ff; 1882, pp. 264–285.

[45] *Trans. H. and A. Soc.*, 4th Ser. XVI, 1883, pp. 168–176.

[46] *ibid.*, 4th Ser. VI, 1886, pp. 154–156.

[47] *Implement and Machinery Review*, Dec. 1890, p. 13464; July 1892, p. 15628; Oct. 1896, p. 20823.

[48] *Jour. R.A.S.E.*, 1891, p. 525 ff.; 1893, p. 703 ff.

[49] James Edwards, *Reaping Machines past and present*, Jour. R.A.S.E., 1900, pp. 292–299.

[50] J. B. M., *Farming fifty years ago*, Mark Lane Express, June 5th, 1922.

CHAPTER IV (B)

[1] John Middleton, *View of the Agric. of Middlesex*, 1798, and 2nd ed. 1807. Anon., *Brit. Husbandry*, 1834, i, p. 491, f.n. *Baxter's Library of Agric. Knowledge*, 1837. Rev. John M. Wilson, *Rural Encyclopaedia*, 1849, ii, p. 607, cf., Ernle, *English Farming past and present*, 1932, p. 357.

[2] Robert Scott Burn, *Outlines of Modern Farming*, 1888, Pt. I, pp. 207–211.

[3] *New Royal Encyclopaedia*, c. 1820, Art. Agric. Sect., xx.

[4] W. Cashmore and J. E. Newman, *The Development of Haymaking Machinery*, Empire Journal of Experimental Agric., 1933, i, p. 58.

[5] Arthur Young, *General View . . Agric. Essex*, 1807, i, p. 152.

[6] J. C. Loudon, *Encyclopaedia of Agric.*, 2nd ed., 1831, p. 420.

[6a] cf. Dan Pidgeon, *The evolution of Agric. implements*, Jour. R.A.S.E., 1892.

[7] Loudon, *ibid.*, and p. 904. Ransome, *op. cit.*, pp. 134, 135.

[8] *Brit. Husb.*, 1834, i, pp. 494, 495.

[9] *Implement and Machinery Review*, 1930–31, p. 1029.

[10] Martin Doyle, *Cyclopaedia of Husbandry*, 1839, p. 267.

[11] *Rural Cyclo.*, 1849, ii, p. 607.

[12] Copland, *Agric. Ancient and Modern*, 1866, i, p. 641. Donaldson, *Brit. Agric.*, 1866, iii, p. 685.

[13] *Jour. R.A.S.E.*, 1842, p. 340; 1843, p. 456; 1845, p. 307.

[14] *ibid.*, 1842, p. 347.

[15] *Jour. R.A.S.E.*, 1895, p. 476.

[15a] *Jour. B. and W. Soc.*, 1853–54, Vol. I–II, pp. 188–219; 1855, Vol. III, pp. 1–30; 1859, Vol. VII, pp. 1–18.

[16] *Jour. R.A.S.E.*, 1851, p. 616.

[17] Andrews, *Agricultural Engineering*, 1852, cited in Cashmore and Newman, *op. cit.*

[18] Slight and Burn, p. 333.

[19] See Note 16.

[20] *Implement and Machinery Review*, May 1880, p. 2888–2890.

[21] *Jour. R.A.S.E.*, 1865, pp. 382; 393–398.

[22] *ibid.*, 1869, p. 542–554.

[23] *Implement and Machinery Review*, 1922–23, pp. 1383 and 1494.

[24] *ibid.*, Sept. 1921, pp. 687–689.

[25] *Practical Agric.* in Jour. R.A.S.E., 1878, p. 642.

[26] *Jour. R.A.S.E.*, p. 630 ff.

[27] Cashmore and Newman, *op. cit.*, p. 59.

[28] John Algernon Clarke, *op. cit.*, p. 642.

[29] *Jour. R.A.S.E.*, 1880, pp. 673, 677.

[30] *ibid.*, 1885, pp. 738–739.

[31] *ibid.*, 1889, p. 504.

[32] *ibid.*, 1892, p. 539 ff.

[33] *ibid.*, 1890, pp. 626–633.

[34] *Implement and Machinery Review*, Sept. 1892, p. 15808.

[35] *Jour. R.A.S.E.*, 1895, p. 477.

[36] *ibid.*, 1896, pp. 446–447. *ibid.*, 1903, pp. 239, 240.

[37] *ibid.*, 1907, pp. 121–129.

[38] Cashmore and Spencer, *op. cit.*, p. 60.

[39] *Trans. H. and A. Soc.*, 1879, 4th Ser., XI, App. A., p. 7. *Jour. B. and W. Soc.*, 1901–02, 4th Ser., XII, pp. 18–35; 1904, 5th Ser., XVI, pp. 1–10. *Implement and Machinery Review*, Oct. 1893, p. 17115.

CHAPTER V

[1] Deuteronomy, xxv, 4.

[2] Judges, vi, 11.

[3] Martin Doyle, *Cyclopaedia of Prac. Agric.*, 1839, art. *Threshing*.

[4] Ernle, *op. cit.*, p. 358.

[5] Robert Somerville, *General View of the Agric. of E. Lothian*, 1805, p. 75, cf. Robert Forsyth, *Principles and Practice of Agric.*, 1804, i, p. 296.

[5a] George Buchan Hepburn, *Gen. View . . . East Lothian*, 1794, p. 174.

[5b] Robert Maxwell of Arkland, *Select Transactions . . . of the Society*, 1743, pp. 276–277.

[6] Donald McDonald, *Agricultural Writers, 1200–1800*, 1908, p. 209.

[6a] Alexander Lowe, *Gen. View . . . of Berwick*, 1794, p. 121.

[6b] George Buchan Hepburn, *loc. cit.*

[7] Robert Somerville, *loc. cit.* Robert Forsyth, *loc. cit.*, cf. Robert Brown, *Treatise of Rural Affairs* 1811, i, p. 318.

[8] *Gen. View. of Agric. . . . Northumberland*, 1794, p. 47 and 48.

[9] Somerville, *loc. cit.*, cf. Brown, *loc. cit.*

[10] Brown, *ibid.*, pp. 319–321.

[11] Bailey and Culley, *Gen. View . . . Northumberland*, 1794, p. 48.

[12] *loc. cit.*

[13] *Political Essays*, art. *Agriculture*, 1772, cited in Russell M. Garnier, *History of the English Landed Interest*, 1893, ii, p. 298.

[14] *loc. cit.*

[15] Somerville, *loc. cit.*, cf., John Sinclair, *Analysis of the Statistical Account of Scotland*, 1825, p. 274.

[16] Bailey and Culley, *loc. cit.*

[17] *Book of Farm Implements*, p. 360.

[18] *Annals of Agric.*, Vol. III, 1785.

[19] *ibid.*, Vol. IV (1785), p. 33.

[20] George Buchan Hepburn, *op. cit.*, p. 145.

[21] *Description of . . . utensils in husb. sold by James Sharp*, 1773. Agricola Sylvan, *Farmer's Magazine*, 1777, ii, p. 311.

[22] William Marshall, *Rural Economy of Yorkshire*, 1796, i, pp. 281–284.

[22a] cf. Spencer and Passmore, *op. cit.*, pp. 69–70.

[23] John Bailey and George Culley, *Gen. View . . . of Northumberland*, 1794.

[24] *ibid.*

[25] James Donaldson, *Gen. View . . . Carse of Gowrie*, 1794, pp. 19, 20.

[26] John Francis Erskine, *Gen. View . . . Clackmannan*, 1794, p. 34.

[27] Sir John Sinclair, Bt., *Gen. View . . . Northern Counties and Islands*, 1795, p. 261.

[28] See each *General View*.

[29] See each *General View*, 1st ed., cf., *Annals of Agric.*, 1794, xxii, p. 426.

[30] *A Cardiganshire Landlord's Advice to his Tenants*, 1800, p. 53.

[31] *Annals of Agric.*, 1802, Vol. XXXVIII, p. 94; 1803, Vol. XXXIX, p. 29.

[32] Robert Forsyth, *loc. cit.* Robert Somerville, *loc. cit.* Slight and Burn, *loc. cit.*

[33] J. L. and Barbara Hammond, *The Village Labourer*, 1920, Chap. X.

[34] Martin Doyle, *loc. cit.*

[35] *Farmer's Magazine*, 1846, xiii, pp. 9 and 496.

[35a] *Jour. R.A.S.E.*, 1844, p. 384; 1842, p. cxvii.

[35b] William Heard, *The Threshing Machine*, Jour. B. and W. E. Soc., 1858, Vol. VI, pp. 114–130. Trials by the Bath and West Society had very much the same results as those of the R.A.S.E., see *Jour.*, 1855, Vol. III, pp. 1–30; 1857, Vol. V, pp. 97–110; 1858, Vol. VI, p. 15; 1859, Vol. VII, pp. 1–18.

[36] *Jour. R.A.S.E.*, 1847, pp. 335, 348 and 352.

[37] Letter of September 23, 1949, from Mr. J. F. Cooch.

[38] Advt. in C. W. Johnson and Edward Cressy, *The Cottages of Agricultural Labourers*, 1847.

[39] *Implement and Machinery Review*, 1921–22, p. 1660.

[40] *Jour. R.A.S.E.*, 1848, p. 412 ff.; 1849, p. 553 ff.; 1850, p. 470 ff.

[41] *Jour. R.A.S.E.*, 1852, p. 322.

[41a] *Implement and Machinery Review*, 1913–14, Vol. XXXIV, p. 1067; 1928–29, Vol. LIV, p. 197.

[42] *Trans. Highland and Agric. Society*, July 1849–51, pp. 124–129, cf., Slight and Burn, *op. cit.*, pp. 360–384.

[43] *Mechanics Magazine*, Nov. 13, 1852.

[43a] Spencer and Passmore, *op. cit.*, p. 70.

[44] H. S. Thompson in *Jour. R.A.S.E.*, 1852, pp. 311–323.

[45] *Implement and Machinery Review*, Feb. 1891, p. 13855.

[46] *Jour. R.A.S.E.*, 1852, p. 324.

[47] *Jour. R.A.S.E.*, 1853, pp. 347–355.

[48] *ibid.*, 1854, pp. 369–378.

[49] *Implement and Machinery Review*, March 1888, p. 10371; July 1899, obit. Thomas Nalder.

[50] *ibid.*, 1926–27, p. 511.

97. Root Cutter. From J. C. Morton, *Cyclopaedia of Agriculture*, 1856.

98. Root Cutter. From J. C. Morton, *Cyclopaedia of Agriculture*, 1856.

99. Up-to-date Barn Machinery in 1866. From Samuel Copland, *Agriculture, Ancient and Modern*, 1866.

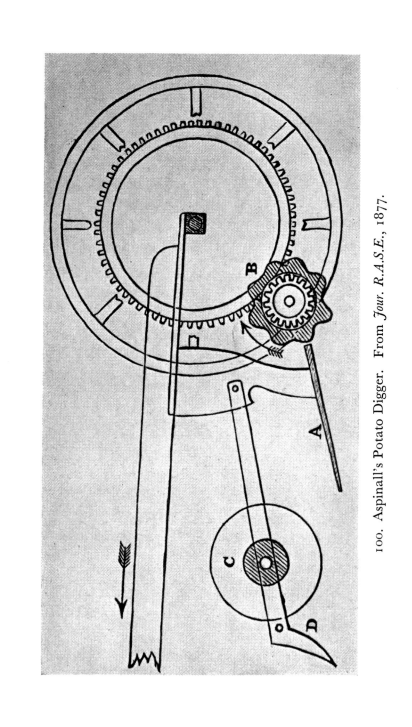

100. Aspinall's Potato Digger. From *Jour. R.A.S.E.*, 1877.

101. Holt's Potato Digger. From *Jour. R.A.S.E.*, 1893.

102. Ransome's Potato Digger.   From *Jour. R.A.S.E.*, 1893.

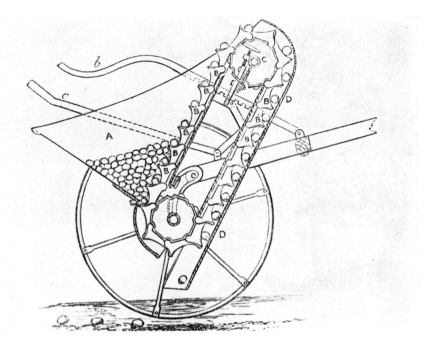

103. Murray and Co.'s Potato Planter. From *Jour. R.A.S.E.*, 1882.

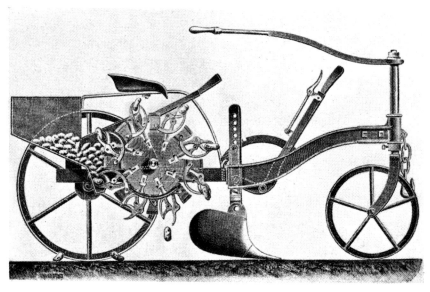

104. Ransome's Double Row Potato Planter. From *Jour. R.A.S.E.*,
1898.

105. East Yorks. Waggon Co.'s Potato Separator. From *Jour. R.A.S.E.*, 1882.

106. Lightfoot's Improved Potato Riddle. From *Jour. R.A.S.E.*, 1883.

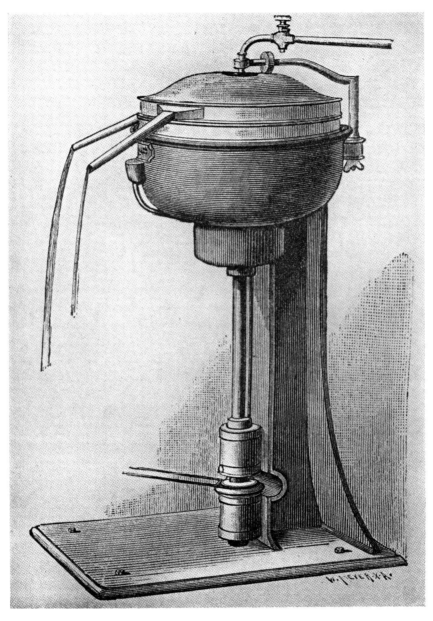

107. Laval's Improved Cream Separator. From *Jour. R.A.S.E.*, 1882.

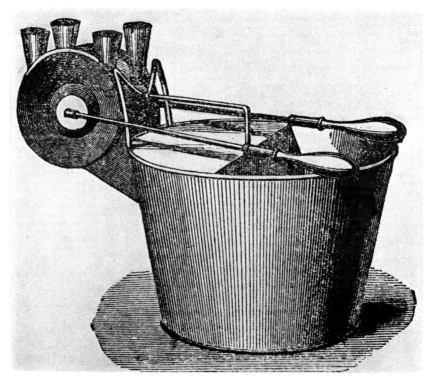

108. Milking Machine of 1862. From *Illustrated London News*, 1862.

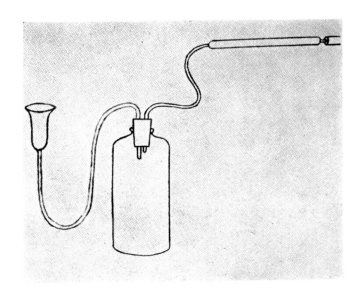

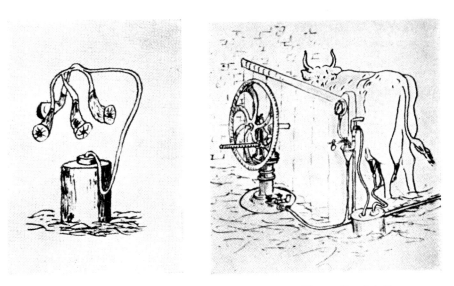

109. Nicholson and Grey Milking Machine. From *Scottish Farmer*,
6 July, 1946.

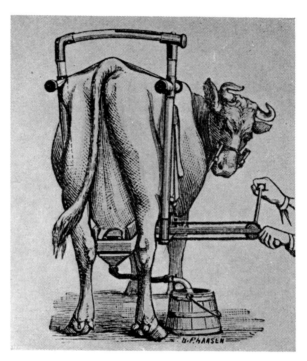

110. Danish Milking Machine. From *Jour.*
R.A.S.E., 1892.

111. Thistle Milking Machine. From *Jour. R.A.S.E.*, 1895.

[51] *Jour. R.A.S.E.*, 1860, p. 498; 1861, p. 451; 1863, p. 496–498; 1867, p. 593

[52] *On the wear and tear of agricl. steam engines and threshing machines. ibid.*, 1862, p. 323–337.

[53] I am indebted to Spencer and Passmore, *op. cit.*, pp. 70–72, for the whole of this description, as well as for that of Shearer's and Ransome's machines that follow.

[54] *Jour. R.A.S.E.*, 1863, p. 499; 1867, p. 595.

[55] *Trans.*, Vol. I, 4th Ser., 1866–67, pp. 367–370.

[56] *Jour. R.A.S.E.*, 1867, p. 601

[57] *Jour. R.A.S.E.*, 1872, pp. 404–475; 1873, p. 606 ff.

[58] *Jour. R.A.S.E.*, 1874, p. 729; 1875, p. 669.

[59] *Trans. H. and A. Soc.*, Vol. IX, 4th Ser., 1877, pp. 334–335 and 340–341.

[60] *Jour. R.A.S.E.*, 1878, p. 642; 1880, p. 664–665.

[61] *Jour. R.A.S.E.*, 1881, p. 604; 1882, p. 641; 1883, p. 584.

[62] *ibid.*, 1888, pp. 570–608.

[63] *ibid.*, 1883, p. 602; 1885, p. 719; 1886, p. 538.

[64] *Jour. R.A.S.E.*, 1891, pp. 482–496. *Implement and Machinery Review*, July, 1891.

[65] J. E. Thorold Rogers, *Six centuries of work and wages*, 1884, ii, p. 541.

[66] *Pat. Specs.* No. 3036 of 1866; No. 50 of 1874; No. 1380 of 1876 and No. 1857 of 1880.

[67] *Jour. R.A.S.E.*, 1869, pp. 554–557, cf., *Trans. H. and A. Soc.*, 1870, 4th Ser., Vol. III, pp. 291–298. *Implement and Machinery Review*, Sept. 1875, p. 153.

[68] *Jour. R.A.S.E.*, 1882, pp. 647–728. *Implement and Machinery Review*, Nov. 1882, p. 4690.

CHAPTER VI

[1] *Museum Rusticum*, 3rd ed., 1766, i, pp. 258–260; v, pp. 208–213.

[2] *ibid.*, v, pp. 386–387.

[3] Agricola Sylvan, *Farmer's Magazine*, 1777, ii, pp. 352, 391, cf. Sharp's *Description*, 1773.

[4] R. W. Dickson, *Practical Agric.*, 1805, i, pp. 32, 40

[5] Spencer and Passmore, *op. cit.*, p. 33.

[6] p. 384, Fig. 269.

[7] *Jour. R.A.S.E.*, 1841, p. cxi; 1842, p. 352; 1843, p. 487; 1844, p. 380; 1845, pp. 316, 691.

[8] Samuel Copland, *Agric. Ancient and Modern*, 1866, i, pp. 644–645.

[9] Letter of Dec. 9, 1949.

[10] John Donaldson, *Brit. Agric.*, 1866, iii, p. 687.

[11] Spencer and Passmore, *op. cit.*, p. 34.

[12] *Trans. H. and A. Soc.*, 1889, 5th Ser., Vol. I, pp. 131-132.

[13] *Encyclo. of Agric.*, 1831, p. 386.

[14] *Jour. R.A.S.E.*, 1841, p. cxv; 1910, p. 211.

[15] *ibid.*, 1842, p. 346; 1844, p. 382; 1845, p. 321.

[16] J. C. Morton, *Cyclopaedia of Agric.*, 1856, p. 1037, ff. Art. turnip slicers.

[17] Donaldson, *op. cit.*, p. 237.

[17a] Copland, *op. cit.*, p. 645–647.

[18] Spencer and Passmore, *op. cit.*, p. 37, and Sharp's *Description*.

[19] *Jour. R.A.S.E.*, 1842, p. 486; 1844, pp. 383–385; 1845, pp. 317–321; 1846, pp. 349–358.

[20] *ibid.*, 1860, pp. 500–506; 1867, pp. 603–615; 1870, pp. 468–497.

[21] Letter of Dec. 9, 1949.

[22] *Trans. H. and A. Soc.*, 1891, 5th Ser., Vol. III, p. 180.

[23] *Jour. R.A.S.E.*, 1890, pp. 604–623.

[24] *Patent Spec.* No. 1732 of 1855.

[25] *Patent Spec.* Nos. 1999, 2193, 2503 of 1858.

[26] *Trans. H. and A. Soc.* 1872, 4th Ser., Vol. IV, pp. 14–15.

[27] *ibid.*, 1877, pp. 339–340, *Implement and Machinery Review*, June 1875, p. 43.

[28] *Jour. R.A.S.E.*, 1877, p. 281; 1884, p. 740; 1887, pp. 665–666; 1888, pp. 216–224. *Implement and Machinery Review*, Nov. 1879, p. 2570; Jan. 1882, p. 4050 ff.; Nov. 1887, pp. 9995–9996.

[29] *Jour. R.A.S.E.*, 1893, pp. 560–570; 1894, p. 476; 1895, p. 466; 1902, p. 210; 1910, p. 205. *Implement and Machinery Review*, Oct. 1893, p. 17113.

[30] Spencer and Passmore, *op. cit.*, pp. 27–28.

[31] *Patent Spec.* No. 22 of 1857.

[32] *Trans. H. and A. Soc.*, 1877, 4th Ser., Vol. IX, pp. 337–339. *Implement and Machinery Review*, June 1875; Nov. 1875.

[33] *Jour. R.A.S.E.*, 1873, p. 635; 1874, pp. 627, 661; 1880, p. 661; 1887, p. 665; 1891, p. 531; 1892, pp. 547–549; 1893, p. 553; 1898, pp. 501–502. *Implement and Machinery Review*, Jan; 1896; Oct. 1897.

[34] *Jour. R.A.S.E.*, 1863, p. 503; 1882, p. 633; 1883, p. 629.

[35] *Implement and Machinery Review*, 1930–31, p. 510.

[36] *Jour. R.A.S.E.*, 1879, pp. 691–707; 1882, p. 616; 1883, p. 629; 1885, p. 41; 1887, p. 665; 1889, pp. 98–99; 1890, pp. 626–632; 1891, pp. 497–501; 1894, pp. 471, 480; 1895, pp. 452, 454, 468; 1898, p. 500; 1899, pp. 525–544; 1904, pp. 203–204; 1908, pp. 183–184; 1910, pp. 203–204. *Jour. Bath and W. Soc.*, 3rd Ser., 1889–90, xxi, pp. 57–67 and pp. 221–223. *Implement and Machinery Review*, Nov. 1879; Feb. and Sept. 1889; Aug. and Nov. 1890; March and June 1892; July and Nov. 1894; July 1895; July 1899.

[37] *Scottish Farmer*, July 6, 1946, p. 834.

[37a] See issue of Aug. 30, 1862, a copy of which was kindly lent me by Mr. Hilary Phillips of the *Farmer's Weekly*.

[38] Hilary Phillips, *A century of machine milking*, Farmer's Weekly, Oct. 28, 1949.

[39] *Jour. R.A.S.E.*, 1891, p. 525. *Scottish Farmer, op. cit.*

[40] *Trans. H. and A. Soc.*, 1875, 4th Ser., Vol. VII, p. 269.

[41] *Jour. R.A.S.E.*, 1890, pp. 645–652. *Pat. Spec.* Nos. 15, 210 of 1890.

[42] *Trans. H. and A. Soc.*, 1892, 5th Ser., Vol. IV, pp. 19–33.

[43] *Jour. R.A.S.E.*, 1895, pp. 460–464. *Cyclopaedia of Agric.*, p. 25. Mr. Allsebrook, who was employed as erector and trained by the company to whom I was introduced through the good offices of Mr. J. B. Knox of Gascoignes (Reading) Ltd.

[44] *Trans. H. and A. Soc.*, 1898, 5th Ser., Vol. X, pp. 166–181. *Implement and Machinery Review*, Feb. 1898.

[45] *Jour. B. and W. Soc.*, 1905–06, 4th Ser., Vol. XVI, pp. 80–82.

[46] *Jour. R.A.S.E.*, 1905, pp. 81–84; 1908, p. 187.

[47] See Spencer and Passmore, Plates XV and XVI.

CHRONOLOGY OF THE FARMER'S TOOLS

1523.   Fitzherbert mentioned various designs of the ploughs used in different counties. The harrow was the only other implement he described.

1577.   Light two-wheel plough used in Norfolk and Lincoln mentioned by Barnaby Googe.

1601.   Plat mentioned "setting" corn. Maxey depicted the setting board.

1614.   Barnaby Googe mentioned the Gallic reaping cart that had been known in classical times.

1623.   Alexander Hamilton patented a seeding machine.

1634.   David Ramsey patented a method of sowing corn and grain "for making the earth more fertile."

1639.   Gabriel Plattes patented a seed drill.

1646.   J. Sha described his seed barrow, manuring plough, waggon and roller.

1649.   Walter Blith's Trenching Plough.
            Hertfordshire wheel plough.
            Double-furrow plough.
            One wheel plough.
            Foot or swing plough.
            Suggested plough with a seed dropper behind it and a harrow behind that.

1657.   Sha's manuring roller, manuring plough and manuring waggon, probably only ideas.

1669.   Worlidge described and illustrated his seed-drill.

c. 1700. Danish iron being imported for making plough tackle.

c. 1700. Jethro Tull made his seed drill and horse hoes. After this very many people designed seed-drills and combined drills for sowing manure and seed at one operation, and special designs for sowing different seeds.

1707.   Mortimer saw an iron ploughbreast in use in Essex, and a double mouldboard plough.

1716.   Cambridgeshire draining plough.

c. 1720. James Meikle designed a winnowing machine.

1724.   Switzer suggested hollow drain made of loose bricks and hollow drain made with a wooden cylinder in clay soil.

1730.   Rotherham plough—in Scotland the Dutch plough.

1732.   Michael Menzies designed a threshing machine, a series of flails driven by a water wheel. A similar machine was made at a little later date by Craw of Netherbyres, Berwick.

1758. Stirling of Dunblane made a thresher on the principles of a flax mill.

c. 1760. The cutting box, a primitive chaff cutter.

1763. Small's improved plough—made in his factory at Blackadder—with a cast-iron mouldboard.

1766. Cuthbert Clarke's draining plough.
Duckett's trenching plough.

1766. John Randall's spiky roller. Ellis described one in 1736.

1767. Francis Moore's patent for "a fire engine to supplant horses."

1768. Knowles's draining plough.

1770. Bush's Warwickshire improved double-furrow plough. A double furrow was used in a good many counties where the soil permitted.

1770. Richard Lovell Edgeworth patented a "sort of endless railway."

c. 1770. James Edgill made a spiral knife chaff cutter.
James Sharp advertised a hand mill for splitting beans, grinding malt, etc.

c. 1770. James Sharp made a winnowing machine that cleaned and sorted grain.

1774. Smart of Wark, Ilderton of Alnwick, and Oxley of Flodden, Northumberland, designed threshing machines to rub out the grain, or scutch it out.

1784. Spring dynamometer used in comparative plough trials organized by the Society of Arts—Brand's iron plough was included in these trials, and Arbuthnot's with the share and breast in one "inclined plane."

1785. Ransome's patent for tempering cast-iron ploughshares.

1785. William Winlaw made a threshing machine that rubbed out the grain.

c. 1786. Andrew Meikle made a threshing machine that beat out the grain.

1787. William Pitt of Pendeford, Stafford, made a drawing to show how the Gallic reaping cart could be built.

1794. James Cooke patented a chaff cutter with blades on the spokes of a wheel. This is the system of the modern machine. By 1845 there was an immense number and variety of these machines, one of them driven by a steam engine.

c. 1795. Read's cylindrical pipe for land drainage.

1797. William Spencer Dix made a threshing machine that rubbed out the grain.

1797. Henry Watts's patent for a mole plough.

1798. Lord John Somerville's improved West of England double-furrow plough.

1800. Richard Lumbert's patent for a mole plough.

1800. Plenty's friction wheel plough patented.

1800. Mr. Cartwright of Brothertoft, Lincs, tried to design reaper scythes.

1800.   Joseph Boyce patented an elementary type of reaper.
         Robert Meares patented a shears type of reaping machine.
c. 1800. Salmon patented his hay tedder. This was the basis of all later haymaking machines.
c. 1800. Thomas Wigful of Norfolk showed a portable threshing machine at Woburn Agricultural Meeting.
1801.   Plug draining—like Switzer's.
1803.   Ransome's second patent for ploughshares.
1805.   Plucknett designed a reaper with circular plate knife made to revolve.
1807.   Ketcher of Burnham, Essex, owned a horse rake, but his implement may have been of earlier date than this.
         A little later there were several types. Weir's (1825) was fitted with a lever to raise and lower it.
1808.   Ransome's patent plough with standardized replaceable parts.
1810.   Major Pratt patented a system of steam cultivation.
c. 1811. Gladstone designed a reaper with a cutter like Plucknett's.
         Salmon designed a reaper with a clipping mechanism and apparatus for collecting and delivering the cut corn.
         Smith of Deanston designed a machine with a rotary cutter and side delivery.
         David Cumming designed one with revolving knives—others were also active.
1812.   Messrs. Chapman patented a steam carriage with a rigger and anchors for hauling ploughs.
c. 1820. Root slicer for cutting up turnips, etc. Such devices may have been made thirty or forty years earlier. Several different types were very quickly designed. Root pulpers were also made. Grain and cake mills were rapidly developed.
1822.   Finlayson's patent rid, or self-cleaning plough, and self-cleaning harrows.
1822.   Roberts patented a rotary digging machine. Many designs of rotary cultivator were constructed later in the nineteenth century.
1823.   Smith of Deanston's subsoil plough.
1825.   Bedford wheel plough with an iron frame.
1826.   Grey's draining plough.
1828.   Bell designed his reaping machine with reciprocating cutters and side delivery.
1832.   Joseph Saxton patented a system of ploughing with an endless rope moved by a windlass.
1834.   (or slightly earlier). An American hay sweep was imported. There has been little change in later designs.
1836.   John Heathcote produced a system of steam cultivation with tracklaying traction, etc.

1840.   Sir Edward Strachey's Rackheath subsoil plough. Many others were designed.

1841.   Competitive trials of threshing machines were held by the Royal Agricultural Society. At this date the threshing machine included most of its modern features.

1843.   Lowcock's patent turnwrist plough.

1843.   Machines for making draining tiles (tubular), both manual and mechanical.

1846.   Boydell patented a primitive tracklaying system of endless rails.

1847.   Cooch and Son won a prize for their seed dresser and winnowing machine that the firm had been making for a good many years.

1848.   Trials of threshing machines driven by steam power.
         First combined threshing and dressing machine produced by Charles Burrell and Sons, Ltd., of Thetford, Norfolk.

1849.   Barrett and Exall made Hannam's system of steam ploughing using a portable engine and wire rope—the original roundabout system.

c. 1850. Paul's rotary trenching machine.

1851.   The American reapers were shown at the Great Exhibition. They were made by McCormick and by Hussey. These, with Bell's machine, are the foundation upon which all later developments have been built.
         There were some other patents, etc., between the date of Bell's machine and 1851. In the century 1851–1951 the simple reaper has been developed into the self-propelled combine.

1851.   Lord Willoughby d'Eresby showed a set of steam ploughing tackle at the Great Exhibition.

1851.   Fowler's mole and pipe-laying draining plough.

1852.   Elevator type potato digger made.

1855.   Messrs. Fisken of Newcastle patented a system of steam ploughing.

1855.   J. Hanson patented a potato digger with revolving forks like the modern spinner. About thirty-five more patents for potato diggers were granted during the following two decades.

1857.   J. Baird patented a potato planter. About twenty more patents were taken out during the following eighteen years.

1857.   Trial of grass mowing machines by the Royal Agricultural Society.

1858.   Fowler awarded a prize of £500 by the R.A.S.E. for his steam plough.
         This was followed by many other systems of steam ploughing, cultivating, etc.

1862.   Milking machine exhibited in America, and the patent bought by a Birmingham firm.

1863.   Hay and straw elevators exhibited, but elevators had been made some time before this date.

1863.   Potato sorter (separator) shown by Maunder.

1865.   Eddington's pipe-laying machine for land draining.

1866.   W. A. Gibbs produced apparatus for crop-drying.

1872.   Safety feeding devices for threshing machines constructed.

1876.   Walter A. Wood exhibited a reaper-binder at the Royal Agricultural Society's Show.

1879.   de Laval cream separator awarded a silver medal at R.A.S.E. Show. This model combined practically all the principles of the modern machine.

1881.   Dederick's Perpetual Hay Press imported from U.S.A.

1883.   Howard won the R.A.S.E. silver medal for a straw trusser.

1889.   William Murchland patented a milking machine.

1890.   Dairy Supply Co's. "Instantaneous" butter maker with a refrigerator between the separator and churn.

1891.   Stewart Nicholson won a silver medal for his milking machine.

1892.   W. N. Nicholson and Son showed Neilson's patent milking machine.

1893.   R.A.S.E. trial of sheep-shearing clippers.

1895.   Thistle Mechanical Milking Machine exhibited at R.A.S.E. Show. This included the pulsator principle, the basis of later machines.

1904.   "Ivel" agricultural tractor driven by an internal combustion engine demonstrated.

GLOSSARY

Awn: The beard of barley.

Beetle: A wooden mallet, e.g. a clodding beetle was used for breaking the clods left behind the plough.

Broad sharing: Ploughing flat and wide with the broad share or paring plough without turning the slice over.

Cavings: Waste resulting from threshing corn; chaff, broken ears and siftings of corn.

Chob: To shake the grain out of the husk.

Clodmaul: A mallet or beetle for breaking up clods.

Clouterly: Clumsy, awkward.

Coulter: A knife-like piece of iron, sharpened at the lower end, fixed by wedges in a mortise hole in the beam. Its purpose is to split the soil for the share to penetrate it more easily. The Dutch coulter was a disc.

Foot plough: A swing plough, i.e. not fitted with wheels.

Gripping plough: A plough with a share fitted with vertical fins or wings on each side that cut a shallow grip or drain.

Hades: Grass-grown divisions between two strips of open field land.

Hales, plough: Plough handles.

Hake: The dentated iron head of the plough.

Haulm: The stalks of green crops, i.e. potatoes.

Hummel barley: To knock off the awns or beard.

Kibble: To crush or bruise dry corn, beans, etc., for cattle feed.

Meares: Balks, or grassy pieces of land separating two strips of open field land; *see* Hades.

Mouldboard: The part of the plough that turns over the furrow.

Nidget: A kind of scarifier or horse hoer.

Rafter: Rafter ploughing is ploughing only every alternate furrow. The same as ribbing or risbalking.

Ridge: see Stetch.

Sarment: Lat. *sarmentum*; twigs, brushwood, a faggot, fascine.

Scutchers: Beaters, e.g. the dry husk of flax was scutched off.

Share, plough: The pointed part that cuts off the earth so that it can be inverted by the breast or mouldboard.

Shelboard: Plough breast; the curved part, shaped like a shield, that turns the furrow over.

Shethe or skeath, plough: A piece of wood $2\frac{1}{2}$ ft. long, mortised into the beam that helped to hold the plough together.

Shim or skim (plough): A horse hoe.

Slade: Part of a plough, fitted beneath it, to make it run smoothly.

Soughe: Adit, (?) as in early mining; an underground drain; occ. a wet ditch.

Stetch: A ridge or land; the ploughed land between two furrows.

Stilt: A plough handle.

Swathe: When cut by the scythe the grass fell in lines or swathes. The swathe was turned to let air dry the hay.

Tailings: The refuse grain left after threshings.

Ted hay, to: To scatter hay about to allow it to dry.

Tedder: A machine for tedding or scattering hay.

Tile draining: Draining with flat or curved tiles used to form a pipe; later pipe draining.

Tine: A harrow tooth, or a tooth on a cultivator, or other hoeing tool.

BIBLIOGRAPHY

1. PERIODICALS.

Museum Rusticum et Commerciale, 1764, *et. seq*, 6 vols.

Annals of Agriculture, 1783, *et. seq*.

Farmer's Magazine, 1800, *et. seq*.

Letters and Communications to the Bath and West of England Society, 1792, *et. seq*. Journal of this Society, 1st to the 5th Series.

Trans. Highland and Agricultural Society.

Quarterly Journal of Agriculture, 1828, *et. seq*.

Journal of the Royal Agricultural Society of England, 1840, *et. seq*.

Implement and Machinery Review, 1875, *et. seq*.

Mechanics Magazine (odd numbers).

Patent Specifications.

Agricultural History.

Economic Journal.

Economic History Review.

Farmer and Stockbreeder.

Farmer's Weekly.

Jour. Min. Agric.

Scottish Farmer.

Scottish Journal of Agriculture.

2. BOARD OF AGRICULTURE, 1793–1819.

General View of the Agriculture (of each county in England, Wales and Scotland. 1st and later editions).

Communications, 6 vols.

3. BOOKS, ESSAYS, ETC.

Amos, William, *Minutes of Agriculture*, 1804.
   Essays on Agricultural Machines, 1810.

Anderson, Russell M., "Grain drills through thirty-nine centuries," in *Agricultural History*, 10 Oct., 1936.

Andrews, G. H., *Rudimentary treatise of agricultural engineering*, 3 vols, 1852–53.
   Modern Husbandry, 1853.

Anon., *British Husbandry*, 3 vols., 1837.

Anon., *A Cardiganshire Landlord's advice to his tenants*, 1800.

Anon., *An easie and profitable order in tilling of ground to improve it and make it fertile*, n.d., *c*. 1657.

Anon., *The Farmer's Complete Guide*, 1760.

Anon., *Overlooked pages of reaper history* (Chicago), 1879.

Anon., *Who invented the sowing machine? Nuova Vita Rurale*, VII, Nov. 1935.

Aubrey, John, *Memoirs of naturall remarques in the county of Wiltshire* (ed. by John Britton), 1847.

Bacon, Richard Noverre, *The agriculture of Norfolk*, 1844.

Bailey, James, *Essay on the construction of the plough*, 1795.

Baxter's Library of Agricultural Knowledge, 1837.

Black, James, *Observations on the tillings of the earth*, 1777.

Blagrave, Joseph, *The epitome of the art of husbandry*, 1669.

Blith, Walter, *English Improver*, 1649.
   English Improver Improved, 1653.

Blome, Richard, *The Gentleman's Recreation*, 1686.

Boswell, George, *A treatise on watering meadows*, 1779.

Bourne, George, *The Wheelwright's Shop*, 1923.

Bowden, Thomas, *The Farmer's Director*, 1776.

Bradley, Richard, *Complete Body of Husbandry*, 1727.
   Riches of a Hop Garden, 1729.

Brayley, W. L., *Some 4730 years of grain drill history*, Farm Implement News,
   May 1, 1930.

Brome, James, *Travels over England*, 1700.

Brown of Markle, Robert, *Treatise of Rural Affairs*, 2 vols., 1811.

Bryant, Arthur, *The England of Charles II.* 1933.

Burn, R. Scott, *Practical Directory for the Improvement of Landed Property*,
   1881.
   Outlines of Modern Farming, 1888.

Cashmore, W. H., and Newman, J. E., *The development of haymaking machinery*,
   Empire Jour. of Experimental Agriculture, 1933.

Clapham, J. H., *An economic history of modern Britain*, 3 vols., 1925., etc.

Clarke, Cuthbert, *True Theory and Practice of Husbandry*, 1777.

Clayton, C. H. J., *Land drainage from the field to the sea*, 1919.

Cooke, Rev. James, *Cooke's Improved Patent Drill and Horse Hoe*, 1789.

Copland, Samuel, *Agriculture Ancient and Modern*, 2 vols., 1866.

Cresentius, *Liber commodorum ruralium* (13th cent.), 1st printed at Augsberg,
   1471.

Darwin, Erasmus, *Phytologia*, 1800.

Day, Thomas, *History of Sandford and Merton*, 1783.

des Carrieres, A. J., *A dissertation on Vergil's description of the ancient Roman
   plough*, 1788.

Devon Agricultural Society, *Rules, orders and premiums of the South Devon
   Division*, 1792.

Dickson, Adam, *Husbandry of the Ancients*, 2 vols., 1788.

Dickson, R. W., *Practical Agriculture*, 2 vols., 1805.

Donaldson, John, *British Agriculture*, 3 vols., 1866.

Dossie, Robert, *Memoirs of Agriculture*, 3 vols., 1771.

Doyle, Martin, *Cyclopaedia of Practical Agriculture*, 1839.

Drummond's Agricultural Museum, Third Report, 1835.

Dubravius, Janus, *A newe booke of good husbandry* (tr. for George Churchey),
   1599.

East Anglian Daily Times, July 6, 1901.

Ellis, William, *Chiltern and Vale Farming*, 1733.

The Modern Husbandman, 1750.

Ellis's Husbandry abridged and methodized, 1772.

Ernle, Lord, *English farming past and present*, 4th ed., 1932.

Essex Farmer, *A letter on the construction and use of the improved foot plough*, 1784.

Evelyn, John, *Discourse of Earth*, 1676.

Finlayson, John, *Treatise on agricultural subjects*, 1822.

British Farmer, 1825.

Fitzherbert, *Boke of Husbandry?*, 1523, } In *Certain Ancient Tracts*, 1767.
Surveyinge, 1523

Forbes, Francis, *The improvement of waste lands*, 1778.

The extensive practice of the new husbandry, 1786.

Forsyth, Robert, *Principles and Practice of Agriculture*, 2 vols., 1804.

Fussell, G. E., *The Breast Plough in Man*, XXXII, 1936, 116.

Garnier, Russell M., *History of the England landed interest*, 2 vols. 1893.

Googe, Barnaby, *Foure bookes of husbandrie*, 1577.

Gray, Andrew, *Ploughwright's Assistant*, 1808.

Hamilton, Henry, *The industrial revolution in Scotland*, 1932.

Hammond, J. L. and Barbara, *The village labourer* (ed. of), 1920.

Hartlib, Samuel, *His legacie, or an enlargement of the discourse of husbandry used in Brabant and Flanders*, 1657.

The Compleat Husbandman, 1659.

Highland and Agricultural Society, *Catalogue of the Museum*, 1844.

Holy Bible.

Horne, John, *The description and use of new invented Universal Sowing Machine*, 1786.

Hoskyns, C. W., *Chronicles of a clay farm*, 1853.

Houghton, John, *A collection of letters for the improvement of husbandry and trade*, 1681–83.

House of Commons Reports of Select Committee on Distress in Agric., 1836.

Hudson, W. H., *The shepherd's life*, 1910.

Hunter, A., *Georgical Essays*, 4 vols., 1770–72.

Hunter, James, *The improved Scotch swing plough*, 1843.

International Harvester Co., *Roots in Chicago one hundred years deep, 1847–1947*, n.d., c. 1947.

Johnson, C. W., and Cressy, Edward, *The cottages of agricultural labourers*, 1847.

Johnstone, John, *An account of the mode of draining land . . . system practised by Mr. Elkington*, 3rd ed., 1808.

Lawson, A., *Farmer's Practical Instructor*, 1826.

Lawrence, John, *A New System of Agriculture*, 1726.

Modern Land Steward, 1801.

Lester, William, *History of British Implements*, 1804.

Letters from: J. F. Cooch, Sept. 23, 1949; J. B. Knox, corres. in 1949 and 1950; Ransomes, Sims and Jefferies, Dec. 9, 1949.

Lisle, Edward, *Observations on Husbandry*, 1756.

Loudon, John Claudius, *Encyclopaedia of Agriculture*, 1831.

Low, David, *Elements of Agriculture*, 1843.

McDonald, Donald, *Agricultural Writers*, 1200–1800, 1908.

Markham, Gervase, *The English Husbandman*, 1616.
  The inrichment of the Weald of Kent, 1625.
  The Whole Art of Husbandry, 1631.

Marshall, T. H., *Jethro Tull and the New Husbandry*, Econ. Hist. Rev., Jan. 1929.

Marshall, William, *Rural Economy of Norfolk*, 2 vols., 1787.
  Rural Economy of Yorkshire, 2 vols., 1796.
  Rural Economy of Midland Counties, 2 vols., 1796.
  Rural Economy of West of England, 2 vols., 1796.
  Rural Economy of Southern Counties, 2 vols., 1798.

Martin, M., *A description of the Western Islands of Scotland*, 1716.

Maxey, Ed., *A new instruction of plowing and setting of corne*, 1601.

Maxwell of Arkland, Robert, *Select Trans. of the Hon. the Society of Improvers in agriculture*, 1743.

Mills, John, *New System of Practical Husbandry*, 2 vols., 1767.

Mortimer, John, *The whole art of husbandry*, 4th ed., 2 vols., 1716.

Morton, J. C., *Cyclopaedia of Agriculture*, 7 vols., 1856.

New Royal Encyclopaedia, c. 1820.

Norden, John, *The Surveyor's Dialogue*, 1607.

Nourse, Tim, *Campania Foelix*, 1700.

Palladius on Husbandrie (Early English Text Soc.), 1873.

Parkinson, Richard, *The English Practice of Agriculture*, 1806.

Passmore, J. B., *The English Plough*, 1930.

Peters, Matthew, *The Rational Farmer*, 1771.
  Agricultura, or the good husbandman, 1776.

Plat, Sir Hugh, *The newe and admirable arte of setting of corne*, 1601.

Plattes, Gabriel, *A discovery of infinite treasure*, 1639.

Plot, Robert, *Natural History of Oxfordshire*, 1677.
  Natural History of Staffordshire, 1686.

Practiser of both the old and the new husbandry. *The modern improvements of agriculture*, 1774.

Prentice, E. Parmalee, *Progress, an episode in the history of hunger*, 1947.

Randall, John, *The construction and use of a newly invented seed furrow plough*, 1764.

Randall, John, *The semi-Virgilian Husbandry*, 1764.
  The construction and use of a newly invented seed furrow plough, 1764.

Ramsome, J. Allen, *The implements of agriculture*, 1843.

Ransome, J. Edward, *Double furrow ploughs*. A lecture to Framlingham Farmer's Club, 1872.

Ransomes Royal Records, 1789–1939, n.d., c. 1949.

Raynbird, William and Hugh, *The agriculture of Suffolk*, 1849.

Reeve, Gabriel, *Directions for the improvement of barren and heathy land*, 1670.

Robertson, George, *Rural Recollections*, 1829.

Rogers, J. E. Thorold, *Six centuries of work and wages*, 2 vols., 1884.

Sha, J., *Certaine plaine and easie demonstrations . . . for improving barren land* 1657.

Sharp, James, *Descriptions of utensils in husbandry sold by James Sharp*, n.d., c. 1773.

Sinclair, Bart. Sir John, *Hints on the Netherlands*, 1815.
    Analysis of the Statistical Account of Scotland, 1825.

Slight, James, and Burn, R. Scott, *The book of farm implements* (ed. by Henry Stephens), 1858.

Small, James, *Treatise of ploughs and wheel carriages*, 1784.

Smith, John, *England's improvement revived*, 1670.

Society of Gentlemen, *The Complete Farmer*, 1766.

Somerville, John, Lord, *Facts and observations relative to sheep, wool, ploughs and oxen*, 3rd ed., 1809.

Speed, Ad., *Adam out of Eden*, 1659.

Spencer, A. J., and Passmore, J. B., *Handbook of the collections illustrating agricultural implements and machinery* (Science Museum), 1930.

Standard Encyclopaedia of Modern Agriculture, 1910.

Strutt, Joseph, *Saxon rarities of the Eighth Century*, cited by Dan Pidgeon, J.A.R.S.E., 1892.
    Complete View of the Manners of England. 1775, cited by Dan Pidgeon, J.R.A.S.E., 1892

Surflet, Richard, *Maison Rustique or the Countrey Ferne*, 1600.

Switzer, Stephen, *Practical Fruit Gardener*, 1724.
    Ichnographia Rustica, 3 vols., 1726.

Sylvan Agricola, *Farmer's Magazine*, 3 vols., 1777.

Tull, Jethro, *New Horse Houghing Husbandry*, 1731.

Tusser, Thomas, *Five hundred points of good husbandry*, 1577, ed. by William Mavor, 1812.

Vaughan, Rowland, *Most improved and long experienced waterworks*, 1610.

Vinogradoff, Paul, *Villeinage in England*, 1892.
    The growth of the manor, 1905.

Walter of Henley's Husbandry, ed. by Cunningham and Lammond, 1890.

Watson, James Scott, and Hobbs, Mary Elliott, *Great Farmers*, 1937.

Watson, Sir James A. Scott, *History of the Royal Agricultural Society of England, 1839–1939*, n.d., 1939.

Williamson, Capt. Thomas, *The Agricultural Mechanism*, 1810.

Wilson, Rev. John N., *Rural Cyclopaedia*, 4 vols., 1849.

Winter, George, *A new and compendious system of husbandry*, 1787.

Worlidge, John, *Systema Agriculturae*, 1675.

Young, Arthur, *Farmers' Letters*, 1767.
    Six Weeks Tour, 1768.

Young, Arthur, *Rural Economy*, 1770.
　Farmer's Tour through the East of England, 4 vols., 1771.
　On the husbandry of three celebrated farmers, 1811.
Young, David, *National Improvements upon agriculture*, 1785.

4.　SELECT BIBLIOGRAPHY OF PUBLICATIONS SINCE 1952

Arnold, J., *Farm waggons and carts*, 1977.
Cawood, C.L., 'The history and development of farm tractors', pts. 1 and II, *Industrial archaeology*, vol. 7, 1970.
Collins, E.J.T., *Sickle to Combine: a review of harvesting techniques from 1800 to the present day*, 1969.
　'The diffusion of the threshing machine in Britain, 1790–1880', *Tools and tillage*, vol. 2, 1972.
　'The age of machinery', in, G.E. Mingay (ed.), *The Victorian countryside*, vol. 1, 1981.
David, P.A., 'The landscape and the machine . . . the corn harvest in Victorian Britain', in, D.N. McCloskey (ed.), *Essays in a mature economy: Britain after 1840*, 1971.
Fraser, C., *Harry Ferguson: inventor and pioneer*, 1972.
Fussell, G.E., *The English dairy farmer 1500–1900*, 1966.
　Jethro Tull: his influence on mechanized agriculture, 1973.
G.E. Fussell: a bibliography of his writings on agricultural history, 1967.
Grace, D.R. & Phillips, D.C., *Ransomes of Ipswich: a history of the firm and guide to its records*
Harvey, N., *The industrial archaeology of farming in England and Wales*, 1980.
Jenkins, J.G., *The English farm wagon*, 3rd edition, 1981.
Jewell, A., (ed.), *Victorian farming: a source book* [Selections from Henry Stephens, *The Book of the Farm*, 3rd edn., 1871.], 1975.
Lane, M.R., *The story of the steam plough works*, Fowler of Leeds, 1980.
Macdonald, S., 'The progress of the early threshing machine', *Agricultural History Review*, vol. 23, 1975.
Morgan, R., *History of agricultural tools, implements and machinery: a bibliography, 1600–1945*, forthcoming, University of Reading, 1982.
Partridge, M., *Farm tools through the ages*, 1973.
Quick, G. & Buchele, W.F., *The grain harvesters*, St. Joseph, Michigan, American Society of Agricultural Engineers, 1978.
Tyler, C., *Digging by steam*, 1977.
Tyler C., & Haining J., *Ploughing by steam*, 1970
Walton, J.R., 'Mechanization in agriculture: a study of the adoption process', in, H.S.A. Fox and R.A. Butlin (eds.), *Change in the countryside: essays in rural England, 1500–1900*, 1979.
Whetham, E.H., 'The mechanisation of British farming, 1910–45', *Journal of agricultural economics*, vol. 21, 1970.
Williams, M., *Steam power in agriculture*, 1977.
White, K.D., *Farm equipment of the Roman world*, 1975.

INDEX

Note : The very large number of types of implement, etc., and of places, inventors, makers, societies and writers mentioned in the text has made it essential to simplify this index. This has been done by adopting a method of naming an implement, e.g. ploughs. Under this heading the names of makers are given in alphabetical order. They are not cross referenced because this would have made the index unwieldy. When several counties are named as using a new implement at some stated time the implement is indexed and the whole passage covered by one entry, e.g. "Threshing machines—distribution of, end of eighteenth century." The great agricultural societies are constantly named, and have only been indexed when specially cited in some particular connection. There are no doubt some disadvantages to this method, as there are to all methods, but it is designed to save space as well as to serve its purpose of being a guide to the contents of the book.

Q